Contemporary Cases in Marketing

Contemporary Cases in Marketing

Second Edition

W. Wayne Talarzyk
The Ohio State University

The Dryden Press
Hinsdale, Illinois

Copy editing by Flora Foss

Copyright © 1979 by The Dryden Press
A division of Holt, Rinehart and Winston, Inc.
All rights reserved
Library of Congress Catalog Card Number: 78-71600
ISBN: 0-03-045436-0
Printed in the United States of America
9 090 98765432

The Dryden Press Series in Marketing

Preface

The preface to the first edition of this book began: "Marketing personnel of today are forced to operate and make decisions in a rapidly changing environment, part of which they have some control over, much of which they have little or no control over. At the same time, marketing concepts are being increasingly and successfully applied to appropriate areas of decision making outside the traditional realm of business."

These words are equally applicable today. Marketers are finding their decisions more and more dependent upon factors over which they have minimal influence. As with most situations, such operating conditions can be viewed as unsolvable problems or unprecedented opportunities. Successful marketers are using their creative skills to develop consumer-oriented strategies that turn potential problems into rewarding opportunities. At the same time, nonbusiness organizations are continuing to find marketing concepts helpful in formulating strategies and tactics to satisfy the needs of their "consumers."

As with the first edition, this book is designed to bring together the key aspects of marketing in an interesting, meaningful, and contemporary fashion. Traditional topics of marketing are covered through real-world, up-to-date cases focusing on innovative product and service offerings in light of emerging issues, problems, and opportunities in marketing. Such topics as minority-owned businesses, social responsibility, conservation marketing, and current legal areas of advertising are illustrative of the coverage. The expanding role of marketing is presented through cases concerning religious organizations, political campaigns, professional associations, government agencies, and nonprofit organizations.

Seventeen of the thirty-six cases are new to this edition. Of the nineteen cases that appeared in the first edition, all but five have been significantly modified through updating and adding of new material.

Cases in this edition continue to represent a comprehensive cross section of marketing topics, wide coverage, and a high level of analysis. Individual instructors can increase the complexity of analysis for each case by requiring special outside investigations on the topics covered or by assigning greater in-depth evaluation of the key issues in each case. Thus the book can be used appropriately and profitably at either the undergraduate or graduate level.

In the development of a book of this type, many companies, organizations, and key executives provide valuable assistance, information, and cooperation. These contributors are gratefully acknowledged individually in a special section of the text. It is appropriate here, however, to express appreciation to a group of present and former colleagues who provided insights, assurances, and evaluations at appropriate points in the progress of this edition and the earlier one. These individuals are Dale D. Achabal, Robert Bartels, Roger D. Blackwell, W. Arthur Cullman, James H. Davis, Terry Deutscher, James F. Engel, Dennis Garber, James L. Ginter, John R. Grabner, Roger Jenkins, David T. Kollat, Michael Levy, H. Lee Mathews, and James F. Robeson.

Special thanks also go to the many students and instructors who used the first edition of the text. My hope is that the second edition will continue to provide a meaningful learning experience for the students of today who will become the marketing leaders and influences of tomorrow.

W. Wayne Talarzyk
Columbus, Ohio
September 1978

Acknowledgments

Many people and organizations were instrumental in the successful completion of this collection of contemporary marketing cases. It is with extreme gratitude that all these individuals and organizations are acknowledged here.

Several professors willingly gave permission for their original case manuscripts to be modified somewhat for inclusion in the text. Appreciation is expressed to the following for their permission: David McConaughy, University of Southern California (Hill Industrial Supply); Donald W. Scotton, Cleveland State University (Warner & Swasey Company); and James D. Taylor and Bert C. Nyman, with the assistance of Terry McClain, University of South Dakota (M-tron Industries, Inc).

Cases on some of the firms and organizations in the text have appeared in other books. Baskin-Robbins 31 Ice Cream Stores, Campus Crusade for Christ, and Simpson's Shoe Store appeared in James F. Engel, W. Wayne Talarzyk, and Carl M. Larson, *Cases in Promotional Strategy* (Homewood, Ill.: Richard D. Irwin, 1971); City National Bank appeared in Roger D. Blackwell, James F. Engel, and David T. Kollat, *Cases in Consumer Behavior* (New York: Holt, Rinehart and Winston, 1969); and Youngs Drug Products, International Telephone & Telegraph, and Wendy's International, Inc., appeared in W. Wayne Talarzyk, *Cases for Analysis in Marketing* (Hinsdale, Ill.: Dryden Press, 1977).

Appreciation is also expressed to the following individuals for their willingness to cooperate in the development of cases based on their organizations and sources:

T. L. Benjamin
Zelma Bishop
N. L. Braun
Lewis R. Brenner
Richard T. Brigham
William R. Bright
Karen L. Brucoli
Milton J. Bryson
Terry L. Casey
J. Ronald Castell
John K. Chance
Douglas Dachenbach
Dorothy C. Davis
Rebecca Dolle
David Dooley
Michael Duvall
Frank T. Fenton

Joel K. Harris
W. Gordon Kearns
Robert L. Lindamood
Julius Litman
John L. Lowden
R. Patrick McCarthy
Fred Poppe
Irvine Robbins
John A. Russell
Tom Santer
Joseph A. Serian
Jim Smith
Joseph A. Sugarman
Stephen J. Waling
Graydon D. Webb
James Wilson
Peter Wiersma

Contents

Part Three
Assessing Marketing Opportunities   101

Part Four
Planning Components of the   163
Marketing Program

Part Five
The Expanding Role of Marketing   227
in Society

Part Six
Developing the Total Marketing Program 291

Contents: An Overview of Cases

Product Service Area	Expanding the Marketing Concept	Legal Considerations	Planning and Strategy	Advertising/Promotion	Product/Service Implications	Franchising	Consumer/Buyer Behavior	Social Responsibility	Market Segmentation	Pricing	Channels of Distribution	Marketing Research	Financial Information
Cosmetics			X	X	X		X	X	X	X		X	
Maple syrup				X				X	X	X		X	
Building structures		X		X			X	X	X	X			
Toys				X				X	X	X	X		X
Banking services			X	X			X						X
Machine tools		X		X	X		X					X	X
Reconditioned merchandise			X	X	X		X	X	X				
Condoms	X		X				X	X					
Contact lenses	X	X	X	X	X	X	X	X		X			
Gasoline	X		X				X						
Advertising	X		X				X	X					
Contact lenses			X				X				X	X	
Toys							X			X	X	X	
Diversified								X				X	
Banking services				X			X					X	
Shoes		X		X			X					X	
Control garments							X					X	
Health care	X						X	X	X			X	
Ice cream			X	X	X	X	X						
Ice cream						X							
Funeral services		X			X		X	X	X	X			X
Industrial supplies			X		X		X						X
Banking services			X		X		X						
Plumbing supplies			X	X	X		X	X			X		X
Control garments							X						
Child care	X	X	X					X					X
Christianity	X	X	X	X				X					
Health care	X	X					X	X			X		
Politics	X	X					X	X	X		X		
Charitable fund raising	X		X					X					X
Energy conservation			X	X	X		X	X	X	X	X		X
Drilling supplies			X	X	X		X		X		X		
Two-way cable TV			X	X	X	X	X	X	X	X			
Electronic air cleaners			X	X	X		X		X	X	X	X	
Collectibles			X	X	X		X		X	X	X	X	
Fast food			X	X	X	X	X		X			X	X

Introduction

Instructors have individual reasons for utilizing cases in their marketing courses. Some introduce them as a vehicle to aid in the understanding of marketing concepts. Others incorporate them for the expressed purpose of developing students' analytical and decision-making skills.

In almost all instances, however, one underlying reason is that of bringing additional realism into a course through the use of current illustrations of actual business problems and situations. This book has been developed to provide the desired realism through a collection of contemporary cases that focus on both traditional marketing issues and the expanding role of marketing in society.

Approaches to the Study of Cases

Just as the reasons for using cases are varied, so also are the approaches to their study. In this regard, the book is designed to be as flexible as possible.

For those who prefer to study the specific functional issues, a list of focal topics is provided at the conclusion of each case. These topics can be utilized as central issues around which class discussions and/or written assignments can be focused.

The cases in the book can also be approached analytically, with an emphasis on problem solving or decision making. Under this plan of study, the focal topics serve mainly as guidelines for investigation by identifying the problems currently facing the organization. These problems range from marketing issues to more general developments of marketing strategy. The text includes recent case histories of certain organizations' marketing strategies. These cases can be analyzed from the perspective of determining the type of marketing strategy that should be adopted for the future.

With the analytical approach, once the problem has been isolated, the decision-making process continues with (a) the identification of problem-solving alternatives open to the organization, (b) a detailed evaluation of each alternative as it relates to the problem and to the organization's objectives and constraints, and (c) specific recommendations about which plan of action the organization should take to solve the problem.

Although there are many different approaches to these steps, certain questions always should be considered in connection with the process, among them:

1. the market and its influence on the problem and decision, including present and potential size and any special characteristics, such as geographic location and seasonality
2. the ultimate consumer, including needs, buying habits, motivations, and key classifications
3. the channels of distribution for the product and their influence on the problem and ultimate decision
4. the types of competition, their present and anticipated future position in the market, and their likely reactions to the various plans of action
5. the legal and political environment and its implications for problem solutions.

Other factors should be evaluated simultaneously. They include the present and future state of the economy, the seriousness and urgency of the problem, the financial position of the organization, the potential risk of the decision, and the effects of the proposed plan of action on key personnel in the company, other product lines, and the company's image.

Organization of the Book

Although many of the cases in the book cover multiple topics and can be expanded or contracted in scope according to the types and levels of analysis desired, six basic sections provide the frame of reference. Part 1 — Introductory Overview of Marketing — involves a set of straightforward, somewhat comprehensive cases. Part 2 — The Changing Environment of Marketing — emphasizes the way marketing reacts to key environmental influences. Part 3 — Assessing Marketing Opportunities — provides insights into marketing research activities. Part 4 — Planning Components of the Marketing Problem — emphasizes some of the functional aspects of marketing. Part 5 — The Expanding Role of Marketing in Society — deals with a variety of types of organizations. Part 6 — Developing the Total Marketing Program — is a group of comprehensive cases that concludes the book.

Part One
Introductory Overview of Marketing

Case 1
Everybody Ltd.

Everybody Ltd. operates a retail establishment located in a student shopping area adjacent to the University of Colorado in Boulder. It sells organic body soaps, lotions, and hair preparations in a low-key environment of old wood and soft lights. The proprietors, a young married couple, have been doing quite well but are interested in expanding their marketing efforts.

The firm is considering the establishment of a broader distribution system for five of their basic products. These products, shown in their display units in Exhibit 1–1, have been formulated to meet the high altitude, dry climatic conditions of the Rocky Mountains. The products are manufactured to Everybody Ltd.'s specifications by a small cosmetics manufacturer in California and shipped in bulk to be packaged at Everybody Ltd.'s warehouse in Boulder.

The Products

Rocky Mountain Shampoo and Rocky Mountain Herbal Rinse

Rocky Mountain Shampoo is an herbal protein shampoo formulated to clean off the outer layer of oil and dirt without removing the natural conditioners found in the hair. Rocky Mountain Herbal Rinse is designed to impart body naturally without coating the hair. It also eliminates tangles and static electricity. Both products contain pure extracts from freshly ground herbs. For example, rosemary gives mild conditioning while releasing tangles and camomile is used to bring out the natural highlights. Apple cider vinegar helps relieve dry itchy scalp and dandruff. Herb nettles are also used in the herbal rinse for dandruff control.

Rocky Mountain Hair Rescue

Conditioning is important for healthy hair, since damage can result from climate, pollution, and improper care. To return hair to its naturally healthy state, Rocky Mountain Hair Rescue replenishes protein with natural amino acids derived from milk and collagen protein. (See the ad for this product in Exhibit 1–2.)

Rocky Mountain Skin Drink

To eliminate dry skin and maintain a healthy skin balance, Rocky Mountain Skin Drink replenishes moisture and nutrients which are removed by the environment. Pure coconut oil and distilled lanolin are the primary moisturizing ingredients. The juice of the aloe vera plant, a natural healing agent, is also used in the lotion.

Lip Trip

Lip Trip was formulated to combine a moisturizer and sun screen in the same lip balm. In a beeswax and lanolin base, Everybody Ltd. has combined a number of natural ingredients, including apricot kernel oil, sesame oil, cocoa butter, peppermint oil, aloe vera, and vitamin E. PABA is used for protection against the sun.

Communication Factors

Packaging

The simple black and white label on the plain plastic bottle is designed to project an image of simplicity, functionality, and quality. The labels list the products' major ingredients and stress that the products are especially formulated for the harsh climate of the Rocky Mountains. The word *biodegradable* and the PH factor—indicating the degree of alkalinity or acidity of the product—are clearly marked.

Point-of-Purchase Displays

Four point-of-purchase displays (shown in Exhibit 1–1) have been designed for retail stores. They are handmade of roughly finished Colorado pine with the Everybody Ltd. logo heavily embossed on the front. The large display case, costing the manufacturer about

$9.00, is a floor model with a generous amount of storage space. The small display case, with a manufacturing cost of $7.50, is usually placed on a counter. A Lip Trip display, also designed for counter use, is small enough to be placed at the checkout area of a store. The Skin Drink counter display is designed to be placed with the skin lotions so the customer can "test" the lotion before purchasing the product. These items' manufacturing cost is $1.50 each.

Since the point-of-purchase displays are a primary communication factor for Everybody Ltd., management is interested in developing an attractive program for inducing retailers to order the displays and use them exclusively for Everybody Ltd. products.

In making policy decisions concerning these displays, Everybody Ltd. is considering two questions. First, should the company retain ownership and, therefore, greater control of the displays, or should it distribute the displays to retailers at no charge, at cost, or with a small markup? Second, to qualify for a display, should retailers be required to purchase enough Everybody Ltd. products to fill the unit?

Samples

Management believes that people who try the products a few times will notice an improvement in hair and skin condition and start buying Everybody Ltd. products. Therefore, the company produces one-ounce sample bottles of the lotion, shampoo, rinse, and conditioner, at a cost of eighteen cents apiece. Providing samples to wholesalers, retailers, and consumers could boost sales of the products at all links in the distribution channel.

In developing its total marketing strategy, Everybody Ltd. is interested in formulating a policy for distribution of these samples. In making such policy decisions the firm is concerned about what prices to charge for the samples and how the samples can best be used with wholesalers and retailers.

Additional Promotional Strategies

Everybody Ltd. has also developed advertisements (see Exhibit 1–2 for an example). However, due to the small size of the firm and the nature of the product, the company is planning to rely heavily on its point-of-purchase displays, samples, retail sales help, and word-of-mouth promotion from loyal customers to sell the products at the retail level.

To help promote its products to wholesalers and retailers, Everybody Ltd. participates in the annual MAHO (Middle America Health Organization) trade show held in Kansas City in the spring and the NNFA (National Nutritional Foods Association) trade show held in Las Vegas in the summer. The firm has developed a package of product samples and product information materials to distribute to potential wholesalers and retailers attending the shows.

Prices

The retail prices for the types of cosmetic products marketed by Everybody Ltd. vary considerably. They range from the relatively low prices found on discounted private label products to the relatively high prices found on exclusive bath boutique and health food store products.

Everyboyd Ltd. has determined that its manufacturing costs of the finished products are as follows:

8 oz.	Rocky Mountain Skin Drink	$.85
8 oz.	Rocky Mountain Shampoo	$.85
6 oz.	Rocky Mountain Hair Rescue	$.80
8 oz.	Rocky Mountain Herbal Rinse	$.70
2 oz.	Lip Trip	$.45

Again, in developing its total marketing strategy, Everybody Ltd. is interested in arriving at suggested retail prices for its products. In addition to manufacturing costs, the firm is evaluating marketing, distribution, and other operating expenses; the profit margins needed by other possible members of the distribution channel; and appropriate levels of profit for itself.

Channels of Distribution

Retail

The types of retail outlets best suited for these products are currently unknown. Everybody Ltd. has gained some knowledge of the market through experience in its own retail store, but that knowledge is limited, since most of the present customers are students. Management is concerned that if they sell their products to stores catering to the "mass" market, the more exclusive health food stores may be less inclined to carry Everybody Ltd. products.

Local health food stores, bath boutiques, women's specialty stores, and college bookstores are all possibilities for reaching the "specialty" products market. Everybody Ltd. has determined that these retailers usually expect a 35 to 40 percent discount from the suggested retail price for health and beauty aid products.

Department stores, grocery chains, and drug chains could also be approached by Everybody Ltd. as possible retail outlets. Initial investigations have determined that it is not unusual for these stores catering to the "mass" market to receive a discount of 50 percent or more from the suggested retail price for these types of products and to try such products only if a "guaranteed sale" is offered.

Wholesale

Currently, Everybody Ltd. employs only one salesperson to call on retail outlets. To obtain adequate coverage of the market, therefore, the firm recognizes that it will be necessary to either hire additional salespeople or use wholesalers.

Preliminary nonrandom, unstructured interviews were made with a number of wholesalers to get some understanding of their possible interest in handling the products. The consensus was that since these wholesalers are constantly asked to represent new lines, initial placement in a few "good" outlets to provide some "success stories" will be necessary before wholesalers will have the incentive to take on the line. It was also found that these types of wholesalers typically expect a 55 to 60 percent discount from the suggested retail price.

Focal Topics

1. What marketing research information would be helpful in developing Everybody Ltd.'s marketing strategy?
2. Identify potential consumer segments for Everybody Ltd.'s products. What are the "best" target markets for Everybody Ltd.?
3. Develop a marketing strategy for Everybody Ltd. Be specific in terms of:
   a. communication factors
   b. pricing recommendations
   c. suggested channels of distribution

Exhibit 1–1
Point-of-Purchase Displays for Product Line

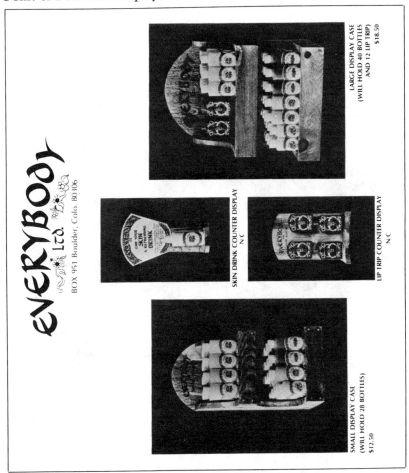

Exhibit 1–2
Proposed Advertisement for Hair Rescue

Case 2
Smith Syrup Company

The Smith Syrup Company, located in Columbus, Ohio, produces and distributes two products—maple flavored syrup and cane flavored syrup. Jim Smith, the company's founder, owner, manufacturer, and salesman, is a black businessman in his early seventies. With the firm's relatively large debt structure, limited product distribution, and annual production capacity about thirty times its actual sales volume, Mr. Smith is trying to decide whether he should try to keep the business going and, if so, what marketing actions he should take.

Origin of the Firm

Mr. Smith started the syrup company in his home in 1958. At that time he produced around five to eight gallons of syrup each week and sold it door-to-door. People liked his syrup, and demand began to increase. A few stores agreed to stock the syrup, and some additional sales were made to local restaurants. In 1961 Mr. Smith registered the trademark "My Syrup So Good" for his products.

For about ten years, My Syrup So Good enjoyed a reasonable level of sales, largely in the vicinity of Mr. Smith's neighborhood. During this time, Mr. Smith generated enough revenue to pay his bills and provide some profit to take care of himself and his family. In 1969 he was approached by two enthusiastic men who had an interest in helping him enlarge the business.

Expansion Moves and Results

Mr. Smith knew he had a superior product and an ability to sell that product on a very personal basis. He also knew, however, that his overall experience in managing a business was quite limited. The two new partners assured Mr. Smith that they had the necessary expertise and that with the proper financial backing success would be imminent.

The partners' first step toward this "imminent success" was to apply for a Small Business Administration loan, which was eventually approved for $26,000. Portions of the loan were used for expanding the facilities and increasing production capacity. A small warehouse was constructed, and two 120-gallon boiling vats were purchased. A bottle-filling and a bottle-capping machine were also acquired to speed up the production process. The firm could now easily produce 200 gallons of syrup a day.

One basic problem remained, however—how to effectively penetrate the highly competitive retail market to achieve the volume of sales necessary to support the new overhead structure. Mr. Smith and his partners had not anticipated this situation properly and found themselves unable to get My Syrup So Good on the shelves of supermarkets. Some distribution was obtained through small grocery stores, but the volume was almost insignificant compared to that needed to meet the payments on the loan and other operating expenses.

The new partners quickly lost interest in the company and moved on to other ventures. Mr. Smith found himself once again a one-man company, only this time he was faced with a relatively large monthly overhead. In an attempt to meet this overhead, he began working longer and longer hours and eventually suffered a heart attack.

After being hospitalized for some time, Mr. Smith returned to his business and found that most of his regular retail customers were no longer interested in carrying his syrup. Understandably discouraged, he returned the unused portion of his loan to the bank, reducing the principal to approximately $15,000, and attempted to rebuild his business back at least to the level of his "prepartners" days.

Situation in 1974

Mr. Smith, in 1974, sold 70 percent of his syrup door-to-door, with the remainder being distributed equally among small grocery stores and restaurants. Exhibit 2–1 shows the packaging of the maple flavored and cane flavored syrup.

In 1974, the Smith Syrup Company sold approximately 1,500 gallons of syrup, resulting in a total revenue of around $5,000. My Syrup So Good was priced competitively, but major brands generally offered both twelve- and twenty-four-ounce containers, while Mr. Smith's syrups were offered in only one size. The company used sixteen-ounce bottles purchased in small quantities from another company that purchased them in large volume for a different product.

Monthly payments on the bank loan cost $315. Assuming an hourly wage of $2.50 for production and bottling, the following figures are estimates of the variable costs for a sixteen-ounce bottle of syrup:

Ingredients	14.4¢
Labor:	
Production	1.7
Bottling	0.5
Packaging Materials:	
Label	0.6
Cap	1.3
Bottle	7.0
Total	25.5¢

To verify consumer statements regarding the superior taste of My Syrup So Good, Mr. Smith hired a local consumer research firm to conduct a taste comparison test between his product and Log Cabin Syrup, the largest selling brand in the area. The results of this study, as presented in Appendix A, indicated an overwhelming preference for My Syrup So Good.

Mr. Smith also reviewed several research articles on why consumers purchase new products or try new brands in order to gain some insights as to how he might increase sales of his products. Some representative results are included in Appendix B.

Focal Topics

1. What alternatives are open to Mr. Smith at this time?
2. Evaluate and discuss the strengths and weaknesses of each of these alternatives.
3. What specific plan of action do you recommend for Mr. Smith?

Exhibit 2–1
Bottles of Maple and Cane Flavored My Syrup So Good

Appendix A
Comparison Taste Test

Purpose

A taste test was run between My Syrup So Good and Log Cabin to determine how the quality, taste appeal, and texture of My Syrup So Good compared with the same characteristics of an established leader in the syrup field.

Procedure

Biscuits were baked, split, and buttered. One half was topped with My Syrup So Good, the other with Log Cabin. Participants were asked to comment on which sample they preferred and why.

Findings

The results were overwhelmingly in favor of My Syrup So Good. Out of twenty-five samples given, only two responses indicated a preference for Log Cabin, and even those preferences were qualified. Both of these stated they preferred Log Cabin taste but preferred My Syrup So Good's thick texture.

The twenty-three favorable respondents preferred My Syrup So Good for a variety of reasons. Its texture was preferred because the thickness lessened the possibility of a soggy biscuit, thus making the primary food (pancakes, waffles, biscuits) more appetizing. The subtle maple flavor and the rich color were also noted.

Conclusions

It was apparent that this syrup combined the three major assets of a good syrup: appealing flavor, texture, and appearance.

Appendix B*
Some Findings from a Progressive Grocer Study

Reasons Why Customers Switch Brands	Percent
Special display and/or store feature	25
Cheaper	21
Just wanted a change	19
Recommended by family/friend	9
Usual brand out of stock	7
Stamps, sample, or coupon	6
Saw or heard it advertised	4
Other reasons	9

Reasons Why Customers Buy New Items	Percent
Special display or store feature	50
Recommendation by family/friend	19
Saw or heard advertised	17
Just wanted a change	5
Cheaper	4
Other reasons	5

*Extracted from "New Items in Action," *Progressive Grocer*, June 1968, p. 54.

Case 3
Spirex Structures, Inc.

Spirex Domes are an effective, economical, and aesthetically satisfying solution to a variety of problems requiring a strong but lightweight dome-shaped structure. These structures have enjoyed an excellent growth rate over the past three years, and management sees a very attractive future for its existing markets of water and sewage treatment plants, as well as possibilities for expansion into other markets.

In order to compete for sales with alternative types of domes on the market, the firm may have to modify its selling and advertising approaches. Many alternative domes are less expensive but of lower quality than Spirex Domes. Nonetheless, some manufacturers are constantly pushing the specifiers (architects, consulting engineers, and so on) to acknowledge that their product is equal in quality.

Product Information

Product Development

The idea for the design of Spirex Domes originated in 1959, when Donald R. Wright, a Dow Chemical Company engineer, was building a snow igloo for his children. Using an inverted trough, which he moved in circles to distribute the snow, he constructed a dome-shaped structure from which the Dow Dome (later the Spirex Dome) was modeled. Extensive development tests carried on by Wright and other Dow engineers showed that by using an 8-inch thickness of Styrofoam[1] bonded by heat, domes up to 90 feet in diameter could be constructed. Later developments, including the addition of reinforced steel wire, allowed for the construction of domes up to 220 feet in diameter. Between 1964 and 1975 over 175 Dow Domes were constructed and sold commercially. Exhibit 3–1 shows a photograph of 27 of these, ranging from 50 to 168 feet in diameter, covering circular structures at a water pollution control plant in Cedar Rapids, Iowa.

In 1975 Dow licensed Spirex Structures to construct domes using this technology and ceased all marketing and construction activities relating to the Dow Dome.

Product Characteristics

The Spirex Dome is a thin shell of reinforced, high-strength, latex-modified cement covering a Styrofoam plastic foam base. These domes are strong enough to withstand high winds and heavy snow loads but light enough to be placed upon most existing foundations. When conditions dictate, Spirex Domes can be constructed in place, with process interruptions at treatment plants measured in days rather than the weeks required for alternative structures. In many cases, Spirex Domes can be constructed near the treatment facility and lifted into place and installed on a circular structure with virtually no process interruption.

The plastic foam possesses extremely effective insulation properties, therefore eliminating the need for hazardous manual deicing techniques usually employed at treatment plants. In addition, Dow Domes are practically maintenance free. There are no moving parts to maintain or replace, and no interior finish is necessary. Since the domes are not affected by moisture, rot, ultraviolet degradation, or corrosion, frequent repainting is not required. Exhibit 3–2 shows some of the structural properties of the domes.

Technique of Construction

The domes are constructed at the customer's location by Spirex's own construction people. Construction begins with the assembly of a steel base tension ring on a site adjacent to the installation site (although in some instances, the domes are constructed in place). A temporary pad of concrete is poured in the center of the ring to support the spinning equipment. The basic form is constructed of Styrofoam

---

[1]Trademark of Dow Chemical Company.

extruded polystyrene foam, utilizing a unique construction process developed by Dow Chemical known as "spiral generation." As the spinning booms move along, as shown in Exhibit 3–3, the operator feeds boards of Styrofoam into the welding machine. The contacting surfaces are heated to the fusion point and pressed together by the weight of the welding machine to form a thermal weld. Steel wires implanted at regular intervals strengthen the structure. With the crane moving at approximately thirty feet per minute, a five-man crew can cover up to seven thousand square feet in a fourteen-hour day.

After each dome is spun, it is lifted by crane onto the existing foundation. The base tension ring is then anchored to the foundation with expansion bolts. Next, openings are cut for doors, windows, and vents, and the frames are set in place. Self-furring, steel reinforcing mesh is then fastened to the dome, and a layer of welded wire fabric reinforcement is placed over that. Additional steel reinforcement is placed near the base region and about openings. Later, layers of a high-bonding, latex-modified concrete are applied to the exterior of each dome to form the structural shell. Some details of typical dome structure are shown in Exhibit 3–4.

Marketing Environment

Market Segments

Today, Spirex Domes are used primarily for covering circular process units at water and sewage treatment plants. In water plants, they provide protective cover for a potable water supply. In sewage treatment plants, they contain odors emanating from various process units. Other equipment then is used to treat the odors and vent the air into the atmosphere. In certain climates, they may also be used to cover sewage treatment facilities in order to control fogging and icing conditions.

Spirex Domes are functional structures for a variety of architectural needs, such as auditoriums, bulk storage facilities, and similar structures, because of the efficiency of Styrofoam in insulating and the integrity of the latex modified shell. Exhibit 3–5 briefly describes some of the varied dome applications.

The Competition

Several other manufacturers produce dome structures, some less expensive than Spirex Domes and some more expensive. Examples of these products include: air-inflated balloon-type structures, glass fiber domes, reinforced concrete domes utilizing conventional construction techniques, steel and aluminum domes built with truss sections and panels, wood domes of similar construction, and geodesic domes utilizing a space frame of aluminum or steel and panels of construction materials such as glass fiber, Plexiglas, aluminum, and steel.

Marketing Strategy

Spirex Domes are currently marketed by company sales personnel technically trained in pollution control and in daily contact with the key influencers of buying decisions (municipalities, consulting engineers, and architects). Sales representatives specializing in pollution control are used on a project-by-project basis on the West Coast, and the company is aggressively pursuing the odor control market, where the needs are relatively well defined.

The architectural market, on the other hand, is vast and very segmented. Each potential application has unique design and functional requirements which demand special engineering and marketing input as the project progresses through the conceptual and design phases. Although challenging, this market is extremely attractive, because an efficient solution to the engineer or architect's problem could mean minimal competition at the bidding stage.

The company uses direct mail programs with personal sales follow-up to market the product, techniques adequate for current production capacity in the sewage and water treatment market, where the requirements are well defined and the buying influences relatively concentrated. They are not adequate, however, for the architectural market, because the number of potential applications is low relative to the vast number of practicing architects and engineers. Spirex is currently evaluating an advertising program for this market which would include key magazine advertising and direct mail programs inviting a response.

Focal Topics

1. What strategies can help Spirex sell Spirex Domes to consulting engineers and architects?
2. What alternative markets for domes are open to Spirex Structures, Inc.?
3. How can Spirex best reach and cultivate these markets?

Exhibit 3-1
Photograph of Installation of Spirex Domes
(Water Pollution Control Plant, Cedar Rapids, Iowa)

Exhibit 3-2
Structural Properties of Spirex Domes

Typical Shell Thickness Selection Table Standard 50° Dome			
Dome Plan Diameter		**LMC Mortar Thickness**	
0-70'		1″	
70-85'		1¼″	
85-100'		1½″	
100-115'		1¾″	
115-130'		2″	
130-140'		2¼″	
140-150'		2½″	
Design Criteria			
Foam Shell		**LMC Shell**	
Dead Load — 2 pcf		Dead Load — 145 pcf (Seldom exceeds 15 psf)	
Construction Live Load — 15 psf (min)		Live Load — Snow — 30 psf Wind — 20 psf (100 mph wind)	
Material Physical Properties			
Material	**Compressive Strength**	**Tensile Strength**	**Elashi Module**
Foam	30 psi	60 psi	2,000 psi
LMC	4,130 psi	790 psi	1,920,000 psi

Exhibit 3–3
"Spiral Generation" Construction of the Dome

Exhibit 3-4
Details of Typical Domes

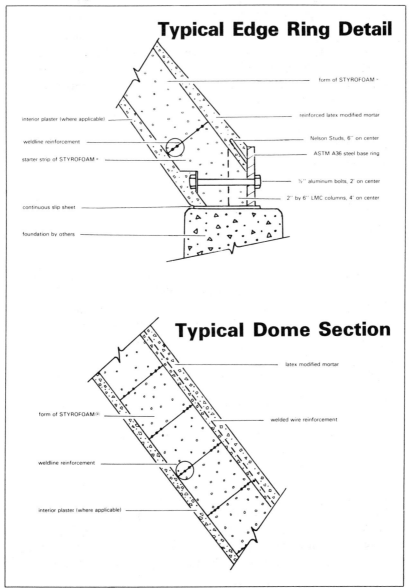

Exhibit 3–5
Some Dome Applications

Sewage Treatment Plant

Two 136-foot, 8-inch diameter domes cover the trickling filter installations for the Chemung County Sewer Authority, located in Elmira, New York. The domes not only play an integral part in the function of the plant but also improve its appearance dramatically. Charles R. Velzy Associates, of White Plains, New York, engineered the project.

Museum

The Neil Armstrong Museum in Wapakoneta, Ohio, contains a 56-foot diameter hemispherical enclosure. The structure is a classic illustration of form following function, as architects Freytag and Freytag (Sidney, Ohio) chose to house the museum's planetarium with a dome.

House

A unique and striking residence in Midland, Michigan, was constructed within a 56-foot hemisphere. Architect Robert E. Schwartz designed the home to provide 5,000 square feet of usable floor space on three cantilevered floor levels.

Medical Clinic

The Women's Medical Clinic in Lafayette, Indiana, consists of seven interconnecting domes, ranging from 26 to 44 feet in diameter. This configuration allows optimum movement of equipment and people, while maintaining the desired privacy. The architect was E. H. Brenner, A.I.A.

Recreation Facility

A recreational and campfire area is enclosed by a 60-foot diameter low profile dome at Camp Nyati, near Farwell, Michigan. The dome is supported by 10-foot columns spaced at 8-foot centers (that is, the columns are spaced 8 feet apart, measuring from center to center). Versatile clear span construction is made possible at a low cost by using a dome.

Case 4

Scioto Company (A)

The Scioto Company manufactures and distributes a rather innovative product called Coloring Rolls. These coloring books in scroll form are 30 feet long when unrolled and are printed the full length without repetition of pictures by means of the firm's unique presses. Coloring Rolls once enjoyed annual sales in excess of 1 million units. In 1972, however, annual sales were only about 200,000 rolls. Management is obviously interested in developing marketing strategy that will return this product's sales to the successful level it once held.

Company Background

The Scioto Company was founded in 1969 through the purchase of the assets of a printing company. The firm manufactures educational devices, such as rapid reading pacers and "teaching machines," and the home game derived from the television show "Concentration." All of these items, however, are marketed by their own firms, and Scioto merely bids on the contracts to produce them. The company is, therefore, quite anxious to increase the sale of its own product, Coloring Rolls, in order to reduce its dependence upon contractual and bid items. Total sales for the company in 1972 amounted to about $250,000, with Coloring Rolls accounting for approximately 20 percent of the total.

Product Information

Coloring Rolls are printed on specially built rotary presses that produce large intermediate rolls 36 inches in diameter. These are then placed on a rewind machine that wraps the Coloring Rolls on a spiral-wound paper core, resulting in a finished roll 10½ inches wide and 30 feet long. The product is then placed by hand into a polyethylene printed bag and packed in cartons for distribution. Exhibit 4–1 shows a promotional piece for distributors featuring the product, packaging, and 1972 prices for rolls purchased directly from Scioto.

Rolls are printed on one side only, and each tells a complete story with no repetitive pictures. The product allows more than one child to color simultaneously on the same roll. The finished product can be displayed as a wall mural in total or in part. A brief description of the nine available rolls is given in Exhibit 4–2. "Noah's Ark" and "Circus" are the best sellers by a wide margin.

Channels of Distribution

Past Methods of Distribution

Coloring Rolls were first marketed by the printing company by means of toy brokers. These brokers, who served as manufacturers' representatives, received a 5 percent commission of sales for their services. Their principal customers were the large chains of variety stores, such as G. C. Murphy, Woolworth, and Kress. Sales were more than a million units per year for the first two years.

Several of the chains carried Coloring Rolls with varying degrees of success. The toy jobbers had little difficulty selling the Coloring Rolls to the purchasing agent of the chain store, but reorders were spotty. Several stores would report a big sale, whereas the majority would never reorder.

The toy broker for the printing company then conducted a survey of some of the stores that were selling the product successfully and compared them to a few that were not. The survey showed that sales were excellent in stores that still had sales clerks who could (or would) explain the product, but the majority of the stores were self-service and the Coloring Rolls just sat in the bins and failed to attract customers' attention, or motivate them to buy. It was concluded that the product was too unusual for the average customer to recognize, and since all the stores were fast converting to self-service, no further attempt was made to promote the product through the toy jobbers.

A few faithful customers continued to buy regular quantities of the product, and two of these, Walter Drake & Son of Colorado and

David C. Cook, religious publisher of Chicago, Illinois, offered Coloring Rolls for sale in their mail-order catalogs. During this time period sales declined to around 40,000 units per year.

Present Method of Distribution

When Scioto assumed manufacture and distribution of the Coloring Rolls, the new company renewed promotional efforts. Noting that the items seemed to sell in catalogs, it made a mailing to all known catalog houses. The response was quite favorable, and a number—notably Breck's, Sunset House, and Spencer Gifts—added the Coloring Rolls to their catalog line. A total of seven mail-order catalogs, with a combined circulation of over 10 million, offered Coloring Rolls.

Each catalog features a photograph or drawing of the product and a short paragraph of copy. Exhibit 4–3 shows the product as featured in the Spencer Gifts catalog. When contracts are signed with the catalog houses, Scioto usually pays an "advertising allowance" of $25 to $50 to cover the cost of photographing the item and including it in the catalog.

The price each catalog house charges depends upon its estimate of the mailing cost for the item, but in every case the price is considerably above the original variety store price. Customers of mail-order houses apparently expect to pay more because of the postage. Sales from these sources amounted to about 140,000 in 1972. The remaining sales were generated by direct orders from retail stores and some unsolicited individual requests from consumers who had evidently previously purchased from catalog houses.

Pricing Information

At an annual volume of 200,000 units, the basic cost of producing a Coloring Roll is around 18.6 cents, about half of which represents allocation of fixed manufacturing costs. An additional average of 2.0 cents per roll is required if Scioto pays shipping expenses.

In reviewing its pricing and distribution strategy, management gathered the following information on the toy industry:

All industries have trade practices that are difficult for the small firm to ignore, and the toy industry is no exception. In determining the price for Coloring Rolls, one of the most important of these practices is the policy of pricing all items in multiples ending in the digit nine (9). For example, a product may be priced at 39 cents or 49 cents for retail sale, but never at, say, 43 cents. Therefore, if a product cannot be made to sell (with all discounts) for 39 cents, it jumps to 49 cents.

The most common discount in the trade is 50 percent off list price. If the suggested price is 49 cents, the retailer pays the manufacturer 24½ cents and earns 24½ cents upon selling the product. If a wholesaler is used he receives approximately 30 percent of the manufacturer's selling price; therefore, it pays the manufacturer to circumvent the wholesaler if possible and go directly to the retailer.

Also of vital importance is the matter of freight allowances which has come to the front in recent years due to the rapidly rising cost of postage and freight rates. Most large buyers expect, even demand, some consideration on freight, and this may take the form of straight cash allowances, usually 5 percent, or a policy of allowing the customer to deduct the freight from the invoice when he pays. Depending upon the mode and distance shipped, this can amount to as much as 15 percent of the selling price.

Last is the cash discount policy that the firm employs. If it is short of cash, a 2 percent discount is usually offered, but with increasing interest rates, many firms have discontinued cash discount policies. Toy purchasers, on the other hand, often insist upon a trade practice known as "datings" where, in return for an early order in slow months, they will not pay for the goods until a later predetermined date.

Focal Topics

1. What channels of distribution would offer the greatest opportunities for the marketing of Coloring Rolls?
2. What type of a pricing strategy should the firm adopt for Coloring Rolls?
3. Are there other segments or marketing opportunities open to this product? How can they best be served?
4. Do you feel that the firm should initiate any marketing research at this time? What type and scope of research should be involved if any is undertaken?

Exhibit 4–1
Promotional Piece for Distributors

Exhibit 4–2
Brief Story Lines for the Product Offering

☐ **Circus Parade**—This story is geared toward the younger children (of Scioto's 4-to-9 market). There are over 200 pictures of circus clowns and animals to color. There is a great deal of free white space on which the child can create.

☐ **Adventures in Space**—This Roll puts the child in the driver's seat of his own space capsule. Each picture is in an individual frame with a sentence describing the scene.

☐ **Daniel Boone**—This Roll tells the story of Daniel Boone from boyhood to manhood. Each picture is in a separately drawn frame with a sentence describing the picture.

☐ **Our American Heritage**—This Roll gives a brief survey of American history from Plymouth Rock to the Sea of Tranquility. Each picture is in a separate frame and has an accompanying explanation.

☐ **Favorite Bible Stories**—This includes pictures of both the Old and New Testaments. Each picture is in a separate frame with a sentence describing the scene. There is an intermittent "connect-the-dots" type picture.

☐ **Adventures of Hattie the Hare**—This Roll is geared toward the younger child. It is a continuous story with occasional frame break. There are no words.

☐ **Around the World with Loco**—This is a story of a trip around the world with Loco, the burro. The pictures and story that go with it are of educational value in that they describe key points of interest like the Taj Mahal in India.

☐ **Headin' West**—This is a continuous picture about the pony express and the problems arising in delivering the mail. There are no words.

☐ **Noah's Ark**—This depicts the story of Noah in separate picture frames with words describing each scene.

Exhibit 4–3
Example of Copy for Coloring Rolls
from the Spencer Gifts Catalog

COLORING BY THE YARD!

COLOR-IN A KING-SIZE 30 FOOT ROLL! Roll out the fun with what could be the world's largest "coloring books!" Keeps a roomful of kiddies happy on rainy days . . . or one pint-size Picasso entertained for weeks! Circus Roll features a merry, seemingly endless circus parade; Noah's Ark Roll tells the ever-fascinating Bible story. Imagine, 360 inches . . . 30 feet of pictures to color-in on each 10" high roll. Get them both & double the fun!
☐ **Circus Color-In Roll** (Z-45963) 79c
☐ **Noah's Ark Color-In Roll** (Z-02105) 79c

Case 5

City National Bank and Trust Company (A)

In the past decade City National Bank and Trust Company (CNB) has built one of the most impressive records of growth and profitability of any bank in the nation. It has accomplished this by aggressive and imaginative programs that serve customers better. Management recognizes that remaining customer oriented will become increasingly challenging as the future brings dramatic shifts in population and income. At the same time, it realizes that the rewards will also be greater for the bank that most effectively develops its consumer offerings.

Background Information

Growth and Profitability

City National Bank has served residents of central Ohio since 1868. As a result of a 1929 consolidation between the City National Bank of Commerce and the Commercial National Bank, City National became the third largest bank in the central Ohio area.

In 1968 CNB applied for and received permission to establish First Banc Group of Ohio, Inc., a registered multibank holding company. By 1978, there were 16 affiliate banks in First Banc Group, with CNB representing almost 45 percent of the total assets. All members of First Banc Group are considered full-service banks, offering a complete line of banking services to their customers.

CNB regularly receives acclaim from banking leaders as one of the most progressive and customer-oriented banks in the United States. Its officers are invited to speak at important conferences and are as frequently quoted in journals and other publications as are officers of banks many times its size.

The bank's profitability has won it equally great acclaim. Since 1960 City National Bank has consistently been among the ten most profitable banks in the nation. In addition, net operating income for First Banc Group increased from about $4.7 million in 1968 to over $22.2 million in 1977. During the same time period, earnings per share increased from $1.61 to $3.52. Exhibit 5–1 provides a financial summary of First Banc Group of Ohio, Inc., for the period 1973 to 1977.

Establishment of Objective

Prior to 1960 City National had been a good, sound bank but had maintained the banking status quo in the community. In 1960, however, a small group of top executives decided to organize the bank in a way that would enable it to become a leader in retail banking in Ohio. The idea was that it become a marketing-oriented bank that would meet the total financial needs of consumers. This group of executives believed that a bank that truly met the needs of its customers could also be a very profitable bank.

The decision to become retail oriented resulted from an analysis of the role CNB played in the community. It was then the smallest of three major commercial banks in Franklin County, with deposits of approximately $100 million in 1960. Although growth had been above average, the future promised to be much the same unless a new force could be introduced in the bank. The executives believed that the new concept of consumer orientation could make City National a driving force in the financial community of central Ohio.

In order to develop the bank into a financial center that would truly serve the needs of the customer and that would further the development of the community, top management leaders were recruited. In 1959, a man respected for his ability to get things done was recruited from outside the bank and elected chairman of the board.

Marketing Program

The chairman first decided that if the bank was to serve the community and consumer, it had to be where the consumer was. City National had seven branches in 1960; by 1978 this number was expanded to 30, with immediate plans for several more. These branches were strategically placed—primarily in the communities surrounding Columbus, having the highest population growth, and in the best traffic positions. Each branch incorporated striking architectural features and had unusually high consumer appeal.

The image of the bank was also affected by a decision of the bank to move into an impressive new twenty-four-story office building in the center of Columbus. On top of the building were large, blue neon signs with the words "City National" visible for many miles in all directions. Research conducted for the bank indicated that many people in Columbus believed that CNB was the city's largest bank, although it was actually the third largest. These people identified CNB with the entire twenty-four-story building, although CNB leased only a few floors. Research also indicated that CNB had the image of a young, progressive, and dynamic bank.

It is also of interest to note that CNB was one of the few banks in the country to have a full-fledged market research department, focusing on image measurement and consumer decision processes as well as the more traditional bank marketing problems of branch analysis and planning.

The chairman's second step was to choose a person to head up an advertising program that would create a distinctive bank image in the eyes of the consumer. The advertising manager, recruited from outside the banking industry, was eventually to become head of a comprehensive marketing department.

Advertising Program

The advertising manager immediately began to develop a marketing program that would (1) develop a specific image for the bank itself aside from the overall banking community, (2) identify specific consumer services that would meet unfulfilled needs, and (3) develop and market the varied services of the bank on a carefully planned, predetermined basis.

The bank's advertising soon came to be recognized as among the most creative and successful of any bank in the nation. In order to develop an image that was personal and distinctive, nationally known personalities were used in the bank's advertising. It also developed continuing campaigns for its services. One of the most successful in bank advertising history was the "Loaningest Bank in Town" campaign. Later research revealed that this campaign not only stimulated loans but also was instrumental in the decision of new residents to open a checking account at CNB. Concurrent with the advertising campaign was an effort to simplify application forms. The bank adopted the slogan, "All you have to do is promise to pay us back."

CNB had been one of the first major banks to aggressively enter the consumer credit field.

The bank's advertising was colorful, artistically advanced through a variety of media. Full-page color ads were frequently inserted into local newspapers, and a heavy television schedule was used. An example of a recent newspaper advertisement is shown in Exhibit 5–2. Exhibit 5–3 is an advertisement for CNB's Honor Bonds.

Implementation of the Marketing Concept

In addition to improving existing banking services and promoting them creatively, CNB executives felt that adoption of the marketing concept called for strong involvement of the marketing department. Marketing could no longer be merely selling or communicating. It should be the *fundamental force in deciding what the bank should offer.* In describing the function of the bank, the President articulated the reasons for the bank's rejection of a narrow concept of banking:

At City National Bank, as we presently see it, our business is much more broadly conceived than the traditional business of banking. We believe our business is to analyze the total needs of individual and corporate consumers relating to the making, possession and expenditure of money or money substitutes and to satisfy all those needs which we are qualified to profitably and legally serve.

He also commented on the role of top management and its relationship to the role of marketing:

The job of top banking executives is developing systems geared to reaching fundamental management objectives. In our modern conception of a bank as a total service and information system, marketing occupies a much different role. It should be the integrating force which interprets the environment to the bank, defines objectives to guide the entire system, and provides guidelines for long-range corporate development.

Offering of New Services

BankAmericard

In 1966 City National Bank senior management initiated a meeting with the Bank of America to determine if they had ever considered franchising their BankAmericard Credit card program (now called VISA) to other banks outside of California. Bank of America had not considered the possibility of franchising but was very interested in pursuing the concept with CNB, and so City National became the first bank in the nation to franchise BankAmericard service. This was a very bold move, since bank credit card acceptance had never been tested outside of California.

Acceptance of BankAmericard in Columbus was excellent, and management quickly realized that plastic card services were going to play a very important role in future customer service. By the end of the second year of operation, over 100,000 customers carried and used the BankAmericard service in the 8,000 merchant outlets in central Ohio. CNB's marketing plan included establishing Bank-Americard as a leading service in all advertising and began to develop other services that could be made accessible to customers through the use of a plastic card.

Line O'Credit

As part of its plan to improve and expand credit card services, CNB developed a service called Line O'Credit, which permitted customers to write their own loans with their checkbooks for whatever purpose the money was needed. When the check reached the bank, it was added to the BankAmericard outstanding balance as a loan. This added value to the BankAmericard account, since it permitted customers to borrow money for short periods without having to call or visit the bank. The program became an instant success.

Entree

Anxious to continue to expand plastic card services for its customers, management worked on a plan to issue a nationally accepted card that would permit customers access to checking account deposits from any outlet honoring the VISA card. The card was called Entree (now called a VISA checking account card), and CNB was again one of the first banks to offer this new service to customers. The Entree card offered a much more convenient way to complete banking transactions. It was issued to multiple-account customers only, and therefore, customers who wanted to get an Entree card had to bring most of their banking business to CNB. Therefore, the program accomplished two objectives. First it provided more convenient service for customers, and as a result it also added profitable customers to the bank.

Expanded Convenience

By 1976 plastic card services had become one of the major ways customers completed transactions through their bank accounts at CNB. Virtually every CNB customer carried one of the bank's cards to access some or all of their bank accounts whether at a merchant outlet, through the bank's automatic banking machines, or even over the teller counter in any of the branch offices.

Management began planning strategy to expand access to CNB accounts in locations other than the traditional branch banking offices. It decided that limited service capabilities in major grocery stores would provide customers with a service benefit. After negotiations, CNB installed electronic banking terminals in all major grocery stores in Columbus. The 125 electronic devices permitted customers to guarantee checks as well as to complete VISA (BankAmericard) transactions. Management viewed this new service as having many benefits. First, it permitted the grocery stores to more readily accept checks from customers since they were guaranteed by CNB. Second, it introduced VISA services into the grocery stores, which did not previously let customers charge groceries. Third, the service proved so successful that other banks' customers asked for cards to access the terminals, a trend which would eventually have market share impact. After the first year of operation, the electronic terminals were processing 300,000 transactions a month.

Honor Bonds

In early 1978 CNB developed and introduced a new certificate of deposit called the Honor Bond. This program was developed after research had shown that customers wanted the benefit of high certificate of deposit interest, but also wanted more flexibility, i.e., to be able to use the money on deposit without government penalty for early redemption of the certificate.

CNB's Honor Bond was developed as a true bearer instrument. Therefore, customers who purchased the Honor Bond could transfer it from one person to another to pay debts or to make purchases. Therefore, the bond had both benefits of high interest and flexibility. In addition, since the bank had no idea who held the bond after purchase (since it could be transferred without notifying the bank) no government 1099 tax forms were issued. Therefore, customers were "honor bound" to report the interest on CNB's new savings certificates, just as they are required to do on all other bearer instruments, including government issues.

The Honor Bond program was another instant success. Banks all over the country either introduced similar programs or had plans to do so when they could be supported by their operations departments. The program caused such interest that the Congress of the United States began to examine the Honor Bond. In addition, the Internal Revenue Service was concerned that people would use the instrument as a means of avoiding taxes. After several weeks of hearings, the Internal Revenue Service decided that even though other bearer instruments were available in the market, the banking industry could be helping people avoid taxes by mass marketing the

Honor Bonds. Therefore, it changed the law, essentially eliminating all benefits of the Honor Bond.

Potential New Services

Banks have traditionally been very conservative and have lacked consumer orientation. However, CNB prided itself on working a lot harder to make banking a little easier for customers. It continued to look at developments taking place in both the financial industry and other areas that might affect the way customers view their relationship with a financial institution. Along those lines they considered several new services described in the following paragraphs.

Gas and Go

In 1977 state law changed to permit customers to pump their own gas in gasoline stations. This was not a new concept, and, in fact, Ohio was one of the last states in the nation to permit self-service in service stations. This change had dramatic effect on the way customers purchased gas for their cars, and after six months under the new law, over 35 percent of all gasoline in the state was pumped by the owner of the car rather than an attendant in the station. It seemed logical that if a customer stopped to buy gas once a week, maybe it would be beneficial to have some type of access to banking services within the gas station complex.

Management began to develop a plan to provide a mini-branch facility right on the gas station lot. This facility was designed to include both one person who could provide all transactions and also one automated teller machine that would provide all routine services on a twenty-four hour a day basis. The bank then negotiated with several major oil companies having stations in Columbus and decided to install two test mini-branches sometime during the last half of 1978.

In-Home Banking

Management also realized that a time would come when customers might like to complete banking transactions right from their homes. This conclusion was based on several major factors. First, it appeared that the home was becoming a more important focal point for all types of activities. This trend was developing because the price of both cars and gasoline was making nonessential travel very expensive. Second, great developments were taking place in microelectronics. Application of these devices was making it possible for customers to communicate directly via their TV sets with a wide range of consumer services, including purchasing, education, and information.

Because Columbus had developed into a major national test city, Warner Communications (a subsidiary of Warner Corporation) decided to install a major two-way cable television system to determine customer reaction to accessing routine services in that manner. This experiment looked like an answer to providing in-home banking services, and CNB management began to consider introducing some types of services in 1979 or 1980.

Focal Topics

1. Evaluate CNB's marketing objectives.
2. Discuss the primary reasons why a consumer chooses a particular bank in preference to a competitor to serve his financial needs.
3. What new services should CNB provide for its customers? Justify your recommendation in terms of maintaining the bank's excellent past profit performance.
4. In what other ways could CNB assist its consumers from a public-service information point of view?

Exhibit 5–1
5-Year Comparisons of Financial Summary of Operating Ratios for
First Banc Group of Ohio, Inc., and Subsidiaries

First Banc Group of Ohio, Inc., and Subsidiaries

Consolidated Financial Summary
Key Operating Ratios

	1977	1976	1975	1974	1973
		(Data based on daily averages)			
Profitability					
Net Operating Earnings To Assets	1.26%	1.21%	1.15%	1.17%	1.20%
Net Operating Earnings To Equity	15.96	15.43	14.31	15.21	15.11
Earnings Efficiency (1)	39.58	39.00	36.89	38.54	40.34
Coverage of Fixed Charges (2)	4.28x	5.34x	4.47x	3.78x	5.71x
Capital Adequacy					
Loans To Deposits	68.09%	63.40%	66.24%	68.38%	68.16%
Equity To Deposits	9.35	9.03	9.36	8.90	9.15
Equity To Assets	7.88	7.83	8.07	7.66	7.94
Long Term Debt To Equity Plus Long Term Debt (3)	23.59	19.88	14.76	16.09	14.56
Imputed Equity Growth Rate	10.43	9.95	9.00	9.76	10.42
Loan Losses and Reserves					
Valuation Reserves To Net Loans	1.05	1.12	1.12	1.11	1.22
Net Charge Offs To Loans	.43	.60	.78	.61	.38
Recoveries To Gross Charge Offs	39.52	33.42	28.40	31.89	36.61
Non-Performing Assets (4) To Loans (3)	.55	.76	.84	.45	N/A
Earnings Coverage of Loan Losses (5)	7.50x	5.31x	4.03x	5.18x	8.59x
Employee Data					
Full-Time Equivalent Staff (3)	2468	2427	2376	2286	2118
Gross (FTE) Revenue Per Employee $(000)	$66.11	$59.91	$55.57	$55.67	$48.87
Net Operating Earnings Per Employee $(000)	9.03	7.95	7.04	6.99	6.89
Miscellaneous					
Effective Tax Rate	16.51%	13.28%	14.04%	22.51%	30.40%
Dividends To Net Income	34.35	35.57	37.28	35.22	31.16
Per Share Data (6)					
Net Operating Earnings	$ 3.54	$ 3.06	$ 2.65	$ 2.54	$ 2.32
Net Income	3.52	3.07	2.66	2.51	2.32
Historic Net Operating Earnings (7)	3.54	3.06	2.65	2.54	2.33
Dividends: Cash (7)	1.21	1.09	.99	.91	.75
Stock	10%		10%		10%
Stockholders' Equity (3)	$23.25	$20.94	$18.79	$17.54	$15.93

NOTES:
(1) Pre tax net (FTE) divided by (net interest margin plus other income)
(2) Excluding interest on deposits
(3) Year end total
(4) Includes non accruing loans, renegotiated loans and other real estate owned
(5) Pre tax net operating earnings plus provisions for loan losses divided by net charge offs
(6) Per share data is based on average number of shares outstanding (6,300,389) after giving effect to pooling and all stock dividends including the 10% stock dividend declared 1/16/78
(7) Not restated for pooling

Exhibit 5-2
Example of Newspaper Advertising

Exhibit 5–3
Newspaper Advertisement for Honor Bonds

CNB helps.

INTRODUCING A NEW WAY TO EARN A HIGH INTEREST RATE.

AND IT'S NOBODY'S BUSINESS BUT YOURS.

The Honor Bond, issued only in "bearer" form — without a customer name, has just been introduced by our bank. It is available in two types — a one-year bond paying 6% annual interest (6.27% when compounded daily) and a four-year bond paying 7.25% annual interest (7.63% when compounded daily). Both will earn interest for up to twelve years.

The Honor Bond can be transferred to anyone.
Since Honor Bonds are "bearer bonds", the only record the bank keeps is the bond serial number and the amount. That means the bond can be transferred from one owner to another — just like cash — without notifying the bank. They can be used as gifts or to pay debts. Upon presentation and surrender of the bond by the bearer, the bank will pay the face amount, along with accumulated interest, during a ten-day redemption period at maturity (annually on one-year bonds and each four-years on four-year bonds). Final maturity occurs at the end of twelve years and the bond earns no additional interest from that time on. Honor Bonds may be cashed anytime at any of our banking offices, subject to federal regulations covering early redemption.*

The Bank will not issue an IRS 1099 form.
Since no name appears on the bond and no customer identification number is required, the Honor Bond you buy is completely anonymous. For that reason, no 1099 tax reporting form can, or will, be issued by the bank. The person holding the bond is honor bound to report the interest received. (Because the bank keeps no records, we recommend you keep your Honor Bonds in a safe deposit box.)

They're easy to buy.
Both types of Honor Bonds can be purchased in one hundred dollar

multiples up to $10,000 per bond with a minimum of $100 for the one-year certificate and $1,000 for the four-year certificate. The two bonds work under slightly different ground rules.

As its name suggests, the one-year bond matures annually. Unless redeemed, it will automatically renew each year and continue to earn interest for a period of twelve years. That means, from the first anniversary of its purchase on through the twelfth, you can redeem it on any anniversary date for the face amount and all interest earned to date. Or you can leave it in the bank and let the interest accumulate. After twelve years, the final maturity date, the bond stops earning interest.

The four-year bond matures in four years. It too, if not redeemed, will automatically renew and continue to

earn interest for two additional four-year periods. By law, the four-year bond can earn a higher rate since it has a longer maturity.
NOTE: The anniversary is determined by the date of original purchase from the bank, **not** when the "bearer" acquires it.

They're as good as gold.
Honor Bonds provide a unique savings opportunity. First of all, the interest rates paid on the two types of Honor Bonds are the highest permitted by law and the interest is compounded daily. The face value of the certificate remains unchanged. You don't have to listen to the radio or read small print in a newspaper to find the asset value of your investment. The interest rate printed on the Honor Bond is positively fixed as far as twelve years into the future. There's no guess work, no questions about future earnings, no changing conditions to consider — the bank will honor the Honor Bond as agreed for the face value plus interest. That's a guaranteed investment. It's even insured by the FDIC like all other bank deposits.

Honor Bonds are another great way to save.
Our bank has nearly a dozen ways to save money, including the regular passbook savings plan and many different Certificates of Deposit. The Honor Bond has special appeal for customers who particularly want the ease of purchase and the total transferability of special certificate for customers who occasionally receive larger sums of money. Elderly customers, particularly, should find the transferability of special appeal. The highest possible interest rate and variable maturities should be helpful to all our customers.

You may wish to purchase multiple certificates in different denominations and maturities. There is no limit on the number of Bonds that can be issued to an individual.

Federal law and regulations prohibit the payment of a time deposit prior to maturity unless three months of interest is forfeited and interest on the amount withdrawn is reduced to the passbook rate.

CNB
City National Bank
Member First Banc Group / Member FDIC

Case 6
Warner & Swasey Company*

The Warner & Swasey Company's unwavering commitment to the future dates back to the very founding of the company, nearly a hundred years ago, and has taken many forms: product research and development; capital expenditures for machinery and equipment, plant expansion, and modernization; the acquisition of additional and diversified operating units; the development and training of management and production personnel; and a corporate advertising program focusing upon the strengths and weaknesses of the United States—its government, businesses, and people.

Corporate Background Information

Company Formation

The Warner & Swasey Company of Cleveland, Ohio, was founded in 1880 by Worcester Warner and Ambrose Swasey. The firm began operation as a machine tool company and continued to produce and market a sophisticated line of machine tools until the end of World War II. At that time, the company launched major programs of acquisition, diversification, and expansion. By 1972 it had five main areas

---

*Modified and updated for inclusion in this text with the permission of Donald W. Scotton, Cleveland State University, author of the original case.

of activity, including: machine tool operations, construction equipment operations, textile machinery operations, other domestic operations, and international operations.

Today, Warner & Swasey products range from machine tools, cutting tools and tool holders to earthmoving machines, textile machines, and electronic equipment and controls manufactured in twenty U.S. and overseas plants, where more than 5,000 men and women build, sell, and service the firm's products. (See Exhibit 6–1.)

Product Offering

Exhibit 6–1 indicates the diversity of the Warner & Swasey operating units. As illustrated in this listing, the company manufactures and distributes a wide range of machine tools and accessories and specialized equipment and machinery for the construction and textile industries. It also maintains supportive operations such as a Research Division, a Sterling Castings Division, and a leasing and customer financing service, the Warner & Swasey Financial Corporation. An expanding International Operations successfully shares in the metalworking machinery and construction equipment markets in other countries.

Financial Performance

In 1972 Warner & Swasey registered sharp upturns in both sales and earnings, marking a turning point in an industry-wide recession that had caused income to decline for three successive years. This improved performance continued into 1973. While 1974 and 1975 also showed increases in sales, earnings declined in both of these years. Net income of more than $10 million (or $2.90 per share) in 1976 represented a 70 percent increase over 1975 earnings before cumulative effect adjustment. This increase was achieved on essentially level sales. The company's total performance for the past five years is shown in Exhibit 6–2.

Selling Operations

Overall corporate philosophy maintains that each area should operate on an individual profit center basis. Therefore, each of the product areas has responsibility for its own sales force and advertising effort.

Warner & Swasey has traditionally marketed its turning machine products directly to the industrial consumer. However, over the past 25 years, as new products have been added, many have been sold through distributors or through a combination of direct and distributor selling.

Corporate Advertising Program

While all divisions and/or subsidiaries plan and execute their individual product advertising programs, the central office has been involved in a corporate advertising program since 1936.

Program Strategy

The program was initiated by Clifford Stilwell, then sales manager. At that time, the machine tool industry was recovering from its most severe depression, in which sales had fallen to as low as 4 percent of capacity. Mr. Stilwell asked the sales force for suggestions as to what the corporate office could do to stimulate sales. They responded that the company should institute an advertising program that would reach the top men in industry.

The company was aware that its product advertising was reaching production executives and those men in the factories that the salesmen contacted. It also knew, however, that the Warner & Swasey story was not reaching the treasurers, vice-presidents, general managers, presidents, directors, or combinations of these people who were passing on appropriations for new machine tools and were often involved in the decision as to which tools to purchase. The strategy then was to develop an advertising program that would make the company and its products known to top management.

Prewar Advertising

The first corporate advertisements were introduced during the middle of 1936 and focused on the economics of modernizing the production plant. A recession in late 1937 and early 1938 necessitated revision of this economics of plant modernization advertising. Still aimed at top executives, the second phase of corporate advertising was designed to instill confidence in the American economic system. The first advertisement in this series, shown in Exhibit 6–3, contained the headline, "The Sun Always Rises."

In an address to the National Industrial Advertisers' Association in Chicago, July 2, 1952, Mr. D. M. Pattison, vice-president in charge of sales, described the campaign: "(It) sets the theme that America is too great, too powerful, too dynamic to sell short; that the wise businessman should not throw in the sponge but should have complete faith that business would rise again, and that he should use the interim to modernize his equipment and so get himself in a stronger low-cost position." Mr. Pattison stated further, "This advertisement caused so much comment that from that day on our campaign has become broader and broader along this and similar lines."

World War II Advertising

At the beginning of World War II, Warner & Swasey had to decide what long-run product direction the company should take. It was clear the firm's reputation was of sufficient stature that the company would sell large volumes of machine tools during the war. It seemed probable, however, that product diversification would be mandatory after the war, since it was quite possible that the firm would sell so many machine tools during the war that there would be virtually no demand for years after the cessation of the war.

Clifford Stilwell felt that the firm must be made known to other industries, such as those using metal turning equipment, and not just to users of machine tools. He knew that Warner & Swasey had a successful advertising program aimed at making the company better known to top executives of a specific industry, so his goal was to modify this program and make the company known to all groups that might possibly do business with it in the future. The theme of this program was to promote unity and appreciation of the American way of life within the country and go about the business of coping with the war. Each of these messages contained a picture and note about the contribution of The Warner & Swasey Company.

Postwar Advertising

By the end of World War II, Warner & Swasey's advertising program had become an American institution, and management elected to continue it. After the war its theme was concerned with perpetuating the American system through analysis of its strengths and weaknesses and suggesting corrective actions. The advertisements were designed to encourage people to be responsible for the continued well-being of the United States. They continued to achieve the primary goal of selling Warner & Swasey products to business executives, and the readership and acceptance of the program gradually extended to other groups.

Current Advertising

In 1977, Warner & Swasey continued to speak out on current issues, problems, and opportunities. Recent advertisements from the corporate advertising program appear in Exhibit 6–4.

Thus far, approximately 1,000 print advertisements have appeared in magazines such as *Time* and *Newsweek* (in which the company has placed a series running for 33 years), *U.S. News and World Report, Dun's Review, Forbes, Business Week,* and the *Wall Street Journal.*

In its first departure from printed advertising, the company used radio in early 1977 for a special six-week campaign promoting free enterprise. The prototype campaign involved nine radio stations in Cleveland, running a total of 222 spots. The editorial-type messages were placed on stations spanning the spectrum of listenership—rock stations, black stations, and others devoted to news, soft music or general programming, both AM and FM.

The spots were scheduled around the clock, based on the desire to reach housewives, college students, inner city residents, waiting room patients, and shift workers, including the firm's own employees. The advertisements were vignettes focusing on ordinary people involved in business situations. Each message concluded with an announcer saying, "Even the worst critics of business use business principles and practices every day. And we'd like you to think about that. We're The Warner & Swasey Company, makers of machinery to improve your life. And we think that what happens to business is your business, too."

The firm is currently evaluating the results of the radio test. It is considering making radio advertising an adjunct to its continuing print campaign in order to reach even farther beyond the business community.

Changing Industrial Environment

In today's rapidly changing environment, Warner & Swasey has found that it is necessary to combine the efforts of the sales force, the product divisions' advertising programs, and the corporate advertising program in order to sell in the competitive markets. This combined marketing effort is the result of the recognition of the significant changes that have occurred during the last decade.

For example, today's purchase decision makers are often younger, better educated, and better trained than their predecessors. While purchases have always been made on the basis of cost and analysis, the current system of analysis has become more comprehensive. Even though the final approval for purchase is still often made at executive levels, many key decisions are made by equipment engineers, who analyze profit potential considering initial cost, integration of machines with all elements of production systems, and maintenance costs. They work closely with the production foreman, who may help determine suitability and the rate of return on investment and is therefore an important influencer in the buying process. Also, past purchase audits are frequently made by users to ascertain how successful the machines are in use and in their contribution to profit.

Evaluation of Advertising Effectiveness

Warner & Swasey evaluates the merit of its corporate advertising program largely on information received from customers and the public at large. For example, some of the items used to measure the success of the program include:

1. Reports from the divisional salesmen and letters received by them from their customers.
2. Direct reports to the corporate office from product users.
3. Up to five thousand letters per year received from ranchers, teachers, students, bankers, persons in government, and so on, which attest to the fact that Warner & Swasey is performing a desired service in promoting the American system, and at the same time is creating favorable attitudes toward the company and its products.

Focal Topics

1. Discuss and evaluate the real objectives of Warner & Swasey's corporate advertising program. Do you think the objectives are being met?
2. What are the roles, responsibilities, and contributions of the decision makers (both as individuals and as a group) who purchase products like those of Warner & Swasey?
3. Evaluate the effectiveness of Warner & Swasey's corporate advertising program.
4. In light of the changing environment of industrial marketing today, would you recommend the continuance of, or any changes in, Warner & Swasey's corporate advertising?

Exhibit 6-1
Warner & Swasey Operations

Machine Tools

Controls Division
Solon, Ohio
  Robert E. Clague
  Division Manager
  *Numerical controls, drives
  and related electronic equipment*

The G. A. Gray Company
Cincinnati, Ohio
  Graham E. Marx
  President and
  General Manager
  *Horizontal boring, vertical turning
  and deep-hole drilling machines*

Grinding Machine Division
Worcester, Massachusetts
  Martin A. German
  General Manager
  Precision grinding machines

Sterling Castings Division
Wellington and Sandusky, Ohio
  William L. Buckingham
  General Manager
  Gray and ductile iron castings

Turning Machine Division
Cleveland, Lima and Solon, Ohio
  Richard D. Erickson
  Group Vice President and
  General Manager
  *NC turning machines
  Single-spindle automatics
  Turret lathes*

Warner & Swasey Turning
Machines Limited
Halifax, England
  Leslie Harkness
  Managing Director
  *NC turning machines
  Single-spindle automatics*

Wiedemann Division
King of Prussia, Pennsylvania
  Richard L. Wirsing
  General Manager
  *Turret punch presses
  Automatic shearing systems*

Construction Equipment

Badger Division
Winona, Minnesota
  David L. Taylor
  Plant Manager
  *Hydraulic backhoes
  Hydraulic cranes*

Gradall Division
New Philadelphia, Ohio
  Calvin W. Hunter
  Vice President and
  General Manager
  Telescoping boom excavators

Warner Swasey (Switzerland) Inc.
Baar, Zug, Switzerland
  Rene Chapuis
  Vice Chairman and
  Managing Director
  *Distribution of construction
  equipment products*

Other Manufacturing Operations

Balas Division
Cleveland, Ohio
  Donald Esarove
  General Manager
  Machine tool accessories

Computer Division
Minneapolis, Minnesota
  Robert R. Moore
  Manager of Operations
  *Microcomputers for general
  industrial control applications*

Manchester Division
Akron, Ohio
  Raymond E. Novkov
  Vice President and
  General Manager
  Metalcutting tools

Midwest Machine & Tool Co.
Brook Park, Ohio
  Andrew A. Hornik
  President
  *Precision contract machining
  and assembly*

The Warner & Swasey Textile
Machine Company
Bessemer City and Gastonia,
    North Carolina and
    Philadelphia, Pennsylvania
  Raymond O. Perrault
  President
  *Worsted, cotton, and synthetic yarn
  preparation machines
  Wire, cord, and rope-twisting
  machines*

Additional Units

Research Division
Solon, Ohio
  John H. Hubbard
  Vice President and
  General Manager
  *Research and development services
  for operating units*

Warner Swasey DISC, Inc.
Eastham, Massachusetts
  Robert L. Groves
  President
  Export agent for domestic products

Warner & Swasey Financial
Corporation
Cleveland, Ohio
  George B. Kozak
  President
  *Leasing and customer
  financing service*

Murata Warner Swasey
Company, Ltd.
Affiliated with Murata
Machinery, Ltd.
Kyoto, Japan
  Junichi Murata
  President
  *Single-spindle automatics
  NC turning machines*

Exhibit 6–2
Five-Year Performance Summary for the Warner & Swasey
Company and Consolidated Subsidiaries

	1977	1976	1975(A)	1974(B)	1973
		(In Thousands Except Per Share Amounts and Shareholder/Employee Totals)			
Operations					
Net sales	$261,613	$251,185	$251,888	$242,921	$212,637
By segment(C):					
Machine tools	165,613	167,592	176,079	148,756	118,163
Construction equipment	69,138	58,140	53,483	67,053	69,511
Other	26,862	25,453	22,326	27,112	24,963
Cost of products sold	167,986	164,962	175,518	162,865	135,346
Interest expense	3,844	4,625	6,947	7,168	4,191
Income before income taxes	18,354	15,974	8,077	12,534	20,273
Income taxes	8,200	6,850	3,050	5,200	9,100
Net income of finance subsidiary . .	1,392	1,090	996	1,019	1,248
Net income	11,546	10,214	7,050	8,353	12,421
Net income applicable to					
common stock	11,450	10,118	6,954	8,257	12,324
Net income per common share. .	3.27	2.90	2.02	2.39	3.52
Cash dividends per share:					
Series A preference stock	5.50	5.50	5.50	5.50	5.50
Common stock.	1.25	1.20	1.20	1.20	1.10
Property, Plant and Equipment					
Gross capital additions	$ 11,103	$ 6,569	$ 7,688	$ 16,146	$ 13,841
Capital additions, net of retirements .	10,270	3,524	5,986	15,530	12,064
Depreciation expense	8,059	7,815	7,734	7,184	6,641
Net investment at year end	65,725	63,514	67,805	69,553	61,208
Financial Position at Year End					
Net working capital	$ 90,939	$ 95,071	$105,781	$ 88,764	$ 77,696
Per common share	26.20	27.06	30.37	25.83	22.39
Long-term debt	38,155	37,394	59,537	49,916	38,597
Shareholders' equity	134,686	128,588	121,968	118,499	114,921
Per common share	38.30	36.11	34.52	33.97	32.61
Other Year End Data					
Common shares outstanding	3,471	3,513	3,483	3,437	3,470
Shareholders	8,083	8,499	9,053	8,853	8,382
Employees	5,305	5,177	5,738	7,016	6,819

(A) *1975 net income includes $1,027,000 or $.30 per share cumulative effect adjustment arising from a revaluation of inventories effective January 1, 1975.*

(B) *In 1974, the Company changed to the LIFO method of inventory valuation.*

(C) *In 1977, the Company restructured its business segments consistent with current disclosure guidelines and 1973-76 data reflect this change.*

Exhibit 6–3
Example of Early Warner & Swasey Advertising,
Appearing May 1938

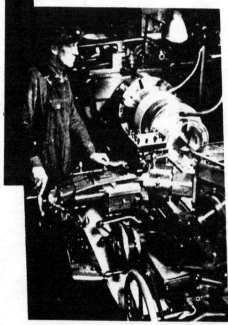

"The Sun Always Rises"

● You and we have lived through many periods like this. They all follow the same pattern:

People get the idea the world is coming to an end. They stop buying. That makes business worse. Then they're sure it's all over. But miraculously the world doesn't end. A few get sensible again and buy a little. Then with a rush everybody wants to buy, and there's a shortage.

If you are one of the sensible executives who knows perfectly well he's going to continue doing business, now is the time to put your plant on a low-cost basis.

Later, when the rush begins, you'll have to wait for deliveries, you won't have time to make sure you're getting the best buy, you'll have a tight production schedule you may hesitate to interrupt. Then you pay a penalty in higher costs and lower profits for years.

Far-sighted concerns are buying improved, faster, more accurate Warner & Swasey Turret Lathes now, and making a profit on them even on today's reduced production. Tomorrow they'll make enormous profits because their costs are low. And tomorrow you'll have to compete with these concerns — and they'll dictate price because they control costs. Isn't it sound to let us discuss with you today, when you have time, a low-cost basis for your plant, too?

WARNER & SWASEY
Turret Lathes
Cleveland

You can turn it better, faster, for less . . . with a Warner & Swasey.

Exhibit 6–4
Current Examples of Warner & Swasey Corporate Advertising

America is 200 years old; Too many Americans act like it.

Timid, weak, too ready for easy compromise—instead of eager, honorable, strong, self-respecting. We're having a birthday because Jefferson, Franklin, Washington and their kind risked their lives, fortunes, futures, and *worked* for that future which we have now. Where are their counterparts today?

This is no huge, sugar-sweet birthday cake which will last forever, although hordes seem to think they have a right to such a childlike life.

The men we have to thank for being here today made *every* decision not on what was best or safest for them and their fortunes and their home states, but on what was the most honorable for the safe future of their country.

When you vote this year, make certain you vote, not for party and not for rhetoric, but for character.

This 4 cubic yard capacity Warner & Swasey 1900 hydraulic excavator is one of 6 working on the Trans-Alaskan pipeline project.

 **THE WARNER & SWASEY COMPANY**
Executive Offices, 11000 Cedar Avenue, Cleveland, Ohio 44106

Productivity equipment and systems in machine tools, textile and construction machinery

Exhibit 6-4 (continued)

Have you ever faced the possibility that your country could cease to exist?

Nations richer and more powerful in their day than we are in this, have been sabotaged, defeated, enslaved

Babylon was the largest and richest nation of its time, but its lust for luxury made it an easy mark for the Medes and Persians who overran it, and divided its land and enslaved people between them.

Rome was a greater military power than we ever were, but when free bread and circuses became more important to the people than hard work and patriotism, Rome was invaded and looted by the tougher Vandals.

The Incas were the most civilized, richest people in the Americas, but ruthless, better-armed invaders destroyed them as a nation, and looted everything they owned and had spent generations in creating.

In every case it was the self-indulgent weakness of the victim which made the victory of the invader easy.

How strong is a nation which allows foreign competitors to capture the world leadership from one after another of its most vital industries?

How wise is a nation which gives away so much of its substance abroad and at home that it can no longer afford to keep up its own strength and protection?

How intelligent is a nation more careful to protect the criminal than his victim?

How *weak* is a nation which allows bureaucracy and a socialist philosophy to run riot and squander billions?

Undoubtedly there were Babylonians, Romans, Incas who warned against overindulgence and weakness, who warned that *each citizen* is responsible for his nation, and that that responsibility cannot be shrugged off onto officials. But to those who warned of impending trouble there was then as now the smug sneer, "It can't happen here."

But it did.

Machine shops produce parts faster and more accurately on this Warner & Swasey SC-15 numerically controlled turret lathe.

THE WARNER & SWASEY COMPANY
Executive Offices: 11000 Cedar Avenue, Cleveland, Ohio 44106

Productivity equipment and systems in machine tools, textile and construction machinery

Exhibit 6–4 (continued)

What's ~~wrong~~ *right* with America

Ours is still the finest and strongest country on earth, and the best place to live and work. Prove it? You bet!

There are still over 86 million jobs here *(more here than ever before)* and they're better than anywhere else on earth. (There would be even more jobs if every one of us worked at his best efficiency, and so cut costs and prices, increasing sales demand.)

We have the competitive system of free enterprise — companies competing to produce a better product at a lower price, which will increase sales and jobs.

We have some statesmen in government who are working their best to cut waste and provide the best government for your tax dollar. (Have you worked as hard for them as they are working for you?)

We have the most generous taxpayers on earth — generous to the needy at home and abroad, even when they get precious little appreciation.

We challenge you to name any other country on earth with that much going for it. *That's* what's right with America, and we're proud to say it *out loud*.

THE WARNER & SWASEY COMPANY
Executive Offices 11000 Cedar Avenue, Cleveland, Ohio 44106

The new Warner & Swasey G-440 Gradall displaying its unique 90° vertical dig feature.

Productivity equipment and systems in machine tools, textile and construction machinery

Part Two
The Changing Environment of Marketing

Case 7
Consumers Hero

JS&A National Sales Group, a direct mail response marketer, has formed a subsidiary called Consumers Hero. In its advertising, Consumers Hero makes a rather unique claim: "We steal from the rich manufacturers and give to the poor consumer." The firm actually purchases damaged or defective merchandise—such as digital watches, television sets, radios, clocks, and other small appliances—from manufacturers, repairs the items, and then sells them as used merchandise at discounted prices to its members. Shortly after its inception, Consumers Hero expanded, allowing affiliate companies to market their closeouts, seconds, and refurbished merchandise to members of Consumers Hero as well.

Formation of the Company

Joseph Sugarman, an electrical engineering graduate who had worked as a CIA agent in Germany, returned to Oak Park, Illinois, in 1965 and started his own advertising agency. In 1971 one of his clients, a direct-mail business, decided not to follow Sugarman's advice on the marketing of pocket electronic calculators. Even the manufacturer did not seem to sense the product's vast sales potential at first.

Sugarman eventually convinced the manufacturer, Craig Corporation, to let him introduce the calculator, and then proceeded to raise money for his own direct-mail campaign. Within ten days and $12,000, a full-color flyer extolling the virtues of the country's first pocket calculator, priced at $239.95, was mailed to 50,000 people. After the price dropped to $179.95, Sugarman sent a second mailing to 1 million general business executives.

When these two mailings yielded a profit for the fledgling company, Sugarman began searching for calculators and other products using the microelectronic integrated circuit—the "brain" of the calculator. Today, the firm is the country's largest single source of electronic space-age products, such as calculators, digital watches, personal communications equipment, home computers and pinball machines.

JS&A's marketing of electronic products created a business problem common to most consumer products manufacturers—what to do with defective merchandise. Rather than taking too large a loss on refurbished, used merchandise, Sugarman and Ted Collins cofounded a subsidiary, Consumers Hero, to assume the function of marketing manufacturers' hard-to-sell merchandise.

The Marketing Approach

For the Consumer

A membership fee of $5 purchases a two-year subscription to the Consumers Hero network, during which time the consumer receives monthly or semi-monthly bulletins describing products available to members. If the consumer chooses not to make any purchases during the membership period, Consumers Hero will refund the $5 membership fee plus 6 percent interest.

When insufficient merchandise is available to fill expected orders, demand is estimated and groups of members are randomly selected by computer and notified of their eligibility to purchase. Product offerings range from microwave ovens to clock radios and stereo sets. Each item is priced 25 to 75 percent lower than regular retail price and, if refurbished, carries a five-year warranty, rather than the usual ninety-day warranty offered consumers.

For the Affiliate

In order to offer its members more merchandise more often, Consumers Hero has organized a group of affiliate companies which prepare bulletins similar to the ones offered by Consumers Hero. Each company is screened to make sure it conforms to the requirements and agrees to the responsibilities as outlined by Consumers Hero in Exhibit 7–1. Consumers Hero gathers all of the affiliates' offers together in monthly or semi-monthly mailings and sends them to its members. Members send their orders directly to the affiliate company, and it in turn ships the product directly to the consumer. Consumers Hero, therefore, merely acts as a distributor of special offers and receives its income from consumer membership fees, affiliate membership fees, and payments made by the affiliate companies for mailing and handling costs.

Initial Consumer Response

An initial advertising campaign to recruit members for Consumers Hero was tested in the *National Observer*. Subsequent advertisements, similar to the one shown in Exhibit 7–2, were placed in ten publications, including the *Wall Street Journal, Popular Electronics, Popular Science* and several airline magazines. This campaign has generated over 15,000 memberships.

The first product mailing offered eight different products to members, including: pocket CBs (retail, $40; member, $20); Lasar digital watches (retail, $150; member, $50); clock radios (retail, $50; member, $20); crock pots (retail, $23; member, $10); television sets (retail, $90; member, $40); and 8-track tape decks (retail, $50; member, $20). This mailing generated over 1000 orders.

In describing its membership to prospective affiliate companies, Consumers Hero offers the following insights:

Who Belongs to the Consumers Hero Membership?

The most concentrated selection of bargain oriented consumers who have expressed an interest in purchasing refurbished merchandise.

Who Do They Represent?

They represent a cross-section of the economy. The membership includes everybody from the very rich to the lower and middle income levels. They include everyone from doctors and clergymen to working women and housewives.

Will They Accept My Offer?

They are open minded to practically any good offer. The most unappealing of any offer is a product that was both used, broken, and repaired. Consumers Hero members are not only willing to take the most unappealing of offers but any bargain that represents true value.

Focal Topics

1. What conditions in our society have led to the formation of a firm like Consumers Hero?

2. What types of consumers would be attracted to such a firm? Be specific in terms of consumer characteristics and purchasing motives.
3. Evaluate other possible ways in which Consumers Hero could attract consumer members.
4. What methods could be used to interest more firms in becoming affiliate members?
5. What other types of activities could Consumers Hero initiate?

Exhibit 7–1
Description of Affiliate Company Membership

I. Eligibility:

To become an affiliate member in the Consumers Hero Program, you must have the following:

A. A product either refurbished, or new that represents from 25% to 75% off the legitimate retail price. Legitimate retail price is defined as the actual price for which the merchandise is sold at retail.

B. A system of fulfillment so you can process and ship orders placed by consumers within five days after receipt of order.

II. Costs:

The various costs of participation are as follows:

A. *Affiliate Fee* An initial fee of $250 will be charged for initiation into the program. This will include the preparation costs for the first product bulletin which will be done initially by the Consumers Hero organization.

B. *Mailing Costs* The inclusion of your bulletin will cost you $50 per thousand names for a four-page 8½ x 11 flyer or smaller unit used with a minimum mailing of 10,000 names.

III. Affiliate Responsibilities:

The following are the responsibilities of each affiliate:

A. The creation of the various offers. As many as 12 items can be offered per four page bulletin or a minimum of one item per single page flyer.

B. The fulfillment of each order within five days. If for some reason this is not possible, then Consumers Hero must be advised of the problem which must be resolved by the affiliate. By law, each affiliate must ship within 30 days after receipt of an order.

C. The prompt handling of all correspondence within five working days of receipt.

D. Compliance with the Federal Trade Commission mail order regulations.

E. The supplying of a list of all customers' names with the products they have purchased to Consumers Hero.

IV. Consumers Hero Responsibilities:

A. Assistance and guidance in the setting up of a mail order fulfillment operation for our participants.

B. Approval of all offers, discounts, and products offered to Consumers Hero customers.

C. Organization and mailing of product bulletins to all Consumers Hero members.

D. The active acquisition of additional members.

E. The "cleaning" of the mailing list to keep it constantly updated.

F. The conducting of regular mailings.

G. The coordination of offers to assure no duplication of effort or competitive offers.

Exhibit 7–2
Example of Initial Advertising

HOT

A new consumer concept lets you buy stolen merchandise if you're willing to take a risk.

We developed an exciting new consumer marketing concept. It's called "stealing." That's right, stealing!

Now if that sounds bad, look at the facts. Consumers are being robbed. Inflation is stealing our purchasing power. Our dollars are shrinking in value. The poor average consumer is plundered, robbed and stepped on.

So the poor consumer tries to strike back. First, he forms consumer groups. He lobbies in Washington. He fights price increases. He looks for value.

So we developed our new concept around value. Our idea was to steal from the rich companies and give to the poor consumer, save our environment and maybe, if we're lucky, make a buck.

A MODERN DAY ROBIN HOOD

To explain our concept, let's take a typical clock radio retailing for $39.95 at a major retailer whose name we better not mention or we'll be sued. It costs the manufacturer $9.72 to make. The manufacturer sells the unit to the retailer for $16.

THE UNCLE HENRY PROBLEM

Let's say that retailer sells the clock radio to your Uncle Henry. Uncle Henry brings it home, turns it on and it doesn't work. So Uncle Henry trudges back to the store to exchange his "lousy rotten" clock radio for a new one that works ("lousy" and "rotten" are Uncle Henry's words).

Now, the defective one goes right back to the manufacturer along with all the other clock radios that didn't work. And if this major retail chain sells 40,000 clock radios with a 5% defective rate, that's 2,000 "lousy rotten" clock radios.

CONSUMERS PROTECTED ALREADY

Consumers are protected against ever seeing these products again because even if the manufacturer repairs them, he can't recycle them as new units. He's got to put a label on the product clearly stating that it is repaired, not new, and if Uncle Henry had his way the label would also say that the product was "lousy" and "rotten."

It's hard enough selling a new clock radio, let alone one that is used. So the manufacturer looks for somebody willing to buy his bad product for a super fantastic price. Like $10. But who wants a clock radio that doesn't work at any price!

ENTER CONSUMERS HERO

We approach the manufacturer and offer to steal that $39.95 radio for $3 per unit. Now think of it. The manufacturer has already spent $9.72 to make it, would have to spend another $5 in labor to fix and repackage it, and still would have to mark the unit as having been previously used. So he would be better off selling it to us for $3, taking a small loss and getting rid of his defective merchandise.

Consumers Hero is now sitting with 2,000 "lousy rotten" clock radios in its warehouse.

Here comes the good part. We take that clock radio, test it, check it and repair it. Then we life test it, clean it up, replace anything that makes the unit look used, put a new label on it and presto—a $39.95 clock radio and it only cost us $3 plus maybe $7 to repair it.

Impossible-to-trace ★ ★ Guarantee ★ ★

We guarantee that our stolen products will look like brand new merchandise without any trace of previous brand identification or ownership.

We take more care in bringing that clock radio to life than the original manufacturer took to make it. We put it through more tests, more fine tuning than any repair service could afford. We get more out of that $10 heap of parts and labor than even the most quality-conscious manufacturer. And we did our bit for ecology by not wasting good raw materials.

NOW THE BEST PART

We offer that product to the consumer for $20—the same product that costs us $3 to steal and $7 to make work. And we make $10 clear profit. But the poor consumer is glad we made our profit because:

1) We provide a better product than the original version.
2) The better product costs one half the retail price.
3) We are nice people.

BUT THERE'S MORE

Because we are so proud of the merchandise we refurbish, we offer a longer warranty. Instead of 90 days (the original warranty), we offer a five year warranty.

So that's our concept. We recycle "lousy rotten" garbage into super new products with five year warranties. We steal from the rich manufacturers and give to the poor consumer. We work hard and make a glorious profit.

To make our concept work, we've organized a private membership of quality and price-conscious consumers and we send bulletins to this membership about the products available in our program.

Items range from micro-wave ovens and TV sets to clock radios, digital watches, and stereo sets. There are home appliances from toasters to electric can openers. Discounts generally range between 40 and 70 percent off the retail price. Each product has a considerably longer warranty than the original one and a two week money-back trial period. If you are not absolutely satisfied, for any reason, return your purchase within two weeks after receipt for a prompt refund.

Many items are in great abundance but when we only have a few of something, we select, at random, a very small number of members for the mailing. A good example was our $39.95 TV set (we had 62 of them) or a $1 AM radio (we had 1257). In short, we try to make it fair for everybody without disappointing a member and returning a check.

EASY TO JOIN

To join our small membership group, simply write your name, address and phone number on a slip of paper and enclose a check or money order for five dollars. Mail it to Consumers Hero, Three JS&A Plaza, Northbrook, Illinois 60062, %Dept. PS.

You'll receive a two year membership, regular bulletins on the products we offer and some surprises we would rather not mention in this advertisement. But what if you never buy from us and your two year membership expires. Fine. Send us just your membership card and we'll fully refund your five dollars plus send you interest on your money.

If the consumer ever had a chance to strike back, it's now. But act quickly. With all this hot merchandise there's sure to be something for you. Join our group and start saving today.

CONSUMERS HERO

JS&A NATIONAL SALES GROUP   Consumers Hero has been made possible by grants from the JS&A National Sales Group.

© Consumers Hero, Inc., 1977

Case 8
Youngs Drug Products

In late 1975, representatives of Youngs Drug Products and groups of other contraceptive manufacturers, planned-parenthood advocates, the clergy, and other interested parties met with the National Association of Broadcasters (NAB) to back a position paper, prepared by them with the aid of the Population Institute of New York, requesting a code change. The NAB turned down the request to allow the advertising of contraceptives on television but did agree to study the proposal.

The Company

Youngs Drug Products manufactures and distributes Trojan brand condoms and a variety of other items through drugstores. The company develops, implements, and establishes specific products that best fit in with a sales force contacting only pharmacies.

The firm distributes its products through wholesale drug houses that in turn sell to registered retail pharmacies. Over 50 percent of Youngs's business is done in this manner, with the remainder of sales going direct to certain large and influential drug chains. Youngs's sales force, in excess of 100 people, contacts the country's 47,000 drugstores with a planned frequency during the year. These salespeople write missionary orders which are turned over to the wholesaler for shipment. Sales of the firm's products are also made through additional sales forces working directly for the drug wholesalers.

The total market for condoms in the United States is estimated at over $150 million. Of the total, about $75 million represents sales through pharmacies, with the rest being marketed through vending machines, mail order, and mass merchandisers. Youngs is generally credited with generating over 50 percent of those sales made through pharmacies.

The Advertising

Youngs originated consumer advertising for condoms in 1969, when the company decided it not only had a quality product to sell but a market that needed to know more about the product, both generically and brand specifically. Mention of the family planning aspects of condoms was not acceptable to most media, so the company decided to promote Trojans for their usefulness in preventing venereal disease. The first advertisements ran in *Sports* magazine with later ones appearing in *Playboy, Family Health, Penthouse, Oui, Psychology Today,* and various other magazines.

After advertisements for male birth control devices were pretty well accepted by magazines, the next logical marketing step seemed to be running television commercials. To that end, two 30-second condom television spots were created and produced for Youngs and Poppe Tyson, the firm's advertising agency, by Trio Productions, Inc. For both commercials, the objective was to develop an institutional message in good taste—"one which would remind the viewer that condoms over the years have had a legitimate and helpful place in family planning." Exhibits 8–1 and 8–2 indicate the audio portions of the commercials along with artist's renditions and verbal descriptions of the video portions.

With about 60 percent of the nation's television stations adhering to the NAB code, it was necessary to ask noncode stations to carry the two commercials. During the last week in July 1975, station KNTV in San Jose, California, agreed to run the commercials. The station first ran the commercials during an early evening movie rerun. The station's switchboard received a great many calls, mostly negative, and the commercials were dropped.

The press, however, picked up the story, making it a news item, and the station decided to rerun one of the commercials as part of its news programming. When viewers' opinions were solicited, the response was about 85 percent in favor of running the television spots. The commercials then went back on the air, this time on a late-hour slot, with little adverse viewer response. Several additional television stations then agreed to run the commercials. Radio commercials, using the audio portion of the television spots, were also accepted by several stations.

The Controversy

Reports that the Code Authority of the NAB was canvassing public opinion on the subject of changing its policy to allow contraceptive advertising on television brought opposition to the change from several fronts, most notably the United States Catholic Conferences (USCC). In a statement calling for an end to television commercials for contraceptives, Bishop James S. Rausch, general secretary of USCC, labeled such advertisements "a gross violation of the rights of parents to guide the moral and social development of their children."

With regard to restricting such advertisements to late evening hours he stated: "There is no acceptable compromise approach to this issue" because "recent studies of viewing habits show that many millions of children watch television after the so-called family viewing period." He added: "It would be unrealistic, unfair, and unacceptable to burden concerned parents with the task of monitoring the home television screen for commercial solicitations on behalf of contraceptives."

Fred Poppe, president of Poppe Tyson, in reply, said that viewer reaction to the Trojan commercials had run about twenty to one in favor of showing such advertisements. He indicated three basic reasons, based on viewer responses, why people support the advertisements.
1. They feel that the commercials should be allowed in deference to freedom of speech.
2. Viewers believe the advertisements are in good taste, often in better taste than other commercials and even the programs being offered.
3. They feel that with abortions and unwanted pregnancies becoming growing problems, people should be told about contraceptives.

Recent Developments

Youngs has not taken an aggressive stance in attempting to get its television advertising on the air. In fact, John C. MacFarlane, president of Youngs, has stated that the firm has decided: "There is no sense in fighting city hall. And we feel there are other ways to spend our money, especially since television has become so high priced."

Much of the firm's advertising in recent years has been placed in men's magazines like *Playboy* and *Penthouse*. Advertising copy for Youngs and rival brands has become increasingly competitive in men's magazines, stressing romance, sensitivity, and enjoyment for both partners.

Youngs has asked its advertising agency to write a softer campaign suitable for women's, family, and news magazines. Some of Trojan's family planning advertisements have appeared in *Ladies Home Journal*, *Redbook*, and *Parent's Magazine*.

As part of its overall communications program the firm distributes a variety of public service informational brochures. Covers from some recent brochures are given in Exhibit 8–3.

In early 1977 the television board of the National Association of Broadcasters agreed to talk about development of a test campaign for contraceptive spot advertisements using the theme "responsible parenthood." Code officials indicated, however, that any actual on-the-air test of such an advertising campaign is still a long way off.

The board also decided not to reveal the results of its poll of 200 national organizations, designed to measure public reaction to contraceptive commercials. The board indicated that not every organization responded directly to the issue and that there was no landslide either for or against the television advertisements among those groups that did comment on the idea.

Focal Topics

1. In your objective opinion, should advertising for contraceptives be allowed on television? Why or why not?
2. Should advertising themes for contraceptives focus on family planning, medical considerations, or other types of messages? Should such themes be aimed at females, males, or both?
3. What types of research do you think the National Association of Broadcasters should undertake to help it in deciding about the issue of contraceptive advertisements on television and radio?
4. What specific recommendations would you make to Youngs Drug? Support your recommendations with a rationale.

Exhibit 8–1
"Young Couple" 30-Second Spot Television Commercial for
Youngs Drug Trojans

AUDIO
Voice over: (Man)

To everything there is a season. And a time to every purpose under the heaven.
   . . . a time to weep.
   . . . a time to laugh.
   . . . a time to mourn
   . . . and a time to dance.[a]
The makers of Trojans Condoms believe there is a time for children. The right
time. When they are wanted. And Trojans have helped people for over half a
century safely practice responsible parenthood.

VIDEO

Young boy and girl running along the beach. We use slow motion, soft dissolves,
facial closeups to establish a graphic poetic mood. Music over voices through to
end when logo appears.

[a]*Quotation from Ecclesiastes III.*

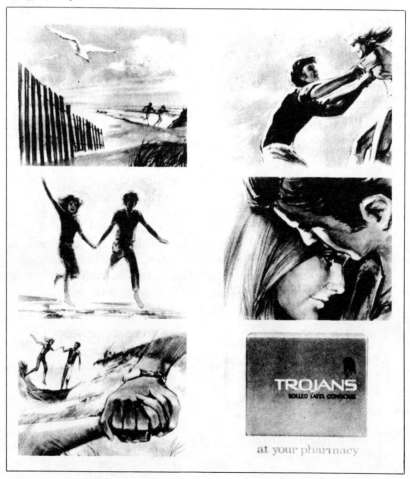

Exhibit 8–2
"Cradle" 30-Second Spot Television Commercial for
Youngs Drug Trojans

AUDIO
Voice over: (Tenderly)

People today know the importance of responsible parenthood.... So they plan.
Carefully. Thoughtfully. And with a great deal of love.

There is a time for having children. And when that time comes, nothing is
more joyous.

The makers of Trojans condoms have been helping people for over half a
century safely practice responsible parenthood.

VIDEO

Open Tight on wooden pieces being glued and assembled. Soft lighting. Through
a series of soft dissolves, we reveal that a cradle is being built by hand; we never
see the person who is building it. Only the hands. Finally, we see a hand polishing
one of the cradle rungs, then widen to see the cradle. A hand touches it and it
begins to rock back and forth. Soft guitar instrumental over voice.

To logo.

at your pharmacy

Exhibit 8–3
Examples of Covers from Informational Brochures

Case 9

20/20 Contact Lens Service (A)

In an interview, Dr. Joseph S. Serian, president of 20/20 Contact Lens Service, stated:

As an optometrist, I saw many patients who couldn't afford to replace damaged or lost contacts. As a result, many people were wearing only one lens, or reverting to their old, unwanted glasses. I knew that the real expense was in the eye examination and fitting the first pair of lenses. Since there was *no medical reason* why replacements should be so expensive, I felt I could offer them for a very moderate cost.

This philosophy led to the formation of 20/20 Contact Lens Service, a nationwide mail order business designed to offer replacement contact lenses at advertised low prices. 20/20 does not intend to replace the personal eye doctor; in fact, it encourages its customers to see their local eye doctors regularly. As many contact lens wearers realize, however, it is not always necessary to see an eye doctor to replace or order a spare pair of contact lenses. Basing price on laboratory and handling costs only, 20/20 is able to provide replacement lenses and spare pairs at significantly lower prices than those typically charged by eye doctors.

The Changing Environment

As of 1976 a variety of factors were influencing the market for all types of products and services. Individual consumers were demanding more information to assist them in making purchasing decisions. Fair trade laws had been removed, allowing retailers to set their own prices for all goods sold. The Supreme Court had rendered a decision concerning prescription drug prices. In the words of the Court: "The particular consumer's interest in the free flow of commercial information may be as keen if not keener by far than his interest in the day's most urgent political debate." For the first time, prescription drug prices could be widely advertised.

The Justice Department had recently filed suit against various bar associations which restricted advertising in the legal profession. Attorneys were limited in terms of what they could communicate to consumers about services and prices. The Justice Department wanted the restrictions eliminated so that the consumer might receive more information and thus, presumably, be able to choose a lawyer and desired services more efficiently.

In addition, the Federal Trade Commission was conducting hearings as part of its investigation of the entire field of optometric services. It seemed likely that the results of the hearings would lead to rulings concerning advertising and the right of consumers to have possession of their optical prescription.

Formation of 20/20

Against this backdrop of a changing, more consumer-oriented business environment, Dr. Serian brought together several other interested parties and formed 20/20 Contact Lens Service. The basic objective was to be the first nationwide, mail-order firm to offer replacement and spare contact lenses at inexpensive prices. Management of 20/20 reasoned as follows:

After the Federal Trade Commission's ruling is enacted, optical prescriptions will have to be released by the doctor for no additional charge. Advertising will also be completely legalized by the ruling. It is felt that the consumer must be educated as to the pricing and quality of goods and services in the optical field. This will have a dramatic effect in changing the consumer's buying habits. They will then have the complete alternative of purchasing their eyewear needs through the optician or retail outlet of their choice. This can be directly related to the development of drug stores which gradually replaced the doctor as a major dispenser of medicine. This change in buying habits took place in the medical profession and will take place in the optical profession.

The specific product and service offering of 20/20 is contained in the fact sheet on contact lenses presented as Exhibit 9-1.

Initial Marketing Efforts

As its first advertising vehicle, 20/20 selected *Cosmopolitan* magazine to reach the primary users of contact lenses—young women. A full-page, four-color advertisement ran in the April 1976 issue, with a guaranteed circulation of 2,095,000. Creative strategy emphasized price and color tints that go with fashion clothing.

Within one week after the issue reached readers, 20/20 had received over 6,000 inquiries via its national toll-free telephone number and 550 sales orders. Exhibit 9–2 shows the outside and inside of a four color brochure about 20/20 sent to individuals requesting additional information about the firm. By the end of two months, the firm had received in excess of 10,000 inquiries and over 2,000 orders.

Future Plans

Based upon the success of the initial advertisement, 20/20 began to plan an expanded media program for August and September. The specifics of this plan are shown in Exhibit 9–3. The firm had not decided what creative strategy to use in the broadened print schedule. Exhibit 9–4 shows one proposed advertisement which focuses on the replacement aspects of 20/20's product and service offering. A second advertisement, shown in Exhibit 9–5, emphasizes the spare pair theme.

20/20 hoped to be able to expand its media schedule even farther in later months to pick up a wider spectrum of women's magazines. The firm was also trying to decide if it should move into men's magazines and attempt to reach young males between the ages of sixteen and thirty-five.

Focal Topics

1. What potential problems do you see in the marketing strategy being pursued by 20/20?
2. What recommendations would you make to 20/20? Be specific in terms of:
   a. market segments
   b. channels of distribution
   c. media strategy
   d. advertising themes
   e. market research

Exhibit 9–1
Contact Lens Fact Sheet

I Wear Contact Lenses ... What Can 20/20 Do for Me?
20/20 Contact Lens Service provides contact lenses identical in quality and fit to the ones you now have at a fraction of the cost you are now paying. Hard lenses for $19.95 EACH (39.90 per pair) in any of our 31 fashion tints, including clear. For soft lens wearers 20/20 offers both the Bausch & Lomb Soflens®, polymacon (61.4% poly (2-hydroxyethyl methacrylate) 38.6% water) and the Hydrocurve® (hefilon-A) poly (2-hydroxyethyl methacrylate) soft lens for only $49.95 EACH ($99.90 per pair).Soft lenses are available in clear only.

How Do I Know They Will Fit the Same?
Think of 20/20 as your contact lens pharmacy. We call your doctor, get your prescription and duplicate your lenses exactly to your doctor's specifications. To insure exactly the same fit we use your current contact lens prescription, the record that your eye doctor would use to reorder your contact lenses. Our lab inspects them, then we re-inspect them just like your doctor would do. Our quality control procedures exceed all government, industry and professional standards and are backed by a 100% moneyback guarantee.

What About the Quality of the Materials You Use to Make My Contact Lenses?
20/20's lab is one of the largest contact lens laboratories in the country. For hard lenses, 20/20 uses the same type and quality material that your doctor uses— polymethyl methacrylate, the standard hard lens material used today by labs and doctors all over the country. For soft lenses we offer the Soflens®, polymacon (61.4% poly (2-hydroxyethyl methacrylate) 38.6% water) made for us by Bausch & Lomb which produces most of the soft lenses in the United States. 20/20 also offers the Hydrocurve® (hefilon-A) poly (2-hydroxyethyl methacrylate) soft lens made by Hydrocurve Soft Lenses, Inc. Bausch & Lomb and Hydrocurve standards exceed all FDA requirements and all professional guidelines. So hard or soft, you get lenses duplicated exactly to your doctor's specifications.

How Can 20/20 Sell Contact Lenses at Such a Low Cost?
Most of the expense of contacts should go to pay for your doctor's time for initial examination and fitting. Since none of this is necessary to replace a lost or damaged lens, or to add a spare pair for fashion (or just peace of mind), you shouldn't have to pay a high price. Now you have a

choice. It's your prescription and it's your right to have it filled where you choose.

How Long Will It Take to Get My Contacts through 20/20?
20/20 will send your lenses to you within two weeks from the time we receive your prescription. They are sent via first class mail, just as your doctor would receive them from the lab. This saves you a lot of time and an expensive visit to your eye doctor's office.

Can 20/20 Fit Me for Contact Lenses?
No ... only your eye doctor can do that. 20/20's purpose is not to replace your eye doctor. Your eye doctor must make the initial examination and prescribe your lenses. In fact, think of 20/20 as a contact lens pharmacy, a personalized service which duplicates your contact lens prescription exactly to your doctor's specifications.

Should I Get Re-Examined Before I Order from 20/20?
No, since your contact lenses are made of plastic and may be showing a little age by being scratched or warped, you might do what many contact lens wearers are doing; The perfect way to take care of this warping or scratching is to get a new pair of contact lenses. They will be made from your eye doctor's prescription. Very rarely will your eye doctor change your contact lenses prescription, but if he should, 20/20 agrees to change any hard contact lens prescription that was purchased from 20/20 at no charge within the first six months, if for any reason your eye doctor makes a change in your prescription other than tint.

Through 20/20 Can I Switch from Hard to Soft Lenses or Vice Versa?
No ... your eye doctor must prescribe both hard and soft lenses individually. Once you have been fitted for hard or soft lenses then 20/20 can take this prescription and duplicate or fill it for you at a fraction of the original cost.

Are My Old, Damaged Bausch & Lomb Soflens® or Hydrocurve Lenses Worth Anything?
Yes they are. As an added service, 20/20 will purchase from you defective or otherwise unusable Bausch & Lomb Soflenses®, polymacon (61.4% poly (2-hydroxethyl methacrylate) 38.6% water) or Hydrocurve (hefilon-A) poly (2-hydroxyethyl methacrylate) lenses. Send your old, unusable soft lenses along with your order and we will deduct $5.00 per returned lens from the purchase price of your

new lenses. In addition to the lenses, we must have the approximate date you received them.

If I Order Hard Lenses from One of 20/20's 31 Fashion Tints, Will They Change the Color of My Eyes?
Any of our 31 fashion tints (except clear) will accent or change your natural eye color. Of course, the fashion tints will have a more dramatic effect in altering the appearance of an eye with lighter natural color, but now at last fashion tints are inexpensive enough to indulge your fancy a little without upsetting your budget. Totally coordinate your dress or mood.

Is It Necessary to Carry Contact Lens Insurance?
Think of 20/20 as an alternative to expensive contact lens insurance. In many cases 20/20's prices for lens replacement are less than the deductible cost you would pay if you lost a lens and with 20/20 there is no premium. You pay only when you actually need a new lens. Many of our customers have in fact elected not to carry insurance. Now, at last, you have a choice.

What Care Should Be Taken When Wearing Contact Lenses?
We at 20/20 encourage you to take excellent care of your eyes. As you are already contact lens wearers, your eye doctor has prescribed your lenses to enhance your vision. Your eye doctor has already instructed you on the correct and proper method of wearing, storing, and hygienic cleaning. We would like to stress that contact lenses should not be worn while sleeping, swimming or in the presence of irritating vapors. Care should be taken to avoid exposing lenses to substances such as cosmetics, lotions, soaps and hair sprays. Your eye professional is always ready to assist you with your vision needs and answer any questions concerning contact lenses or eye glasses. Consult him immediately if you ever encounter any abnormal eye condition such as irritation. We at 20/20 believe everyone should have a professional eye examination semi-annually to protect the priceless miracle of sight.

How Can I Order Lenses From 20/20?
It's easy ... just call toll-free 1-800-848-7573—(in Ohio call 1-800-282-7510) or fill in the enclosed order blank and mail it to 20/20 Contact Lens Service. Enclose with your order blank your hard or soft contact lens prescription and payment (check, money order or bank charge account number). If you don't have your contact lens prescription, call us toll-free and we will arrange to obtain it from your eye doctor.

Exhibit 9–2a
Outside of Informational Brochure about 20/20

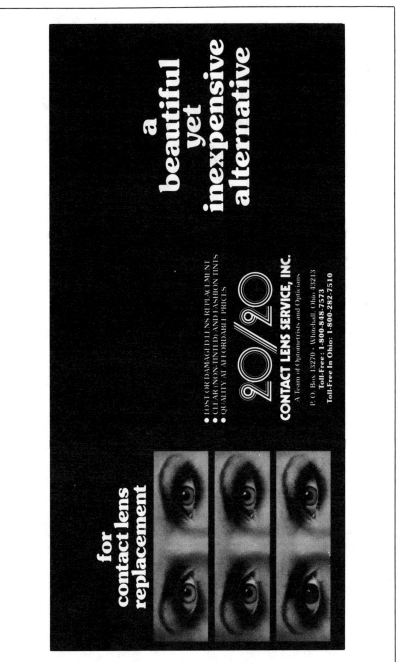

Exhibit 9–2b
Inside Left Panel of 20/20 Brochure

"I want to tell you about a practical, quick new way to replace lost or damaged contact lenses or build a wardrobe of fashionable tinted lenses . . . 20/20 Contact Lens Service, Inc. Its purpose is to provide replacement and duplicate lenses . . . clear or tinted . . . at a fraction of the cost you normally would pay . . . and your lenses are delivered to your door within 10 days. This service is in no way intended to take the place of your present eye doctor. In fact, I personally recommend that you see your own doctor at least once a year. 20/20 is here to fulfill a specific need . . . to make replacement lenses and fashion tints available at an extremely reasonable price!"

Dr. Joseph Serian is a Columbus, Ohio, Optometrist, Optician and Director of the 20/20 Contact Lens Service. The concept of a replacement lens service, offering the highest quality of lenses at affordable prices, began with Dr. Serian's own practice.

Dr. Serian found that many of his patients were doing without their contacts because they could not afford to replace damaged or lost lenses. Dr. Serian realized that the greatest expense involved was his time to examine, fit and adapt the initial set. So he started providing replacement lenses and fashion tints — duplicates of the original prescription — at very reasonable prices based on material and laboratory costs alone. As a result, Dr. Serian's practice has expanded throughout Ohio and beyond. Now as Director of 20/20 Contact Lens Service, he is making quality, low-cost replacement lenses and fashion tints available to contact wearers all over the country.

you pay only $19.95 per lens for hard lenses, $49.95 per lens for Bausch & Lomb Soflens®.

Exhibit 9-2c
Inside Center Panel of 20/20 Brochure

You'll save a lot of money. Only $19.95 for hard lenses, $49.95 for Bausch & Lomb Soflens ′, and all you have to do is send us your contact lens prescription; or if you prefer, call Toll Free 1-800-848-7573 (1-800-282-7510 in Ohio), and we will contact your doctor and obtain the necessary information.

We feel you shouldn't have to pay a premium for good vision; nor for a more attractive appearance. You've already paid the largest single expense involved with contacts — your doctor's time to examine, fit and adapt the initial set. So now 20/20 can take your current hard or soft lens prescription and duplicate it exactly to your doctor's specifications . . . at a fraction of the original cost. Our precise 15-point quality control program guarantees perfect duplication of your prescription. Our laboratory standards exceed all FDA (Federal Food and Drug Administration) requirements and are equal or superior to all professional guidelines.

we use exactly the same materials your own eye doctor uses. and we guarantee 100% money back — that your new lenses will be duplicated exactly to your doctor's specifications.

For hard lenses, 20/20 uses the same type and quality of material that your doctor uses — polymethyl methacrylate. It's the standard hard lens material used today by labs and doctors all over the country. For soft lenses, we exclusively use the Soflens ′, made for us by Bausch & Lomb. So, hard, or soft, you get lenses duplicated exactly to your doctor's specifications. We guarantee it! Your new lenses from 20/20 will be delivered to you via first-class mail, as any pair of contacts would be shipped.

you might also think of 20/20 as an alternative to expensive contact lens insurance.

In many cases 20/20 prices for lens replacement are less than the deductible cost you would pay if you lost a lens. And with 20/20 there is no premium. You pay only when you actually need a new lens. Many of our customers have, in fact, elected not to carry insurance. Now, at last, you have a choice.

buy several pairs in clear or fashion tints for less than you'd normally pay for one pair.

20/20 offers clear hard lenses in addition to 30 fashion tints, which are available at no extra cost. Still just $19.95 per lens. So you can buy several pairs in different color tints for less than you'd normally pay for just one pair. And what opportunity have you had in the past to change the color of your eyes to match your dress or mood . . . a new direction in total fashion. Use any of our 31 fashion tints of hard lenses to accent or change your eye color. Of course, a fashion tint will have a less dramatic effect in altering the appearance of an eye with darker natural color. But now, at last, fashion tints are inexpensive enough to indulge your fancy a little without upsetting your budget. You can totally coordinate your dress . . . and mood.

Choose from any of our 31 fashion tints.

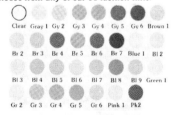

Exhibit 9–2d
Inside Right Panel of 20/20 Brochure

as an added service 20/20 will purchase from you defective or otherwise unusable Bausch & Lomb Soflens®. $5.00 each, applied to the cost of your order.

Send your old unusable Soflens® along with your order, and we'll deduct $5.00 per returned lens from the purchase price of your new lenses. In addition to your Soflens®: we must have the approximate date you received them. So that's what 20/20 Contact Lens Service can do for you. Provide attractive tinted or clear lenses — or replace lost or damaged ones — identical in quality and fit to the ones you now have. And at a fraction of the normal cost.

To order, simply call toll-free or fill in the order blank and send it with your hard or soft contact lens prescription and payment (check, money order or bank charge card account number). If you don't have the prescription, call us toll-free, and we will arrange to obtain it from your doctor. You'll receive your new lenses via first-class mail within 10 days from the time we receive your prescription.

20/20 CONTACT LENS SERVICE, INC.
A Team of Optometrists and Opticians
TOLL-FREE   1-800-848-7573

TOLL-FREE In Ohio: 1-800-282-7510

- -

NAME_____   EYE DOCTOR'S NAME _____

ADDRESS _____   ADDRESS _____

_____   BUSINESS PHONE NUMBER _____

PHONE NUMBER _____   MY NAME WHEN I WAS FITTED _____
                                        (If marital status changed)

SIGNATURE_____   DATE WHEN I WAS FITTED (approx.) _____

Please order my hard lenses in the following shades:

Clear   Gray 1   Gy 2   Gy 3   Gy 4   Gy 5   Gy 6   Brown 1   Br 2   Br 3   Br 4   Br 5   Br 6   Br 7   Blue 1
Bl 2   Bl 3   Bl 4   Bl 5   Bl 6   Bl 7   Bl 8   Bl 9   Green 1   Gr 2   Gr 3   Gr 4   Gr 5   Gr 6   Pink 1   Pk 2

ATTACH HARD OR SOFT LENS SPECIFICATIONS

Order for me _____ hard lens(lenses) @ $19.95 per lens. = _____.

Order for me _____ soft lens(lenses) @ $49.95 per lens. = _____.

I HAVE ENCLOSED THE FOLLOWING: (please check)

Check in the amount of $_____ (Allow 5 additional days for check processing).

Make checks or Money Orders payable to 20/20 CONTACT LENS SERVICE, INC.

Money Order in the amount of $_____

BankAmericard # _____Expiration Date _____

Master Charge # _____Expiration Date _____

C.O.D._____ All C.O.D. orders, add additional $3.50 for handling and C.O.D. charges.

MAIL TO: 20/20 CONTACT LENS SERVICE, INC.
P.O. BOX 13270 • Whitehall, Ohio 43213

Exhibit 9–3
Media Plans for August and September

August media schedule:		
Cosmopolitan	4-color full page ad	2,095,000 circulation
Playgirl	4-color full page ad	1,042,000 circulation
Playgirl/Forum	Inside cover	250,000 circulation
	Total	3,387,000 circulation
September media schedule:		
Cosmopolitan		2,095,000 circulation
Brides		308,000 circulation
Seventeen		1,521,000 circulation
New Dawn		600,000 circulation
Redbook		4,562,000 circulation
Playgirl		1,042,000 circulation
Viva		508,000 circulation
Campus newspapers (40 major college campuses)		1,200,000 circulation
	Total	11,836,000 circulation

Exhibit 9–4
Proposed Print Advertisement for 20/20
(Replacement Pair Theme)

I LOST MY CONTACT LENS!

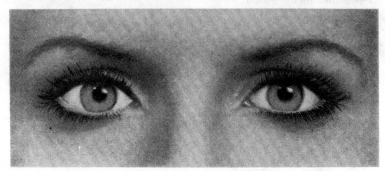

"LESS THAN 10 DAYS AND $20.00 LATER MY GUARANTEED REPLACEMENT ARRIVED."

A UNIQUE NEW SERVICE

There is only one place in the world where contact lens wearers can get this kind of service . . . 20/20 Contact Lens Service. Just call **TOLL FREE** to replace lost or damaged lenses quickly and inexpensively. Hard lenses for **$19.95 EACH** ($39.90 per pair). For soft lens wearers we offer the Bausch & Lomb Soflens® (polymacon) exclusively for **$49.95 EACH** ($99.90 per pair). Hard lenses are available in any of our 31 fashion tints (including clear) at no extra cost. (Sorry, soft lenses are available in clear only).

31 FASHION TINTS

31 fashion shades

OUR PHILOSOPHY . . . YOUR CHOICE

Our philosophy is not to take the place of your eye doctor, but to provide replacement lenses at a fraction of the cost you have been paying. It's just as though we were a contact lens pharmacy and you have chosen us to fill your doctor's contact lens prescription. It's your prescription and **IT'S YOUR RIGHT** to have it filled where you choose. We believe that contact lens wearers should enjoy contact lens beauty and convenience without the worry of unnecessarily high replacement costs. Many people think of 20/20 as an alternative to expensive contact lens insurance.

QUALITY SERVICE . . . FULLY GUARANTEED

Your lens prescription is duplicated exactly, using the specifications provided by your doctor. Our lab serves thousands of eye doctors across the country and uses exactly the same materials used by your doctor. Since we use your current hard or soft lens prescription, you save examination and fitting costs and pay only for the lenses. You receive your lenses just as

your doctor would . . . by First Class Mail . . . within 10 days of the receipt of your prescription. Our lenses exceed all government, laboratory and professional standards and guidelines and are backed by a **100% MONEY-BACK GUARANTEE.** It won't cost you a thing for our consumer brochure — but not having one might be very costly the next time you need a replacement or want to add another fashion tint to your wardrobe.

For a Free Full-color Brochure or to order, call

TOLL FREE 1-800-848-7573 or in Ohio call **1-800-282-7510. We are open 7 days a week 9 a.m. to 9 p.m. (E.D.T.)** or write: **20/20 Contact Lens Service, Inc.** P.O. Box 13270 Whitehall, Ohio 43213.

CONTACT LENS SERVICE, INC. "A Team of Optometrists & Opticians" **Member Better Vision Institute** BankAmericard & Master Charge Accepted Offer void where prohibited by law.

Exhibit 9–5
Proposed Print Advertisement for 20/20 (Spare Pair Theme)

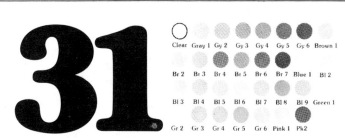

beautiful ways contact lens wearers can choose a spare pair to dress up your eyes!

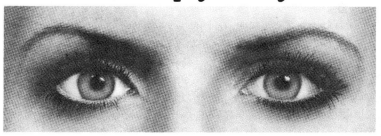

1-800-848-7573 (toll-free) and $39.90 can give you your choice!

It's easy, just call TOLL FREE and 20/20 will contact your eye doctor, get your prescription and duplicate your lenses.

At 20/20 you pay only $19.95 per lens for hard lenses and $49.95 per lens for Bausch & Lomb Soflens® (Polymacon). (Soft lenses available in clear only).

We use exactly the same materials used by your doctor and we guarantee 100% money back that your lenses will be duplicated exactly to his prescription.

Think of 20/20 as a contact lens pharmacy. It's your prescription and your right to have it filled wherever you choose.

There is only one place in the world where contact lens wearers can get this kind of service . . . 20/20 Contact Lens Service.

For a Free Full-color brochure or to order just call:

TOLL FREE 1-800-848-7573
or in Ohio call: 1-800-282-7510. We are open 7 days a week 9 a.m. to 9 p.m. (EDT) or write: 20/20 Contact Lens Service, Inc. P.O. Box 13270, Whitehall, Ohio 43213

CONTACT LENS SERVICE, INC.
"A Team of Optometrists & Opticians"
DR. JOSEPH S. SERIAN,
Optometrist-Director
Member Better Vision Institute
BankAmericard & Master Charge Accepted
Offer void where prohibited by law.

Case 10

Standard Oil Company of California

On January 9, 1970, the Standard Oil Company of California began marketing its Chevron gasoline with a new patented gasoline additive—Formula F-310.[1] According to the company, this additive was designed to remove and prevent harmful deposit buildup on critical engine parts, particularly in areas such as the carburetor and the PCV valve, and to contribute effectively toward cleaner air by reducing exhaust emissions from dirty engines. In its advertising Standard presented F-310 as a significant step toward solving one of today's major problems, namely, the reduction of exhaust emissions that waste gasoline and add to air pollution. In a formal complaint issued on January 11, 1971, the Federal Trade Commission (FTC) accused the Standard Oil Company of making false and misleading advertising claims for Chevron gasolines with F-310.

Standard Oil Research and Testing of F-310

Prior to and in support of the introduction and publication of the first advertisement of F-310, the following testing had been conducted:
1. A total of 2,256 individual laboratory engine tests were conducted at Chevron Research Company, consuming a total of 39,870 test hours.

---

[1]F-310 is Standard Oil's trademark for polybutene amine gasoline additive.

2. Field test programs were conducted with taxicab fleets and with Chevron Research employee cars. A total of 205 vehicles, covering a distance of 4,875,000 miles, were involved.
3. Laboratory engine tests were also conducted by the independent Southwest Research Institute between 1968 and 1970.
4. Extensive testing on F-310 was conducted in Europe by Chevron Central Laboratories (a subsidiary of Chevron Research).
5. Scott Research Laboratories, a nationally recognized research firm, conducted fourteen controlled tests on eight cars, which included "before" and "after" field testing of F-310's ability to reduce exhaust emissions and to improve gasoline mileage.

In addition, the actual research leading up to this development covered a span of some fifteen years.

FTC's Initial Investigations

Less than two weeks after the introduction of Chevron gasoline with F-310, the FTC began its investigation, accompanied by constant publicity in the news media. Standard met with the FTC's staff on January 26, 1970, and agreed to provide it with all the information it requested. On February 14, 1970, Standard submitted to the Los Angeles office of the FTC copies of television films, radio tapes, and newspaper and magazine advertisements for Chevron gasolines containing F-310, together with a substantial amount of supporting information, technical materials, and test data. Exhibit 10–1 shows two of the print advertisements delivered to the FTC at that time, which were eventually used as attachments in the formal complaint against Standard.

In several meetings between Standard and the FTC that occurred during the ensuing months, further advertising and test information was transmitted. At the meeting on May 19, 1970, the FTC's staff advised Standard's counsel that the staff did not challenge the quality of F-310 or claim that there was insufficient scientific data to substantiate the claims for it but recommended the issuance of a complaint because certain advertisements with "before" and "after" demonstrations did not make it sufficiently clear, in the staff's opinion, that the "dirty" test car was an extreme case and that the degree of improvement from using gasolines containing F-310 would vary depending on the condition of the car's engine.

To meet these objections, Standard delivered to the commission on May 25, 1970, an Assurance of Voluntary Compliance, assuring the commission that Standard would cease and not resume the criticized advertisements unless they clearly disclosed (a) that a test car with a very dirty engine was purposely used to provide a severe test for F-310, and (b) that the degree of benefit to be expected by a user of gasolines with F-310 would depend on the condition of the car's engine. As shown in Exhibit 10–2, Standard changed the visual portion of television commercials by superimposing explanatory statements such as "Very dirty engine purposely used to provide severe test," "Only dirty engines emit black smoke," "Degree of improvement in your car depends on condition of engine," on the screen at appropriate points.

On September 29, 1970, after additional meetings, presentations, and interchanges between the commission and Standard, and without having made any reply to Standard's Assurance of Voluntary Compliance, the FTC publicly announced that a "proposed" complaint was to be issued against Standard and published the contents thereof. The actual complaint against Standard was issued formally by the commission on January 11, 1971, and the charges differed in a number of material respects from the "proposed" complaint.

FTC's Actual Complaint

The commission's complaint stated that Standard Oil and Batten, Barton, Durstine & Osborn, Inc. (BBD&O), the agency preparing and placing the F-310 advertisements, had used false, misleading, and deceptive statements, representations, and demonstrations for Chevron gasolines with F-310. It was further stated that these practices prejudiced and injured the public and Standard's competitors and constituted unfair methods of competition in commerce and unfair and deceptive acts and practices in commerce in violation of Section 5 of the Federal Trade Commission Act. Paragraphs five and six of the complaint (which reflect the FTC's interpretation of the advertising) were as follows:

Paragraph Five: By and through the use of the statements, representations, and demonstrations set out in Paragraph Four above, and others of similar import not specifically set out herein, respondents have represented and are now representing that

1. F-310 additive in Chevron gasolines is a revolutionary development in the reduction of air pollution;
2. Chevron gasolines containing F-310 additive produce motor vehicle exhaust which is generally pollution-free;
3. The use of Chevron gasolines containing F-310 additive will significantly reduce the total amount of air pollution;
4. The use of Chevron gasolines containing F-310 additive will significantly reduce air pollution caused by motor vehicles;
5. The use of Chevron gasolines containing F-310 additive will significant-

ly reduce emissions of carbon monoxide and unburned hydrocarbons from every motor vehicle in which they are used;

6. The balloon and bag demonstrations pictured in respondents' advertising attached hereto as #1 and #2, and in certain of respondents' television advertisements, constitute proof or accurately or visually demonstrate that Chevron gasolines containing F-310 additive reduce motor vehicle emissions of unburned hydrocarbons and carbon monoxide, and significantly reduce air pollution caused by motor vehicles;

7. Every motor vehicle will emit black exhaust in the manner pictured in respondents' advertisements attached hereto as #1 and #2, and in certain of respondents' television advertisements, if operated on motor fuel other than Chevron gasolines containing F-310 additive;

8. The building identified as Standard Oil Company of California Research Center attached hereto as #1 and #2, and in certain of respondents' television advertisements, is owned, occupied, or used for research by respondent Standard Oil Company of California;

9. The machine pictured in certain of respondents' television advertising is used by the federal government to measure the total amount of pollution emitted by a motor vehicle;

10. Respondents had conducted or had had others conduct tests or demonstrations which proved or substantiated representations made for F-310 additive in their advertisements attached hereto as #1 and #2, and in certain of their television and radio advertisements, before publication or dissemination of such advertisements; these representations include, but are not limited to, the following:

    a. Chevron gasolines containing F-310 additive produce motor vehicle exhaust which is generally pollution-free;

    b. The use of Chevron gasolines containing F-310 additive will significantly reduce the total amount of air pollution, and will significantly reduce air pollution caused by motor vehicles, and will significantly reduce emissions of carbon monoxide and unburned hydrocarbons from every motor vehicle in which they are used;

    c. Every purchaser of Chevron gasolines containing F-310 additive will obtain significantly better mileage by or through the use of such gasolines than can be obtained by or through the use of any other commercially available gasoline;

11. F-310 additive or Chevron gasolines containing F-310 additive will clean or keep clean all engines and engine components.

Paragraph Six: In truth and in fact;[2]

1. F-310 additive in Chevron gasolines is not a revolutionary development in the reduction of air pollution;

2. Chevron gasolines containing F-310 additive do not produce motor vehicle exhaust which is generally pollution-free; such exhaust contains,

---

[2]That is, in the opinion of the FTC relative to FTC interpretation of the advertising.

among other things, unburned hydrocarbons, carbon monoxide, nitrogen oxides, and particulates, all of which are pollutants;

3. The use of Chevron gasolines containing F-310 will not significantly reduce the total amount of air pollution; F-310 additive has no effect upon industrial and other non-motor vehicle sources of air pollution, and does not significantly reduce air pollution caused by motor vehicles;

4. The use of Chevron gasolines containing F-310 additive will not significantly reduce air pollution caused by motor vehicles; F-310 additive has little, if any, effect upon, for example, nitrogen oxides and lead particulates, which are air pollutants; in addition, exhaust from motor vehicles using Chevron gasolines contains, among other things, unburned hydrocarbons and carbon monoxide, which are air pollutants;

5. The use of Chevron gasolines containing F-310 additive will not significantly reduce emissions of carbon monoxide and unburned hydrocarbons from every motor vehicle in which they are used;

6. The balloon and bag demonstrations pictured in respondents' advertisements attached hereto as #1 and #2, and in certain respondents' television advertisements, do not constitute proof or accurately or visually demonstrate that Chevron gasolines containing F-310 additive reduce motor vehicle emissions of unburned hydrocarbons and carbon monoxide; motor vehicle emissions of unburned hydrocarbons and carbon monoxide are relatively colorless. Neither do such demonstrations constitute proof or accurately or visually demonstrate that Chevron gasolines containing F-310 additive significantly reduce air pollution caused by motor vehicles; among other things, the black exhaust pictured is not generally free of air pollutants; it contains, among other things, unburned hydrocarbons, carbon monoxide, nitrogen oxides, and lead particulates, all of which contribute to air pollution;

7. Every motor vehicle will not emit black exhaust in the manner pictured in respondents' advertisements attached hereto as #1 and #2, and in certain of respondents' television advertisements, if operated on motor fuel other than Chevron gasolines with F-310 additive;

8. The building identified as Standard Oil Company of California Chevron Research Center in respondents' advertisements attached hereto as #1 and #2, and in certain of respondents' television advertisements, is not owned, occupied, or used for research by respondent Standard Oil Company of California; the building pictured is the Riverside County Court House, located in Palm Springs, California;

9. The machine pictured in certain of respondents' television advertising is not used by the federal government to measure the total amount of pollution emitted by a motor vehicle;

10. Respondents had not conducted or had others conduct tests or demonstrations which proved or substantiated representations made for F-310 additive in their advertisements attached hereto as #1 and #2, and in certain of their television and radio advertisements, before publication or dissemination of such advertisements; these representations include, but are not limited to, the following:

   a. Chevron gasolines containing F-310 additive produce motor vehicle exhaust which is generally pollution-free.

b. The use of Chevron gasolines containing F-310 additive will significantly reduce the total amount of air pollution; and will significantly reduce air pollution caused by motor vehicles; and will significantly reduce emissions of carbon monoxide and unburned hydrocarbons from every motor vehicle in which they are used;

c. Every purchaser of Chevron gasolines containing F-310 additive will obtain significantly better mileage by or through the use of such gasolines than can be obtained by or through the use of any other commercially available gasolines;

11. F-310 additive or Chevron gasolines containing F-310 additive will not clean or keep clean all engines and engine components; F-310 additive reduces the accumulation of deposits in the carburetor and in or on certain other engine components.[3]

Standard Oil's Response

On learning of the FTC's "proposed" complaint, Mr. O. N. Miller, chairman of the board of Standard Oil Company of California, publicly stated:

Our company intends to take immediate and strong action to defend itself against the Commission's accusations, which are erroneous and unfounded.

The Commission has issued a false and misleading complaint that blindly ignores overwhelming scientific proof, developed by independent testing laboratories, of the exceptional ability of F-310 additive to reduce automotive emissions.

Standard will continue to market the product as aggressively as possible.

Standard Oil continued to defend its claims for Chevron with F-310 by placing double-page advertisements in major metropolitan newspapers charging the FTC's accusations were "unfounded and wrong." An example of these advertisements is shown in Exhibit 10–3.

The company also prepared what it referred to as a Factual Guideline and a Legal Guideline for the interpretation of F-310 advertising. Both of these guidelines were introduced into the formal proceedings by Standard and became a part of the court record for the case. The Factual Guideline, keyed to the numbered statements in paragraphs five and six of the FTC's complaint, posed the following questions:

1. Does the advertisement claim that F-310 is a "revolutionary development in the reduction of air pollution"? (Compl. *Five-1, Six-1*)

---

[3]Standard Oil of California, et al., FTC Docket No. 8827, January 11, 1971. The referred-to attachments #1 and #2 are presented as Exhibit 10–1 in this case.

2. Does the advertisement claim that F-310 produces motor vehicle exhaust which is "generally pollution-free"? (Compl. *Five-2*)
   a. Does it claim that such exhaust is free of, "among other things, unburned hydrocarbons, carbon monoxide, nitrogen oxides, and particulates"? (Compl. *Six-2, Six-4, Six-6*)
   b. Do the bag and balloon advertisements claim that the clear exhaust is "generally free of air pollutants"? (Compl. *Six-6*)
3. Does the advertisement claim that F-310 will reduce air pollution from "industrial and other non-motor vehicle sources"? (Compl. *Five-3, Six-3*)
   a. Does it claim that it will reduce the "total amount" of air pollution? (Compl. *Five-3*)
4. Does the advertisement claim that F-310 will "reduce" emissions from "every motor vehicle" in which it is used? (Compl. *Five-5, Six-5*)
5. Do the bag and balloon advertisements "constitute proof or accurately or visually demonstrate" that F-310 reduces vehicle emissions of unburned hydrocarbons and carbon monoxide? (Compl. *Five-5, Six-6*)
   a. Was the black exhaust "produced by an atypically dirty engine"? (Compl. *Six-6*)
   b. Do the bag and balloon advertisements claim that "every motor vehicle will emit black exhaust in the manner pictured" if operated on other fuels without F-310? (Compl. *Five-7, Six-7*)
6. Did the use of the Riverside County Courthouse or the sign placed thereon affect the "results of the demonstrations"? (Compl. *Five-8, Six-8*)
   a. Did the use of the courthouse building or the sign misrepresent the "qualities or characteristics of F-310"? (id.)
7. Does the meter commercial claim that the meter shown "is used by the Federal Government to measure the total amount of pollution emitted by a motor vehicle"? (Compl. *Five-9, Six-9*)
8. Does the advertisement claim that tests had been conducted to substantiate the representations made for F-310? (Compl. *Five-10, Six-10*)
9. Does the advertisement claim that "every purchaser" of F-310 will obtain "significantly better mileage" than can be obtained from "any other commercially available gasoline"? [Compl. *Five-10(c), Six-10(c)*]
10. Does the advertisement claim that F-310 "will clean or keep clean all engines and engine components"? (Compl. *Five-11, Six-11*)

FTC Judge's Decision

On May 9, 1973, Judge Eldon P. Schrup, an Administrative Law Judge of the Federal Trade Commission, dismissed the complaint against Standard Oil. He stated that the complaint counsel for the FTC had failed to prove the charges that Standard Oil had falsely advertised the F-310 additive in its Chevron gasoline. Shortly after this decision, the complaint counsel filed an appeal with the FTC Commission.

Focal Topics

1. How do you think the average consumer interpreted the advertising for F-310?
2. Were the Factual Guidelines for the interpretation of the F-310 advertising helpful in understanding the issue?
3. Do you agree with the judge's decision to dismiss the FTC complaint? Why or why not?

Exhibit 10–1
Examples of Print Advertising Introducing Chevron
Gasolines with F-310

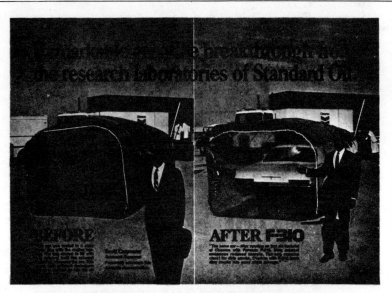

New **F·310** *in Chevron gasolines* turns dirty exhaust into good clean mileage.

Now, research scientists at Standard Oil Company of California have achieved the most long awaited gasoline development in history! It's a new gasoline additive—Formula F-310*—that sharply reduces dirty exhaust from dirty engines. And helps toward cleaner air.

Tests conducted by Scott Research Laboratories, an independent research group, showed that Chevron gasolines with F-310 reduced unburned hydrocarbon and carbon monoxide exhaust emissions dramatically. Clearly, this is a major step towards solving one of today's most urgent problems.

F-310 also improves mileage, because dirty exhaust is really wasted gasoline. So F-310 literally keeps good mileage from going up in smoke.

How does an engine produce dirty exhaust in the first place? As a car accumulates mileage, deposits build up. The amounts of gasoline and air fed into the engine get out of balance. This causes the engine to "run rich", wasting gasoline. As a result, excessive unburned hydrocarbons and carbon monoxide exhaust emissions go into the air. F-310 can correct this condition. Just six tankful can do the job.

Formula F-310, a patented gasoline additive, is now available in all three grades of Chevron gasolines at all Chevron Dealers Standard Stations in the greater Los Angeles area and southward. As soon as additional supplies are available, we'll be introducing this remarkable development elsewhere throughout the West.
F-310 trademark for Polybutene Amine gasoline additive.

Chevron with **F·310.** There isn't a car on the road that shouldn't be using it.
STANDARD OIL COMPANY OF CALIFORNIA

Exhibit 10–1 (continued)

Exhibit 10–2
Television Storyboard for Chevron with F-310

Exhibit 10–3
Newspaper Advertisement by Standard Oil Responding
to the FTC's Complaint

If every motorist used Chevron with F-310 for 2000 miles, air pollutants would be reduced by thousands of tons in a single day.

The Federal Trade Commission doesn't seem to think that's significant. We think it is.

A recent test conducted in Pasadena, California, demonstrated that the use of Chevron gasolines with F-310 could result in the decrease of thousands of tons of exhaust emissions every day from America's car population.

297 cars, using 21 competitive brands of gasoline, and specifically selected to be representative of the total California car population, were tested for exhaust emissions by an independent research laboratory.

Then they were switched to Chevron with F-310, driven by their owners approximately 2,000 miles each, and tested again.

The automobiles showed an average reduction of 13.9% in unburned hydrocarbon emissions, and a drop of 11.6% in carbon monoxide emissions.

If Chevron with F-310 were used in all the cars in Los Angeles County alone, reductions of this size would have the effect of cutting back these emissions by over 1,000 tons per day.

This single test alone is conclusive proof of the effectiveness of F-310, and it is strong to refute the Federal Trade Commission's recent charge that Standard's F-310 makes no significant contribution to the air pollution problem.

The FTC says that F-310 is similar to competitive additives and that it will not significantly reduce automobile emissions of carbon monoxide and unburned hydrocarbons, and that claims made for the additive have not been proven or fully substantiated by reliable testing.

The FTC accusations are grossly in error and unfounded.

F-310 is in fact new and different. The U.S. Patent Office has approved a U.S. patent on F-310 on gasoline. Patents are awarded only for new inventions. Competitive oil companies have made similar claims for the effectiveness of their detergent additives, but no one has come forward with independent proof that we have seen.

F-310 does significantly reduce automobile exhaust emissions of carbon monoxide and unburned hydrocarbons. Proof of this is provided in results of tests which are covered in detail on the opposite page.

The testing of F-310 is accurate, scientific, and reliable. F-310 has been extensively and repeatedly tested in the laboratory and in the field, utilizing independent automotive testing laboratories and testing procedures widely used and accepted throughout the automotive research field. Standard Oil Company of California has spent years in the development of F-310, and in testing to prove that it does exactly what we say it does. F-310 is undoubtedly one of the most thoroughly tested and documented additives in gasoline history.

Because the FTC's allegations may tend to lessen confidence in F-310, Standard Oil Company of California is taking strong and immediate action against these accusations.

We will continue to advertise and market Chevron with F-310, and continue to let the public know the exceptional ability of this additive to reduce automotive exhaust emissions of unburned hydrocarbons and carbon monoxide. We have complete faith in our product, its superiority, in the scientists and laboratories who have helped develop and test F-310, and in the remarkable results it has achieved. F-310 is, in fact, a genuine and significant contribution to air pollution control.

We have not just made claims. We have offered proof.

Standard Oil Company of California

Chevron

F-310 TESTS BY INDEPENDENT RESEARCH LABORATORIES

Scott Lab Tests

Los Angeles County Sheriff's Cars

Pasadena Tests

Orange County Test

Case 11

Federal Trade Commission: Television Advertising to Children*

This report addresses the large volume of current television advertising which is directed to children. Many young children—including an apparent majority of those under the age of eight—are so naive that as this commission and the Federal Communications Commission have previously recognized, they cannot perceive the selling purpose of television advertising or otherwise comprehend or evaluate it and tend, as the FCC has observed, to view commercials simply as a form of "informational programming." The youngest children tend to be even more naive and thus even less capable of comprehending the influence which television advertising exerts over them. For example, it appears that a large proportion of preschoolers think that the persons or animated figures on television are addressing them personally, and that the animated figures are "real" and in some sense appropriate objects for emulation. Apparently, the youngest preschoolers think that there are "real little people" inside the set.

The largest single part of the television advertising addressed

---

*This case is an adapted version of the summary and recommendation sections of the FTC Staff Report on Television Advertising to Children (1978). Some of the section headings have been added to provide additional organization. Footnotes have been omitted to conserve space.

specifically to children is for sugared foods, consumption of which poses a threat to the children's dental health, and possibly to other aspects of their health as well.

The commission now has pending before it two petitions on this subject, both of which urge that a major portion of the advertising to children for such sugared products is unfair and deceptive within the meaning of the FTC Act. Both petitions request that the commission promulgate a trade regulation rule (1) banning what they describe as the worst of that advertising during hours when children are an especially large proportion of the audience, and (2) granting certain related relief.

The Petitions

The petitioners are Action for Children's Television, a nonprofit Massachusetts corporation with 10,000 members which works to eliminate commercial abuses from television advertising addressed to children, and the Center for Science in the Public Interest, a nonprofit District of Columbia corporation with 4,000 members which works to improve domestic food policies. The petitions point out that sugar consumption, especially between meals, is commonly understood by experts to be a principal cause of tooth decay; that tooth decay is a disease that afflicts virtually every person (and more than half of all adult teeth) in the United States; that it is so widespread that at any given moment there are an estimated 1 billion unfilled cavities in American mouths; and that there is some medical evidence that excessive consumption of sugar probably contributes to obesity, and possibly contributes to heart disease.

The petitions also point out that the great volume of televised advertising which urges children to eat sugar is not balanced by any remotely comparable volume of advertising which urges them to consume other foods—or impresses on them the risks they take by eating the advertised products.

The petitions contend that the special naiveté, suggestibility and vulnerability of children have long been recognized by the commission, so that advertising practices which might be neither unfair nor deceptive as to adults can be both unfair and deceptive to children.

ACT's petition, received on April 16, 1977, seeks a ban on televised "candy" advertising addressed to children. Specifically, ACT asks that such advertising be prohibited (a) before 9:05 p.m.; or (b) where the dominant appeal of the advertising is to children; or (c) during any periods when children make up at least half of the audience. ACT does not define the word "candy," but proposes that the commission obtain the aid of an expert body such as the American

Dental Assn. in arriving at an appropriate definition for regulatory purposes.

CSPI's petition, received on April 26, 1977, seeks a ban, during any periods when children make up at least half of the audience, on televised advertising for between-meal snacks which derive more than 10% of their calories from added sugar. CSPI also seeks mandatory affirmative disclosure of the added sugar content of foods permitted to be advertised, as well as of the dental health risks posed by eating sugared products, during periods when children make up at least half of the audience.

Support for Regulation

Regulation of televised advertising of sugared products to children has obtained broad expert and public support. On Dec. 19, 1977, Dr. Donald Kennedy, Commissioner of Food & Drugs, wrote to chairman [Michael] Pertschuk of this commission that:

In view of the large amounts of advertising—particularly television advertising—that are directed to children urging them to consume a seemingly endless variety of sugared products and the substantial likelihood that children will be unable to appreciate the long-term risks to dental health that consumption of these products will create, I strongly support action by the Federal Trade Commission to regulate the advertising of these products directed to children.

Likewise, the Council on Dental Health of the American Dental Association has endorsed "the elimination of advertising of sugar-rich products on children's television." Similarly, the Council of Foods & Nutrition of the American Medical Association has characterized present televised food advertising to children as "most distressing," and as "counter-productive to the encouragement of sound [nutritional] habits."

On July 20, 1977, representatives of the following organizations met with chairman Pertschuk to express their endorsement of the petition: The American Academy of Pediatrics, the American Parents Committee, the Dental Health Section of the American Public Health Association, the Association for Childhood Education International, the Black Child Welfare League of America, the East Coast Migrant Head-Start Program, the Latino Media Task Force, the National Assn. for the Education of Young Children, the National Assn. of Elementary School Principals, the National Council of Negro Women, and the National Women's Political Caucus.

Significantly, too, the U.S. Department of Agriculture has been exploring ways to curb the overpromotion to children of heavily sugared and otherwise nutritionally poor foods. USDA has proposed that the use of "formulated grain/fruit products" such as specially formulated doughnuts, cream-filled cakes, coffee cakes, oatmeal bars, and peanut butter cookies be prohibited in school breakfast programs. In explaining this proposal, USDA noted that "questions have been raised over the sugar and fat content of the products . . . and their value in teaching good eating habits to children." USDA has also recently issued guidelines for that program "encourag[ing] the service of foods with relatively low sugar content."

Similarly, the Assistant Secretary for Health of the Department of Health, Education & Welfare, Julius Richmond, M.D., recently told the Senate select committee on nutrition and human needs that "there is a need to change current (food) advertising directed to children." He commended this commission for what he described as its present efforts "to bring a reasonable degree of regulatory control to bear on nutrition-related advertising, particularly on television."

These experts and others believe that reform of children's television advertising is needed in part because that advertising induces children to take health risks which they are not equipped to assess. But the potential for health-related risks is not the only reason for such views. Many believe it is unfair to advertise *any* product on television, specifically to children who are so young (evidently below the age of eight) that they cannot understand the selling purpose of, or otherwise comprehend or evaluate, commercials and thus cannot discount them, if they so choose, as adults or older children can. That unfairness is exacerbated when television advertising is directed to the very youngest children who are even more naive. The abuse inherent in advertising directly to such an audience via a medium as powerful and pervasive as television is such that a committee established by the British Parliament has just recommended that "*no* advertisements should be shown within children's programs." (Emphasis added.) The committee explained that:

Children are inclined to believe that what they are told in a television program is not only true, but the whole truth. How are they to distinguish between what they are told in a children's program and what they are told in an advertisement? Yet in singing the praises, and the jingles, of a particular product, a child cannot be expected to know that other, less advertised products may be equally good. . . . That is why the majority of us believe that children should not be exposed during their own programs to the blandishments and subtle persuasiveness of advertisements. Lord Annan, "Report of the Committee on the Future of Broadcasting" 166 (1977).

That view has widespread support throughout the world. Of the major industrialized nations, the U.S. and Britain are part of only a handful that ever allowed television advertising—for *any* product— to be directed specifically to preschool children. The other members of that handful are Australia, Canada and Japan. And experience in those first two countries has led to authoritative proposals now pending to ban such advertising.

At least one advertiser of sugared products recognizes the need for fundamental change in televised advertising directed to children. On Nov. 22, 1977, Kenneth Mason, president of the Quaker Oats Co., appeared as part of a panel of cereal industry representatives to discuss the televised advertising of that industry's products to children. Mr. Mason vigorously defended his company's products, but he conceded that:

We do not believe any reasonable person can view a typical eight to 12 noon Saturday morning period on any of the major television networks and fail to recognize the need for fundamental change in the way our society is using its most powerful and pervasive medium of communication to entertain and enlighten the very young.

Mr. Mason accordingly urged the commission to hold thorough hearings on the present petitions.

Background Information

Children and Television

In 1977, the average American child aged two through 11 was exposed to more than 20,000 television commercials. This came as a result of watching an average of 3-2/3 hours of television per day throughout the year. Those children who attended school spent, on the average, more time watching television over the course of the year than they did in the classroom. Moreover, the amount of time which children spend watching television has apparently increased by a full hour per day over the last 22 years, and is now almost double the amount of time that children spent listening to radio immediately before the advent of television.

Infants are attracted to television almost from the moment they first become aware of the world. Not only are they attracted to television, but they are more attracted to commercials than to programs. This is not surprising, given the resources and the accumulated experiences of advertisers, and given the financial incentives they have to make every second count for the purpose of gaining and holding children's attention. By the early 1970's, $400,000,000 was spent annually on TV advertising to children, and approximately

$80,000,000 was spent annually by the processed cereal industry alone.

Joan Ganz Cooney, president of the Children's Television Workshop, and producer of "Sesame Street" and "The Electric Company," has explained that those educational programs were designed to resemble commercials because this allowed them to employ the same attention-getting devices that advertisers had perfected. Those devices, according to Dr. Kenneth O'Bryan, a child psychologist, are so potent that they make the 30-second commercial the most effective teaching device yet invented for implanting any relatively simple idea in a child's mind—including the idea that a product is desirable.

The effectiveness of television advertising in "teaching" children is especially great among those who are still too young to understand the selling purpose of that advertising. This category takes in an apparent majority of children under the age of eight. Even when children in this category understand that there is some difference between commercials and programming, they tend to explain that the difference is that commercials are "shorter," or "more funny," or to point to some other superficial distinction.

Among preschool children, moreover, confusion about the nature and purpose of television advertising tends to be even greater than among elementary school children up to the age of eight. As we noted in the introduction and recommendations, the youngest children may think that there are actual people inside the television set; and even when they outgrow that illusion they may think that a person speaking from the set is specifically addressing them. Cartoon fantasy figures, such as elves, wizards and the like, tend to be perceived by such children as in some sense real and as appropriate figures to be imitated and learned from.

Legal Aspects

It is both unfair and deceptive, within the meaning of Section 5 of the FTC Act, to address televised advertising for *any* product to young children who are still too young to understand the selling purpose of, or otherwise comprehend or evaluate, the advertising. This conclusion rests, in part, on legal precedents which hold that even adults—a group much less vulnerable than children—are not to be exposed to "disguised" or "hidden" advertising. The policy of those precedents is to proscribe efforts to by-pass the defenses which adults are presumed to have when they understand that advertising is being addressed to them.

For example, Section 317 of the Federal Communications Act, 47 U.S.C. § 317, prohibits the broadcasting of paid advertising which is not clearly identified as such. The FCC has explained that Congress determined it to be "unfair" to broadcast advertising whose selling intent was not made plain to listeners or viewers. The legislative history characterizes such a practice as "a deception." To give another example, the FCC has characterized as "deceptive" the practice of subliminal advertising, which also seeks to influence viewers while bypassing the defenses they would have if they were aware that paid advertising was being addressed to them.

If it is unfair and deceptive to seek to bypass the defenses which adults are presumed to have when they are aware that advertising is being directed at them, then *a fortiori* it is unfair and deceptive to advertise to children in whom these defenses do not yet even exist.

Unfairness also arises out of the striking imbalance of sophistication and power between well-financed adult advertisers, on the one hand, and children on the other, many of whom are too young even to appreciate what advertising is. Such children are at the opposite pole, psychologically, intellectually and economically, from the traditionally assumed "rational consumer" for whom advertising provides a service, by offering him or her information relevant to logical market behavior.

Unfairness in the Section 5 sense is a term which Congress deliberately made broad, leaving it to the commission to supply the term with specific content in the light of changing market practices and public values.

The most elaborate test stated by the commission for determining unfairness—and one cited approvingly by the Supreme Court in S&H, *supra*, 405 U.S. at 244–45 n. 5—appears in the *Cigarette Rule* issued by the commission in 1964. That test looks to three factors: First, whether the challenged practice, even if it has not previously been considered unlawful, "offends public policy" in the sense of being "within at least the penumbra of some common-law, statutory, or other established concept of unfairness"; second, "whether it is immoral, unethical, oppressive or unscrupulous"; and third, "whether it causes substantial injury to consumers (or competitors or other businessmen)."

Present televised advertising for sugared products to children is also "false," "misleading" and "deceptive" within the meaning of Sections 5, 12 and 15 of the FTC Act. These terms, like "unfairness," are to be construed especially broadly where children constitute the target audience and where personal health as distinct from mere pecuniary interest, is at stake.

The advertising at issue is deceptive in that it fails to state facts which are material, either in light of the claims made in the advertising, or in light of the customary or recommended use of the advertised products. All advertising for sugared products makes at least the implicit claim that consumption of the advertised products is desirable. The material but unrevealed fact is that the products can also pose health risks.

Some candy advertising urges that the products are desirable because they last a long time in the mouth, or because they are suitable for between-meal consumption, or because a child can "eat some now, save some for later"—all without disclosing that frequent or sustained between-meal snacking on sugared products is the pattern best calculated to cause tooth decay. Additionally, such advertising has a cumulative deceptiveness greater than that of any single commercial in that it erects what the commission in the *Cigarette Rule* called a "barrier to adequate public knowledge and appreciation of the health hazards" of consuming the advertised products, and is deceptive for that reason.

Summary and Possible Remedies

As we describe in the summary and as we explore in far greater detail in the ensuing sections, we have concluded that the petitions are generally meritorious, that rulemaking proceedings should be commenced under the Magnuson-Moss FTC Improvements Act and that the commission should proceed to rulemaking to determine whether it should:

(a) Ban all televised advertising for any product which is directed to, or seen by, audiences composed of a significant proportion of children who are too young to understand the selling purpose of, or otherwise comprehend or evaluate, the advertising[1];

(b) Ban televised advertising directed to, or seen by, audiences composed of a significant proportion of older children[2] for sugared products, the consumption of which poses the most serious dental health risks;

(c) Require that televised advertising directed to, or seen by audiences composed of a significant proportion of older children for sugared food products not included in paragraph (b) be balanced by nutritional and/or health disclosures funded by advertisers.

---

[1]For purposes of this Report, "young children" refers to below the age of eight. Comments and testimony in the rulemaking proceedings we recommend should address the appropriateness of this age definition.

[2]For purposes of this Report, "older children" refers to a group as old as eleven and as young as eight years of age. Comments and testimony in the rulemaking proceedings should address the appropriateness of the age definition.

The remedy described in paragraph (a) follows from the conclusion that televised advertising directed to children too young to understand the selling purpose of, or otherwise comprehend or evaluate, commercials is inherently unfair and deceptive. The remedy described in paragraph (b) reflects the conclusion that the most cariogenic sugared products should not be advertised to children on television. The remedy described in (c) reflects the view that those products of lesser cariogenicity should be advertised to children only if balanced by nutritional and/or health disclosures addressed to that group.

The remedy in paragraph (a) must be implemented in a way that protects child audiences without unreasonably foreclosing the right of adults to receive otherwise protected commercial speech. Remedies (b) and (c) must be implemented in a manner which fairly differentiates among sugared products in terms of their relative cariogenicity, capturing the worst for remedy (b) and leaving the rest for remedy (c).

In this report, we explore five possible remedies for the unfairness and deceptiveness previously discussed:

(a) Affirmative nutritional and/or health disclosures, presented within the body of the advertisements;

(b) Affirmative nutritional and/or health disclosures presented in other contexts and/or under other auspices than those of the advertisers;

(c) Limitations on the amount of television advertising which can be permissibly directed to children for sugared products;

(d) Limitations on particular techniques used or statements made in television advertising directed to children for sugared products; and

(e) Bans on televised advertising which is

(i) directed to children too young to understand the selling purpose of, or otherwise comprehend or evaluate, the advertising for any product, or

(ii) directed to older children for those products which pose the most severe risks to dental health.

The foregoing remedies, of course, do not have to be considered in isolation from one another; some appropriate combination might be devised. On that point, the present practice in the Netherlands is instructive. There, advertisements for sugared foods are banned before 7:55 p.m. After 7:55 p.m., they can be broadcast, but they cannot be "clearly directed toward influencing children in favor of the recommended product," and during a portion of the commercial the advertiser must show a stylized toothbrush on the screen as a reminder of the health hazards of the product.

Focal Topics

1. Do you believe that televised advertising of sugared foods to children is unfair under any or all of the parts of the *Cigarette Rule* test? Explain your response.
2. How would you go about gathering information to evaluate the potential advantages and disadvantages of each of the proposed remedies? Be specific in terms of types of information needed and methods of obtaining it.
3. What remedy or combination of remedies do you think would be appropriate for FTC to adopt?
4. Considering the present FTC staff report, what advertising recommendations would you make to a manufacturer of cereals with high sugar content?

Part Three
Assessing Marketing Opportunities

Case 12
20/20 Contact Lens Service (B)

20/20 Contact Lens Service is a national mail-order firm specializing in replacement and spare pair contact lenses at advertised low prices. The firm's initial advertisement in *Cosmopolitan* drew a large number of inquiries and sales orders.[1]

In fact, the number of requests for additional information and initial orders from that publication and subsequent ones caused 20/20 to fall behind the planned schedule for delivery. As a result, the firm was very concerned that it might develop an unfavorable image among its early customers. It was also interested in learning more about customers' characteristics, where they first heard about 20/20, etc.

20/20 decided that it could combine a research instrument with a sort of "thank you" and "sorry you had to wait" type of letter. Through some type of special offer, the mailing might also serve to generate additional sales to help cover handling costs.

With all these objectives in mind, the firm put together a proposed letter as shown in Exhibit 12–1. A copy of the proposed questionnaire to be mailed with the letter is presented in Exhibit 12–2.

---

[1]Study of this case should include a careful review of 20/20 Contact Lens Service (A).

Focal Topics

1. What is your evaluation of this approach to communicating with consumers and attempting to obtain information from them?
2. Evaluate the cover letter. How would you recommend it be changed?
3. Evaluate the questionnaire. How would you recommend it be changed?
4. What other types of research do you think should be undertaken by 20/20? Be specific in terms of types of information needed and methodologies suited to obtain such information.

Exhibit 12-1
Proposed Cover Letter for Mail Questionnaire

CONTACT LENS SERVICE, INC.
"A Team of Optometrists & Opticians"

A letter of thanks is not sent often enough but we at 20/20 wanted to be sure you know how much we appreciated the opportunity to serve you. We must also be very honest and admit to you that the response we received from customers all over the country was absolutely incredible. We did the very best we could to keep up with the demand but in some cases we fell behind and lenses were not delivered as quickly as we would have hoped. We have now been able to increase the size of our staff dramatically. Now that we have your contact lens prescription in our files, we can guarantee you that your lenses will be delivered to your door within 10 days of the receipt of your payment.

Many of our customers have ordered numerous pairs of lenses in a wide variety of fashion tints. Not only have these lenses been ordered for fashion purposes, but many have been ordered just because our customers wanted to have a spare pair around. Many soft lens wearers have also ordered duplicate or spare pairs from 20/20.

This month we are offering our customers an exceptional offer to say thanks for being patient with us during our rapid growth. This offer must be used by September 1, 1976.

$10 OFF THE PURCHASE OF ANY PAIR OF CONTACT LENSES FROM 20/20 CONTACT LENS SERVICE. THIS MAY NOT BE USED IN CONJUNCTION WITH THE $5.00 MEMBERSHIP OFFER. TOTAL DISCOUNT WITH THIS COUPON OFF THE RETAIL PRICE IS $10.00. OFFER EXPIRES SEPTEMBER 1, 1976.

To take advantage of this fabulous offer just call us toll-free at 1-800-848-7573 or in Ohio call 1-800-282-7510, or drop this letter in the mail with your payment. (See attached order blank on the reverse side).

We at 20/20 are constantly trying to improve the service to our customers. If you would take a few moments our of your day and complete the questions on the back and return them to us in the postage paid envelope, it would be greatly appreciated.

If we can ever be of any assistance, please feel free to contact us at our office at any time.

Sincerely,

Dr. Joseph Serian, Optometrist
Director

P.O. BOX 13270 • WHITEHALL, OHIO 43213 • 1-800-848-7573 OR IN OHIO 1-800-282-7510

Exhibit 12–2
Proposed Mail Questionnaire

Was the service you received from 20/20 as you expected? _____ Why? _____

_____

What can be done to improve 20/20's service to you? Please explain _____

_____

How did you find out about 20/20?

_____ Cosmopolitan	_____ Redbook	_____ Other
_____ New Dawn	_____ Referred by friend	Please list
_____ Playgirl	_____ Newspaper	_____
	_____ Saw brochure	_____

When did you order from 20/20?

_____ First time I saw your ad and called for more information
_____ After I received your brochure
_____ Second time I saw your ad and called for more information
_____ Third or fourth time I saw your ad and called for information

Why did you order your lenses from 20/20? Please explain _____

_____

When you first learned about 20/20 were you skeptical? Why? _____

_____

What answered your questions about 20/20 and convinced you to order from us?

_____

Have you referred any of your friends to 20/20? _____ How many? _____ If not, why?

_____

Would you like to see 20/20 handle contact lens supplies by mail? Please explain

_____

What magazines do you read and enjoy on a regular basis? _____ Cosmopolitan
_____ Playgirl _____ Viva _____ Brides _____ Redbook _____ Seventeen
_____ New Dawn _____ Other (please list) _____

Please check the categories which apply to you.

AGE		MARITAL STATUS	EDUCATION—Currently in
_____ 17–under	_____ 33–35	_____ married	_____ Jr. high school
_____ 18–20	_____ 36–38	_____ single	_____ high school
_____ 21–23	_____ 39–41	_____ divorced	_____ college
_____ 24–26	_____ 42–45	_____ widow	_____ not currently enrolled
_____ 27–29	_____ 46–50		
_____ 30–32	_____ 51–above	EMPLOYMENT	
		_____ full time	
Male_____		_____ part time	
Female_____		_____ not employed	

Case 13
Scioto Company (B)

The Scioto Company, a manufacturer of unique coloring books in scroll form, called Coloring Rolls, has undertaken some marketing research projects to assist in the evaluation of the firm's total marketing strategy. "Scioto Company (A)" set forth background information on the company and its product and reviewed the current pricing and distribution strategies. This case focuses on the design, execution, and results of some consumer and retailer marketing research.

Consumer Marketing Research Overview

A medium-sized town near Scioto's manufacturing facility was selected as the site for a personal survey on Coloring Rolls. Scioto retained a marketing research firm which designed and implemented the study. Six young female interviewers contacted homes selected at random from the city's telephone directory. The interviewers were instructed to use the following general introduction in asking people to participate in the project:

Good _____ (morning, afternoon, or evening). My name is _____ and I work for a marketing research organization which is doing a research project on a new, unique product for children—Coloring Rolls. Do you have any children between the ages of 3 and 10? If *no*, thank respondent and terminate interview. If *yes*, may I leave a sample of this product with you and return in about a week to ask you a few questions about how _____ (he, she, or they) enjoyed it. If *no,* thank respondent and terminate interview. If *yes,* leave a Coloring Roll (only one, regardless of the number of children in the household) and attempt to schedule an appointment for the return interview.

Only one Coloring Roll (the *Circus Parade*) was left in each household, since more than one child can work with the product at a time. If no one was at home, if there were no children in the home, or if a person refused to cooperate, the interviewers continued in that area until a person agreed to participate. Out of 465 people contacted, 243 did not have children in the proper age range and 77 did not want to participate. Of the 145 accepting the Coloring Rolls, completed interviews were eventually achieved with 110 respondents. If a family had more than one child, the information requested was to be supplied on that child who most often used the Coloring Roll. Exhibit 13–1 shows the questionnaire used in the study. Results of the survey are shown in Exhibit 13–2.

Interviews with Middlemen

In order to get the reaction of trade business people, Scioto asked the marketing research firm to do a series of open-ended interviews with toy wholesalers and toy buyers for retail stores. A total of four interviews were completed with wholesalers and eight with retailers.

Although this was a relatively small sample base, some rather interesting information came out of the interviews. The reactions presented below were fairly typical for both the wholesalers and retailers:

(a) Almost all respondents indicated a need to change the package. The key issue was a need for more information on the package itself to help sell the product. Some suggested putting the product on a description box or adding an appropriate top to the package for rack hanging.
(b) Almost all interviewees thought that a much shorter roll (say, 15 feet) would be better received by the consumer at the same retail price as the present 30-foot roll.
(c) Other respondents suggested the need for such things as advertising support, display units, larger pictures, prepricing, perforated rolls, and recommended age-ranges on the package.

In summary, most of the wholesalers and retailers felt that the product had potential but that it would not be readily marketable with its present form and packaging. They indicated an interest in handling the product if it were packaged differently and/or redesigned, and if the price were right. The "right price" at retail varied from 29 cents to 79 cents with most respondents suggesting 49 cents.

Focal Topics

1. Evaluate the design and value of the research. Should additional analysis or research be undertaken at this time? If so, what type should be done?
2. What marketing strategy do you recommend for the Coloring Rolls? Be specific in terms of product design, packaging, promotion, pricing, and channels of distribution.

Exhibit 13–1
Survey Instrument for Consumer Research

1. What was your child's first reaction to the coloring roll?
   _____ (a) wanted to color the roll immediately
   _____ (b) interested, but did not color right away
   _____ (c) ignored it, almost no interest

2. How much time did the child spend with it the first time it was used?
   _____ (a) less than 10 minutes
   _____ (b) 10 to 30 minutes
   _____ (c) 31 to 60 minutes
   _____ (d) more than 60 minutes
   _____ (e) did not use it (IF CHECKED, PLEASE GO TO QUESTION 10)

3. How much time totally did he spend with it since he received it?
   _____ (a) less than 10 minutes
   _____ (b) 10 to 60 minutes
   _____ (c) 61 to 120 minutes
   _____ (d) more than 120 minutes

4. Where did your child color the roll?
   _____ (a) on the floor
   _____ (b) on a table
   _____ (c) other. Please specify _____

5. How did your child work on the coloring roll?
   _____ (a) by himself
   _____ (b) with other children
   _____ (c) with an adult

Exhibit 13–1 (continued)

6. Following are some factors which may be used to describe Coloring Rolls. Please indicate if each factor is very important, important, or very unimportant to you.

	Very Important	Important	Unimportant	Very Unimportant
(a) It is a roll.	1	2	3	4
(b) It tells a story.	1	2	3	4
(c) It is 30 feet long.	1	2	3	4
(d) More than one can color it.	1	2	3	4
(e) It makes a mural.	1	2	3	4
(f) It is printed only on one side.	1	2	3	4
(g) It has a protective plastic covering.	1	2	3 ˉ	4
(h) It can be painted.	1	2	3	4
(i) Individual pictures can be easily cut out.	1	2	3	4

7. Following are some statements about the Coloring Roll. Please indicate if you strongly agree, agree, disagree, or strongly disagree with each statement.

	Strongly Agree	Agree	Disagree	Strongly Disagree
(a) It held my child's interest.	1	2	3	4
(b) My child enjoyed it.	1	2	3	4
(c) My child liked the story.	1	2	3	4
(d) It is easy to use.	1	2	3	4
(e) It is too short.	1	2	3	4
(f) It is too long.	1	2	3	4

8. How old is the child who used the roll most often?
   _____ 3-4   _____ 7-8
   _____ 5-6   _____ 9-10

9. Is this child a _____ girl or _____ boy?

10. If you would buy the product for your child, what price would you be willing to pay?
   _____ (a) 39 cents   _____ (d) 69 cents
   _____ (b) 49 cents   _____ (e) 79 cents
   _____ (c) 59 cents   _____ (f) would not buy it

Exhibit 13-1 (continued)

11. Where do you usually purchase products of this kind? (Check one.)
    _____ (a) discount house
    _____ (b) department store
    _____ (c) drug store
    _____ (d) supermarket
    _____ (e) toy store
    _____ (f) mail order
    _____ (g) other _____

12. Who usually purchases the coloring book for your child?
    _____ (a) wife
    _____ (b) husband
    _____ (c) child
    _____ (d) other _____

13. Who is usually the major influence behind the purchase of coloring books?
    _____ (a) wife
    _____ (b) husband
    _____ (c) child
    _____ (d) other

14. What do you consider the most desirable features of Coloring Rolls?

    _____
    _____
    _____

15. What do you consider the least desirable features of Coloring Rolls?

    _____
    _____
    _____

16. How many children do you have? _____ total

    Girls   Boys
    _____ under 4   _____ under 4
    _____ 4 to 10   _____ 4 to 10
    _____ over 10   _____ over 10

17. Does the wife work outside the home?
    _____ (a) yes
    _____ (b) no

Exhibit 13–1 (continued)

18. Approximately how many coloring books do your children
    receive a year?
    _____ (a) none
    _____ (b) 1 to 3
    _____ (c) 4 to 6
    _____ (d) over 6

19. Please stop me when I come to that category that best
    describes your total family income last year before taxes.
    _____ (a) under $5,000
    _____ (b) $5,000 to $7,500
    _____ (c) $7,500 to $10,000
    _____ (d) $10,000 to $15,000
    _____ (e) over $15,000
    _____ (f) refused

Thank you very much for your cooperation. I sincerely hope that
your child enjoys the Coloring Rolls.

Exhibit 13-2
Consumer Research Results to Survey

1. Sixty-three percent wanted to use it immediately, 22 percent wanted to color it later, and 5 percent had little or no interest in it.

2. Nineteen percent spent less than 10 minutes with it, 15 percent spent between 10 and 30 minutes, 34 percent spent between 31 and 60 minutes, 10 percent spent more than 60 minutes, and 22 percent did not use it. (Note: The percentages for the following questions are based upon the answers of the 78 percent of the original sample who did use the product.)

3. Nine percent spent less than 10 minutes, 69 percent spent 10 to 60 minutes, 12 percent spent 61 to 120 minutes, and 10 percent spent over 120 minutes.

4. Sixty-six percent used it on the floor, 26 percent on a table, and the remainder used it elsewhere such as on the lap, outside, and so on.

5. Sixty-two percent of the children worked by themselves, 26 percent with other children, and 22 percent with adults.

6.

	Very Important	Important	Unimportant	Very Unimportant
(a) It is a roll.	63%	30%	5%	2%
(b) It tells a story.	42	36	13	9
(c) It is 30 feet long.	15	46	28	11
(d) More than one can color it.	22	51	18	9
(e) It makes a mural.	20	60	17	3
(f) It is printed only on one side.	23	52	21	4
(g) It has a protective plastic covering.	35	42	21	2
(h) It can be painted.	21	48	27	4
(i) Individual pictures can be easily cut out.	18	46	30	6

Exhibit 13–2 (continued)

7.	Strongly Agree	Agree	Disagree	Strongly Disagree
(a) It held my child's interest.	37%	40%	13%	10%
(b) My child enjoyed it.	40	35	17	8
(c) My child liked the story.	20	57	20	3
(d) It is easy to use.	12	43	26	19
(e) It is too short.	14	26	22	38
(f) It is too long.	43	28	20	9

8. Sixteen percent were 3 or 4 years old, 29 percent were 5 or 6, 38 percent were 7 or 8, and 17 percent were 9 or 10.

9. Fifty-six percent were girls and 44 percent were boys.

10. Would pay 39¢: 15 percent; 49¢: 19 percent; 59¢: 29 percent; 69¢: 7 percent; 79¢: 4 percent; would not buy: 26 percent.

11. Thirty-one percent purchase from discount stores, 18 percent from department stores, 22 percent from drug stores, 9 percent from supermarkets, 12 percent from toy stores, 2 percent from mail order, and 6 percent from others.

12. Wives purchase 58 percent of the time, husbands 12 percent, children 12 percent, and others 18 percent (grandparents, friends, and other relatives).

13. Wives influence the purchase 21 percent of the time, husbands 5 percent, children 63 percent, and others 11 percent.

14. The respondents liked the fact that a story was associated with the roll. Also mentioned as desirable were the scroll nature of the product, its interest to the children, and the ability for children to work together on it.

15. The major dislike was that respondents thought it was much too long. Other undesirable features included the ability to manipulate the roll, small pictures, and the fact that children argued over it.

Exhibit 13–2 (continued)

16. Twenty-seven percent had one child, 38 percent had two children, 23 percent had three, and 12 percent had four or more. The rest of the question was not analyzed.

17. Thirty-one percent of the mothers worked outside the home.

18. Twelve percent receive none, 48 percent one to three, 29 percent four to six, and 11 percent more than six.

19. Six percent were under $5,000 in annual income, 7 percent between $5,000 and $7,500, 28 percent between $7,500 and $10,000, 32 percent between $10,000 and $15,000, 20 percent over $15,000, and 7 percent refused to answer.
    Additional analysis on the data brought out the following points:

(a) Girls played with the rolls more than boys.
(b) Children from upper income families tended to play with the rolls less.
(c) Children from families who were heavier receivers of coloring books tended to play more with the rolls.
(d) Older children tended to utilize the rolls more with other children.
(e) Younger children tended to use the rolls more on the floor.

Case 14

International Telephone & Telegraph Corporation*

Some months ago, when I first talked publicly about our advertising campaign, I was surprised that a subject like corporate advertising would draw so many people in our business. Corporate advertising was supposed to be a corporate ego massage, after all, and something you couldn't measure. Also corporate advertising didn't have the appeal (or, frankly, the budget) of a new mouthwash, a new detergent, or a new refrigerator.

But of course times change. Lately, vast new pressures have been directed against virtually all institutions—business organizations included. Corporations have found it necessary to speak their piece to an often hostile community, which is why you and I are here this morning, talking about this business of putting together a corporate advertising campaign.

But there's one difficulty we face in corporate advertising, and I'd like to address these remarks to it: How do we justify corporate advertising expenditures to a disciplined, bottom-line-oriented management? With packaged goods or hard goods, you can follow Niel-

*Adapted and updated from talks given by John L. Lowden, vice president, Corporate Relations and Advertising, International Telephone & Telegraph Corporation, at the 1975 Eastern Annual Conference of the American Association of Advertising Agencies and the 1976 Television Bureau of Advertising Seminar on Corporate Advertising.

sens and factory sales. How do we prove the tangible returns of a corporate campaign, in the absence of such marketplace indicators? I offer the ITT campaign as an illustration of one way to go about it.

Motivation for the Campaign

To begin with, the current corporate campaign was a direct response to a need uncovered by research. I mentioned earlier the hostile climate that has beset corporations in the last few troubled years. At ITT we were and are concerned about this antagonistic public opinion, and so we asked the Yankelovich, Skelly & White organization to find out what people knew about our company.

This was in 1972. ITT was zooming to ninth largest industrial company in the Fortune 500[1] —a major among majors. Yet research found that there was an extraordinary lack of knowledge about ITT (familiar to less than one out of three adult Americans in households with incomes of $15,000 or more), and the vacuum was being filled only by news stories reporting unfavorable allegations about us.

It wasn't a question of our not having advertised before. Through our corporate advertising agency, Needham, Harper & Steers, we had been running a successful print campaign for a number of years. But we had directed this effort at a narrow, carefully-defined target group. We had aimed at people in business, finance, government, and the campus world . . . and we had believed we were getting through.

What our research told us, unmistakably, was that this wasn't enough. It appeared that the so-called influentials weren't communicating downward to others such subjective reactions about ITT as awareness, understanding, and confidence. There were too many people out there—prosperous, relatively well-educated people— who didn't know what ITT was or did. They were voters, people who might be potential buyers of our stock, college students who are the influentials of tomorrow, and so on. The brutal fact was, they didn't recognize our name as they would the familiar consumer goods companies that some of you represent. And lacking knowledge about us, they were ready to believe anything said about us.

Communication Decisions

That is why we decided to shift most of our media dollars into television—taking our message to an audience a good deal larger than the

---

[1]An annual listing of the nation's 500 largest corporations, published by *Fortune* magazine.

audience we had been talking to. We needed both television's reach and its speed of communication.

There would still be a basic print schedule, directed at that part of the audience that watched little TV. But print's role was considered largely supportive of television's.

Our job was to communicate how we could help improve the quality of life through the quality of our R & D, our products, and our services. Television was a perfect vehicle for this not only because it could help us demonstrate dramatically our concern and involvement but because of its speed and efficiency in reaching the large audience we now had in mind.

Also, we knew that many of ITT's products and services—some of them highly complex and unfamiliar to the average consumer—would have to be seen in action to be understood. As you know, one can't feel friendly toward a company unless one understands what it does.

Our basic decision, therefore, was to create better public attitudes toward our company by demonstrating that ITT makes a large and continuing investment in research and development, producing a wide diversity of products and services, many of them in highly technical fields, and that these products and services help improve the quality of life. That was to be Phase I of our communications effort. We had to change our standing in the eyes of a great many people, and do it in a hurry.

Evaluative Marketing Research

Now, we knew that reaching our desired audience and changing minds in a relatively short time would be an expensive proposition. We also knew we had to demonstrate to our management (and to ourselves) that this expense was justified—that a major corporate advertising campaign, on the scale we projected, could fill the identity vacuum and dilute the unfavorable publicity we were getting. As I said, we had no Nielsens to go by; we had to create our own yardsticks.

So in late 1973 we undertook a major research program that had two key objectives:

1. To track changes in awareness, familiarity, and reputation of ITT among people in households with $15,000 plus annual incomes. (The technical specifications called for a national probability sample of such households.)
2. To assess the effectiveness of the campaign in improving attitudes among this target audience.

We developed a questionnaire, carefully pretested it, and administered it before the campaign began to get a benchmark. Then we went back six months after, and again six months after that. We are still continuing to chart our progress at six-month intervals. Each sampling has consisted of 1,500 or more telephone interviews.

The Campaign and Results

We started the campaign in early 1974. Television carried the major thrust. The commercials were backed up by print ads in the major news and business magazines, particularly to reach those people at the higher end of the scale who watch very little television.

As I mentioned earlier, our message was simply that ITT is improving the quality of life through the products and services which are coming out of our extensive R & D programs. Exhibits 14–1a and b show two sample advertisements from the Phase I campaign.

Now, rather than tell you more about our original Phase I approach, let me explain how our direction has changed. Actually, the basic message hasn't changed at all. We're still talking about unusual products and services coming out of our extensive R & D programs that help improve the quality of life. But you probably noticed in those first commercials that the subjects—fiber optics and the undersea cable—are quite unusual.

These products do their job; they are designed with people's needs in mind. But 99.9 percent of the public will never see them in action. And while they're superb for grabbing the viewer's attention, they are obviously not the products which will contribute most to ITT's future as a successful company.

So as soon as we were making real progress in creating awareness and improving attitudes, we made another basic decision: The campaign would have to work harder. Our commercials and our print ads would now have to communicate the fact that ITT has products and services which not only improve the quality of life but also improve the company's prospects for future earnings and profits. That was the direction in which we decided to go with Phase II of our corporate advertising.

Corporate advertising will obviously never market any company as an investment in the same way that consumer advertising sells a product. There are too many restraints on financial advertising for that. But corporate advertising can and will play a much larger role in portraying the advertiser as a successful, viable instrument for the making of profits in the future.

On top of these pressures, the sheer increase in the cost of advertising means that all communications efforts will have to accomplish more. So much for that. A group of corporate commercials that reflect our Phase II approach appear in Exhibits 14–2a and b. Try to keep in mind our earlier basic objective: to improve the quality of life with products and services resulting from ITT research and development. But we hope you'll also see that something new is being said about ITT.

These products are inherently attention-getting, of course. But when was the last time a *weed* really caught your eye—unless you saw, as you did here, that the annual battle doesn't have to be lost. More important, imagine how many people didn't even know we own Scotts, the nation's leader in lawn care products.

From the benchmark research results of early 1974 to the latest research results, ITT's image has shown improvement in all areas. There were some declines, however, from October 1976 to October 1977. Exhibit 14–3 compares awareness percentages from five individual studies.

Summary Comments

When the corporate campaign began, ITT invested $4,000,000 in network television and $2,000,000 in print during the first year. Earlier ITT corporate advertising, stressing the free enterprise system in magazines, cost about $2,700,000 a year. In 1977 the ITT image campaign was supported with about $6,400,000 in media, compared with $4,800,000 invested in 1976. (In foreign markets, ITT corporate advertising has the same basic objectives as the U.S. campaign. The advertisements, however, do add a localized dimension to the country or area where they are used.)

Let me reiterate my opening question: Can a corporate advertising campaign, particularly a rather substantial one, be justified to a financially-disciplined management? In our experience, yes. Skepticism toward business is a fact of our times, and certainly ITT has had more than its share of negative publicity. But a well-thought-out corporate campaign can go a long way toward countering a hostile press and can be justified to management by carefully documented research.

There was much, much more in the way of gratifying results, including a firm vindication of our selection of TV as the primary medium for this effort. But perhaps I've already indicated the success this campaign has achieved. I think what our campaign says about corporate advertising is this:

1. Corporate advertising can effectively change attitudes in specific, predetermined directions.

2. The effectiveness of corporate advertising can be clearly measured.
3. Corporate advertising can be just as exciting as product or service advertising—and often more so.
4. Advertisers will have an increasing need to talk about their growth and prospects, and corporate advertising will grow commensurately—in volume, in quality, and in stature as a management tool.

Focal Topics

1. In your own words, describe the basic objective of ITT's corporate advertising program. Do you agree that this is what the objective should be? Why or why not?
2. To what would you attribute the decline in some of the image measures for 1976 to 1977?
3. Evaluate ITT's image research to date and discuss the specifics of other types of research which you think ITT should undertake at this point.
4. Discuss other types of themes which you feel would be appropriate for ITT's corporate advertising program. What themes would you recommend and why?

Exhibit 14–1a
Examples of Phase I Advertisements

ITT
"Fiber Optics":60

Product: Fiber Optics

ANNCR (VO): In cities all over the world these days, there's congestion even <u>underground</u>.

The cables beneath the streets carry more and more phone calls, computer data, TV signals.

Do we have to keep tearing up streets for bigger and bigger cables?

The people of ITT have an answer: optical fibers. Threads of glass, thin as human hair.

ITT has pioneered a practical way to communicate over these fibers by light—

laser light.

Eventually, today's underground cables...

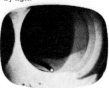

could be replaced by ITT optical fibers...

carrying thousands of times more information in the same space.

We could end that congestion below the streets...

without tearing them up to do it.

ITT
The best ideas are the ideas that help people.

Exhibit 14–1b

ITT
"Cable": 60

PRODUCT: UNDERSEAS POWER CABLE

ANNCR (VOICE OVER): The men and ships of Norway

have been partners for centuries. But for some today, the task is different.

They're laying underwater power cables...bringing electricity to remote villages, hungry for it.

MAN (IN NORWEGIAN): There's a ship coming, hey! etc...
SOUND: CHURCH BELLS BEGIN RINGING.

The cable is a new kind of underwater cable, built and laid by the people at ITT.

And it loses far less energy than other marine cables over far greater distances.

SOUND: CHURCH BELLS RING. TOWNSPEOPLE'S VOICES APPROACHING DOCKS.

With ITT cables, we'll be able to carry electricity underwater 80 miles and more—

from generating plants across a sea, down a river or far offshore.

With this ITT cable, electric power could be brought those extra miles

to a lot of American communities that are running short, too. Perhaps, even yours.
SOUND: CHEERING, HAPPY CROWD.

ITT
The best ideas are the ideas that help people.

Exhibit 14–2a
Examples of Phase II Advertisements

ITT

"Scotts Consumer Advisory Service":60

ANNCR(VO): There's a jungle of strange plants...in Ron Vollrath's office.

RON(VO): It's a shallow-rooted plant. It's chickweed. It's got a smooth, shiny-pointed leaf...(FADES UNDER)

ANNCR(VO): Ron identifies weeds for troubled homeowners who write to O.M. Scott,

the ITT company that cares about America's lawns. 170,000 people come to Scotts each year with lawn problems—

including unfamiliar weeds. RON(VO): It's shepherd's purse. It can be controlled quite easily.

ANNCR(VO): Scotts has helped people grow things for over a hundred years.

Not just providing seeds, fertilizers and weed controls,

but acres of good advice, too.

RON(VO): Nimblewill returns unless it's spot-treated or hand-grubbed... (FADES UNDER)

ANNCR(VO): At Scotts, the lawn people of ITT, Ron Vollrath helps folks all day with their lawns...

Then goes home...and cares for *his.*

Exhibit 14–2b

ITT
"School Lunch":60

Product: Morton School Lunches

ANNCR (VO): Julie Gillespie goes to school in a school district that hasn't a penny to spare these days—

what school district does? They wanted to serve Julie and her classmates hot lunches.

But *how*—without an expensive kitchen and staff?

The answer came from Morton's, the frozen food people of ITT...

who developed compact minikitchens for schools—

and good, nourishing hot lunches for the children.

With the ITT Morton school lunch program,

there are different lunches for every day of the month.

And the cost is well within the school budget.

All of which leaves Julie Gillespie—

and her school—with a nice warm feeling inside.

ITT
The best ideas are the ideas that help people.

Exhibit 14–3
Research on Image of ITT (1974–1977)

	Percent Agreement				
	January 1974*	December 1974	December 1975	October 1976	October 1977
One of largest companies	68	85	86	90	86
Makes quality products	54	75	74	82	77
Very profitable	61	76	73	80	76
Leader in technology	49	72	73	81	75
Develops many new products	46	67	68	75	74
Reliable	48	64	63	73	70
Good stock to buy or own	52	53	62	72	70
Leads in research and development to improve products	46	65	66	71	69
Gives good value	43	56	56	62	58
Cares about its customers	40	56	55	59	58
Pays good wages	34	44	47	50	51
Cares about general public	31	43	42	50	51
Fair to employees of all races	34	42	45	48	48
Gives women equal opportunity	29	40	43	45	44
Good labor relations	29	43	40	46	42
Interesting place to work	26	40	40	45	42
Honest, forthright advertising	27	39	37	44	42
Cares about community near plant	26	40	40	44	40
Makes products safe without regulations	29	40	38	42	39
Protects jobs of U.S. workers	27	38	39	41	36
Good balance—profits/public interest	29	31	33	37	35
Working to curb pollution	21	29	26	31	32
Solves social problems	19	23	21	24	23
Reduces prices when possible	12	18	18	18	19
Tells all about itself—good and bad	11	16	15	16	13

*Adjusted to account for variation in method of asking question.

Case 15
City National Bank and Trust Company (B)

The marketing department of City National Bank and Trust Company (CNB) is charged with the responsibility for developing a comprehensive information and planning system for insuring that the bank maintains and improves its consumer orientation. A key question is: How can this task best be accomplished initially and on an ongoing basis?

Marketing Research Activities

Of the 14,000 banks in the United States in 1970, the number with marketing research departments probably was no more than a few dozen. However, CNB had been conducting research of various kinds for several years and in 1967 appointed a marketing research manager. The marketing research group consisted of a manager and two assisting marketing analysts, who worked on research projects as needed but had other duties. The marketing research group serviced the advertising department and the planning department. All these personnel reported to the vice-president in charge of marketing, who reported directly to the president and the chairman of the board.

Prior to 1968 the marketing research activities had focused on branch analysis and planning and on image measurement among various market segments. There was an increasing need in the 1970s, however, for greater understanding of consumer decision processes as they applied to banking services and to the marketing mix of CNB. Although CNB was possibly the smallest bank in the nation with a major marketing research program, management had already demonstrated its interest in and commitment to research. The task that lay ahead was to determine the organization and research activities that were needed to the bank's offerings in accord with changes in the environment.

Central Data Files

A typical problem in banking is that banks do not know how many customers they have. Each account is recorded separately, and generally there is no record of which checking account customers also have passbook savings accounts, trust accounts, loans, and so forth. Sometimes an individual might have a small checking account but may be an officer in a corporation having large balances with the bank. Most banks have no systematic record of such facts, however. In addition, some customers have more than one account of a given type. CNB felt that it would be useful to establish a customer monitoring system that would permit the bank to know the total banking relationship that existed between a customer and the bank.

Toward this end, CNB began to plan for the total reprogramming of all computer applications so that the bank could move into a completely automated Customer Information File (CIF) program with the fewest possible problems. This process would be a major time and financial investment. It was considered necessary, however, if the bank was to provide the advanced customer services being planned.

The new computer files were being designed to contain almost every conceivable bit of information about the accounts that the customer presently maintained or had previously maintained and to permit inclusion of many items of external data. A small sampling of the information available for consumer research includes the following items:

Sex	SIC of employer
Children (number and ages)	Rent or own home
Marital status	Transaction history (all
Credit rating	accounts)
Occupation	Reason accounts closed
Zip code	Dun & Bradstreet rating
Census tract	Income range
Opening officer	Interest paid last year
Birthdates of family	Real estate taxes paid last year

A software package was available with a complete set of management report options with which the bank could cross-classify the segments of its business by any variable in the CIF. For example, if CNB wanted to know the age distribution of its passbook savings account customers, it could place an inquiry in the computer and receive such a report. If it wanted to determine those with large demand deposit accounts but no other relationships, that could easily be reported. Also, the computer could be programmed to produce promotional outputs such as letters addressed personally to customers on their birthdays or as their children enter college or on other special occasions. Another feature of the CIF was the capacity to treat a customer as a "net account"; that is, the balance and profitability of a *customer* could be assessed rather than the balance and profitability of an *account*, which is only a fractional representation of the customer.

From the customer's perspective, CNB management felt that CIF would provide much improved service as well as more efficient marketing research. CNB's chairman of the board commented:

> It's this computer opportunity that excites me. Imagine, as a customer, getting a statement every month that spells out all of the things the bank did for you that month. You'll receive a complete report on your family financial status, including a listing of all the bills paid for you, the amount added to your savings, the balance on your mortgage loan, or the status of your income tax deductions.

Implementing the CIF program offered no serious technical difficulties; the problem faced by CNB was how best to use the information contained in the file. They needed to decide how to gather the external data, how much of the information to relay to customers, and in what ways the information could be used to solve research questions. Exhibit 15–1 shows an advertisement which was initially used to inform consumers about Total Account Banking, one way that CNB planned to use CIF.

Focal Topics

1. Discuss the marketing programs that could be affected by the CIF and how CIF could contribute to greater effectiveness in achieving the bank's objectives.
2. How much of the available information should be provided, and how should this information be communicated to CNB consumers?
3. What other types of consumer research activities should the marketing department undertake?

Exhibit 15–1
Newspaper Advertisement for Total Account Banking

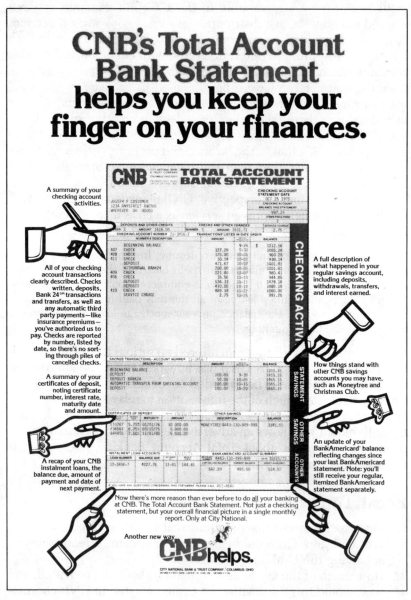

Case 16
Simpson's Shoe Store

The management of Simpson's Shoe Store, located in the downtown area of a large Eastern city, was quite concerned about the performance of its women's department, whose sales and profits had remained fairly steady for the past several years. Because of the following facts, however, management felt that improvements should have been noted: (1) total population in the city had increased about 30 percent in the last ten years, (2) most merchants in the downtown area had reported increased sales and profits during the decade, and (3) sales in the men's department had been increasing at about a 4-percent-per-year rate.

Given this background, in early 1979 the management decided to call in a marketing consulting firm to evaluate operations. As the first phase of its investigation, the consulting firm recommended a replication of a study made ten years earlier, which researched the image of Simpson's and other shoe stores or shoe departments perceived by management to be Simpson's competitors. The material presented here focuses on the relevant background information, the design and execution of the two image surveys, and the comparative survey results. The main problem facing management at this time is to determine how to use the results of the second image study to improve the firm's operations and promotional strategy.

Background and Environment

The Store

Simpson's Shoe Store was founded in 1912 by George A. Simpson, a salesman turned merchant. The store was an immediate success, largely through the personal efforts of Mr. Simpson. He established rapport with his customers by remembering their names and families, their likes and dislikes in shoes, and other consumer characteristics.

Mr. Simpson maintained a file system on all his customers, containing the sizes, styles, and prices of shoes purchased. When he received a particular style or size of shoe, he would often send a penny postcard to certain customers telling them he was holding back a pair of shoes for them. This personal touch, plus a complete line of all shoe sizes, helped the store grow at a rapid rate.

In 1978, with 100 full- and part-time employees, Simpson's achieved a sales volume of slightly less than $3 million. Before-tax profits amounted to about $200,000.

Product Mix

Simpson's has always prided itself on providing the consumer with the greatest shoe value for the dollar spent. The store handles almost all brands of shoes as well as its own private label. Following is a brief description of the four main sources of shoes sold at Simpson's:

Private Brand Simpson's will frequently contract directly with the manufacturer for a particularly popular type of shoe built to its individual specifications. The store can sell these for less than comparable national brands due to the volume of shoes purchased and the direct contact with the manufacturer.

Factory Overstocks Simpson's buyers are always on the lookout for special purchases where the manufacturer has overproduced a particular item. These stocks are usually purchased at very attractive prices, with the savings being passed on to the customer.

Store Buyouts When a store is going out of business, Simpson's will sometimes purchase its entire remaining stock of shoes. Again, these buys are made at very reduced prices.

Factory Irregulars Here Simpson's will contract with a manufacturer to purchase any irregular shoes. These shoes are then clearly marked as such for the consumer and sold at reduced prices.

Competition

While there are many shoe stores and shoe departments within stores in the city where Simpson's operates, management identified four main competitors, feeling that the images of these four competitors could be applied to other, similar stores in their city. Following is a brief description of each of these competitors:

Interstate's Shoe Department Interstate is a major department store chain which enjoys a good reputation based on the quality of its merchandise, competitive prices, and good services. Advertisements for the shoe department are usually included in full-page newspaper ads for the department store as a whole. The shoe department does not do any advertising by itself via any medium.

Mongon's Shoe Department Mongon's is a local department store with an excellent reputation for backing up the merchandise it sells. The store has a "no questions asked" refund policy. The shoe department carries a complete price line of shoes with emphasis on some store brands. Advertising is limited to newspaper space within a larger ad for the entire department store. Some special sales are advertised via radio spots and coupons sent through the mail.

The Balcony Shoes An exclusive women's shoe store with very comfortable surroundings, the store focuses on the better brands of shoes and offers many personal services. Advertising is concentrated in the local newspapers, although the store's infrequent sales are promoted via radio and television spots.

Save-Much Shoe Store The Save-Much Shoe Store features mostly irregulars and low-quality shoes. Its major advertising is done through newspaper ads and some door-to-door distribution of flyers. There is a limited amount of sales assistance in the store, and the customer relies mostly on self-service.

Several of these stores also have branches throughout the city and in suburban shopping centers. Simpson's has attempted to open some branch stores, but they have been unsuccessful. Therefore, Simpson's has preferred to concentrate on a large, easy access, free parking store in the downtown area.

Simpson's Promotional Program

For the past several years Simpson's advertising budget has averaged about 6 to 7 percent of sales. During 1978, the store spent $195,000 on advertising and related expenses. In general, the store's promotional activities can be divided into two main areas—direct mail and newspapers.

Direct Mail Following the tradition established by George Simpson, the store keeps a file card on each customer in the men's and women's departments. This card contains the following information on each purchase: date, amount, brand, and size. In addition, a mailing plate which can be used in an automatic addressing machine is made up for each customer. It contains information on the customer's preferences, including price paid, brand purchased, and size of shoe. Thus, the store can direct a mailing to a very select subset of its customers.

The costs of mailing flyers and operating and maintaining the mailing department during 1978 came to $65,000. These costs covered the rental on addressing equipment ($2,000 per year), salaries to maintain the mailing list and handle mailings ($18,000), and the preparing, printing, and mailing of 400,000 pieces during the year ($45,000). Simpson's has about 200,000 names on file, and each person received two mailings during 1978.

The direct mailings usually consist of a catalog containing pictures and copy on men's, women's, and children's shoes. Frequently, the catalogs or flyers are designed to announce a sale to "Simpson's Select Customers" before the news is relayed to the general public.

Newspaper Advertising The bulk of Simpson's advertising budget is typically devoted to advertisements in the major local newspaper. For 1978, newspaper advertising amounted to $120,000. During the last few years, Simpson's has had a full-page advertisement in each Friday evening's newspaper. A half-page advertisement is also featured each Sunday. (Simpson's is open from noon to eight each Sunday.)

The advertisements are basically designed around the theme "Save 1/4, 1/3, 1/2 and even more at Simpson's," and point out that Simpson's is the largest shoe store in the city, with "over 200,000 pairs of shoes in stock." Pictures of sale shoes and announcements of seasonal sales, buy-outs of stores going out of business, and factory purchases are also frequently included in these weekly advertisements.

Other Promotional Activities The remainder of Simpson's advertising budget in 1978 ($10,000) was devoted to a few spot radio advertisements announcing special sales and advertisements purchased in the publications of local schools and charitable organizations.

Image Study

Following the 1969 recommendation of a marketing consulting firm, management conducted a mail survey to determine Simpson's image and major competitors. A total of 2,000 questionnaires were mailed to female heads of households selected at random from the city telephone directory and to those on Simpson's customer mailing list. The questionnaires were sent out under the letterhead of the consulting firm so that the results would not be biased toward Simpson's. Each respondent was promised a $5 gift certificate for her cooperation in filling out the questionnaire, a portion of which is shown in Exhibit 16–1.

In addition to the data gathered by the questions given in Exhibit 16–1, the survey also asked socioeconomic questions such as age, education, and income of the respondents. The attributes of shoe stores given in questions 1, 2, and 3 of the survey were determined after in-depth interviews with fifty female consumers. These in-depth interviews took the form of a question and answer group session where the women, five at a time, discussed what they looked for in a shoe store or shoe department. The same methodology and questionnaire were used in the 1979 study.

After three weeks, a total of 512 questionnaires had been returned to the consulting firm in 1969, and 490 questionnaires had been returned by this same time period in the 1979 study. The results from these questionnaires are presented in Exhibit 16–2.

Focal Topics

1. Evaluate the surveys conducted. What other kinds of information or analysis would you like to have? How would you go about obtaining this information or doing the analysis?
2. What promotional strategy recommendations do you have for Simpson's? Be specific in terms of media and copy appeals.
3. Should Simpson's continue its emphasis on direct mail? Why or why not? How would you go about studying the effectiveness of its direct mail program?

Exhibit 16–1
Women's Shoe Store Questionnaire

Following are several questions concerning your "feelings" about certain shoe stores and shoe departments in the area. Please be careful to answer each question about each store, EVEN IF YOU HAVE NOT VISITED IT. This is extremely important! Therefore, even if you have not shopped a particular store, please answer each question to the best of your ability based upon your "feelings" about the store.

1. Attributes of shoe stores are listed below. I would like to know how you would rate an IDEAL SHOE STORE on each of the attributes. Please circle one number for each attribute. For instance if you circle a "1" for the attribute PRICE OF SHOES it indicates that your ideal store would have very low prices. A "6" rating means you want the store to have very high prices.

	Low				High			Limited				Large
Price of Shoes	1	2	3	4	5	6	Selection of Shoes	1	2	3	4	5	6

	Low				High			Poor				Excellent
Quality of Shoes	1	2	3	4	5	6	Store Service	1	2	3	4	5	6

	Traditional				Fashion			Unfair				Fair
Style of Shoes	1	2	3	4	5	6	Adjustment Policy	1	2	3	4	5	6

2. Now I would like for you to think about these attributes for the following shoe stores and shoe departments. Circle the rating on each attribute which best describes how you "feel" about the store on that attribute. Again, please note the scales for each attribute. Please indicate your feelings about each store even if you have not visited or shopped it.

	Price of Shoes						Selection of Shoes					
	Low				High		Limited				Large	
Interstate's Shoe Dept.	1	2	3	4	5	6	1	2	3	4	5	6
Mongon's Shoe Dept.	1	2	3	4	5	6	1	2	3	4	5	6
Simpson's Shoe Store	1	2	3	4	5	6	1	2	3	4	5	6
The Balcony Shoes	1	2	3	4	5	6	1	2	3	4	5	6
Save-Much Shoe Store	1	2	3	4	5	6	1	2	3	4	5	6

	Quality of Shoes						Store Service					
	Low				High		Poor				Excellent	
Interstate's Shoe Dept.	1	2	3	4	5	6	1	2	3	4	5	6
Mongon's Shoe Dept.	1	2	3	4	5	6	1	2	3	4	5	6
Simpson's Shoe Store	1	2	3	4	5	6	1	2	3	4	5	6
The Balcony Shoes	1	2	3	4	5	6	1	2	3	4	5	6
Save-Much Shoe Store	1	2	3	4	5	6	1	2	3	4	5	6

Exhibit 16-1 (continued)

	Styles of Shoes		Adjustment Policy	
	Traditional Fashion		Unfair	Fair
Interstate's Shoe Dept.	1 2 3 4 5 6		1 2 3 4 5 6	
Mongon's Shoe Dept.	1 2 3 4 5 6		1 2 3 4 5 6	
Simpson's Shoe Store	1 2 3 4 5 6		1 2 3 4 5 6	
The Balcony Shoes	1 2 3 4 5 6		1 2 3 4 5 6	
Save-Much Shoe Store	1 2 3 4 5 6		1 2 3 4 5 6	

3. Please rank the following attributes of the shoe stores in their order of importance to you in selecting a store to buy from. Write a "1" by the attribute which is most important, a "2" by the attribute which is next most important, and so on until you have ranked *all 6 attributes*. (Please be sure to use all the numbers 1 to 6.)

_____ Price of Shoes
_____ Quality of Shoes
_____ Style of Shoes
_____ Selection of Shoes
_____ Store Service
_____ Adjustment Policy

4. Now I'd like for you to rank the five shoe stores by marking a "1" next to your favorite store, a "2" next to your second favorite *and so on.* IMPORTANT! Rank these 5 stores even if your favorite is not included. (Please be sure to use all the numbers 1–5.)

_____ Interstate's Shoe Dept.
_____ Mongon's Shoe Dept.
_____ Simpson's Shoe Store
_____ The Balcony Shoes
_____ Save-Much Shoe Store

5. Please check the frequency with which you shop the following stores. Check only one blank for each store.

	Have Not	Have Heard of, and Shop		
	Heard of	Never	Occasionally	Frequently
Interstate's Shoe Dept.	_____	_____	_____	_____
Mongon's Shoe Dept.	_____	_____	_____	_____
Simpson's Shoe Store	_____	_____	_____	_____
The Balcony Shoes	_____	_____	_____	_____
Save-Much Shoe Store	_____	_____	_____	_____

6. Please mark a "1" by the item you consider most important in buying a pair of shoes, a "2" by the next most important item, and so on until you have ranked all 5 items.
_____ FIT _____ PRICE _____ BRAND _____ QUALITY
_____ STYLE

Exhibit 16–1 (continued)

7. Please mark a "1" by that medium which you look to first for information about shoes, a "2" by the second most important medium, and so on until you have ranked all 4 media.
   _____ RADIO _____ DIRECT MAIL _____ NEWSPAPERS
   _____ TELEVISION

8. Please check how often you buy your shoes at sale prices.
   _____ NEVER _____ OCCASIONALLY _____ FREQUENTLY
   _____ ALWAYS

Exhibit 16-2
Tabulation of Responses to Women's Shoe Store Questionnaire (1969 and 1979)

Average Rating for Each Attribute of Ideal Store (Question 1)

	1969	1979		1969	1979
Price of Shoes	3.10	2.90	Selection of Shoes	5.01	4.56
Quality of Shoes	5.14	5.01	Store Service	5.61	5.59
Style of Shoes	3.97	3.41	Adjustment Policy	5.65	5.68

Average Rating for Attribute for Each Store (Question 2)

	Price		Quality		Style		Selection		Service		Adjustment	
	1969	1979	1969	1979	1969	1979	1969	1979	1969	1979	1969	1979
Interstate's Shoe Dept.	4.69	4.81	4.54	4.32	4.39	4.31	4.44	4.19	4.73	4.82	4.81	4.72
Mongon's Shoe Dept.	4.73	4.65	4.51	4.21	4.46	4.42	4.87	5.11	4.78	4.52	4.90	4.61
Simpson's Shoe Store	4.31	4.35	4.18	4.01	4.15	4.32	4.95	4.35	3.94	3.81	4.07	4.31
The Balcony Shoes	5.11	4.92	5.04	4.75	4.91	4.75	4.68	4.65	4.89	4.91	4.52	4.50
Save-Much Shoe Store	3.27	3.82	2.75	3.09	3.16	3.51	3.42	3.39	2.97	3.01	3.26	3.20

Percentages of Responses for Most Important and Least Important Attribute Ranking (Question 3)

	Ranking of Attribute Importance*			
	First		Sixth	
	1969	1979	1969	1979
Price of Shoes	12%	14%	20%	16%
Quality of Shoes	20	19	16	18
Style of Shoes	19	15	12	14
Selection of Shoes	25	20	11	18
Store Service	14	18	17	14
Adjustment Policy	10	14	24	20
	100%	100%	100%	100%

*Read: 12 percent of the respondents ranked price as the most important attribute of shoe stores in 1969. 14 percent ranked it first in 1979; 20 percent ranked price as least important in 1969, 16 percent ranked it sixth in 1979.

Exhibit 16-2 (continued)

Percentages of Responses for Favorite and Least Favorite Store Ranking (Question 4)

	Ranking of Store Preference*			
	First		Fifth	
	1969	1979	1969	1979
Interstate's Shoe Dept.	21%	24%	10%	8%
Mongon's Shoe Dept.	30	29	8	10
Simpson's Shoe Store	24	20	20	18
The Balcony Shoes	14	18	24	17
Save-Much Shoe Store	11	9	38	47
	100%	100%	100%	100%

*Read: 21 percent of the respondents ranked Interstate as their favorite shoe store in 1969, 24 percent ranked it first in 1979; 10 percent ranked Interstate as their least favorite in 1969, 8 percent ranked it last in 1979.

Percentages of Responses to Shopping Frequency (Question 5)

	Have Not Heard of		Have Heard of and Shop					
			Never		Occasionally		Frequently	
	1969	1979	1969	1979	1969	1979	1969	1979
Interstate's Shoe Dept.	2%	3%	12%	14%	55%	50%	31%	33%
Mongon's Shoe Dept.	3	4	11	13	58	52	28	31
Simpson's Shoe Store	10	8	26	34	43	40	21	18
The Balcony Shoes	13	13	40	30	28	31	19	26
Save-Much Shoe Store	12	15	53	58	26	17	9	10

Percentages of Responses for Most Important and Least Important Shoe Attributes (Question 6)

	Ranking of Attribute*			
	First		Fifth	
	1969	1979	1969	1979
Fit	18%	24%	17%	15%
Price	10	12	20	17
Brand	17	15	24	27
Quality	28	29	15	16
Style	27	20	24	25
	100%	100%	100%	100%

*Read: 18 percent of the respondents ranked fit as the most important attribute of shoes in 1969, 24 percent ranked it first in 1979; 17 percent ranked fit as least important in 1969, 15 percent ranked it fifth in 1979.

Exhibit 16–2 (continued)

Percentages of Responses for Each Media Ranking (Question 7)

	First		Second		Third		Fourth	
	1969	1979	1969	1979	1969	1979	1969	1979
Radio	18%	19%	40%	41%	38%	37%	4%	3%
Direct Mail	2	2	5	4	13	12	80	82
Newspapers	70	54	25	20	4	16	1	10
Television	10	25	30	35	45	35	15	5
	100%	100%	100%	100%	100%	100%	100%	100%

Percentages of Responses to Sales Purchases (Question 8)

	Frequency of Sales Purchases	
	1969	1979
Never	11%	14%
Occasionally	48	34
Frequently	26	32
Always	15	20
	100%	100%

Case 17
DuPont (A)*

Pantyhose began the assault. They eliminated one function of the
girdle—holding up stockings. Then the attrition accelerated with the
rapid changes in dress which accompanied new casual life-styles
until, by 1975, the girdle—once worn almost universally by women
of all ages and backgrounds—seemed doomed to extinction.

But is the decline of this market inevitable? Or is there a future
somewhere—if only the right direction can be determined? These
questions are of vital importance to a hurting industry; machines,
personnel, facilities, and heavy investments hang on their answers.

Accordingly, DuPont, which has as much at stake in the market as
anyone, commissioned three separate research studies to probe the
problem. These studies, briefly overviewed in the Appendix, yielded
the results discussed in the following sections.

Reasons for the Girdle Decline

There always was resentment toward girdles. Women disliked the
constriction and discomfort girdles cause, but wore them anyway,
because there was no option. Wearing a girdle was "almost a legal

*This case is an edited version of "Control Garments: Do They Have a Future?"
a report prepared by DuPont.

requirement" for young and old, slim and heavy, with sporty or dressy styles. But once a choice was possible (with the alternative of pantyhose) and permissible (with today's "go-natural" life styles and relaxed social standards) women en masse decided: No! To many women, the idea of control in any form is repugnant. Dichter reports that the single most frequent response to the question: "Do you wear a girdle?" was: "Thank God, I haven't worn one for years!"

Many believe that girdles cause physical problems. For whatever reason—old wives' tales or advice from authorities (doctors, spa managers, etc.)—many women are convinced that girdle-wearing causes loss of muscle control and problems with circulation, as the following responses illustrate:

"Girdles are unhealthy. . . . They make your muscles flabby and cause varicose veins."
"To my great joy, my gynecologist suggested I go without a girdle to get rid of an itch. It went away. That was all the convincing I needed not to have to go back to wearing a girdle."
"My gynecologist told me to diet and exercise. He told me never to wear a girdle again."

Changing life styles and changing attitudes toward dress have made girdles optional. Today's emphasis on "naturalness"—the desire to give up artificial aspects of modern life—has persuaded many women to either just be themselves and live with their "natural package" or to control their weight by diet and exercise rather than to rely on a girdle to give them a smooth line under outerwear. Some choose clothes that minimize figure faults. Women are no longer willing to endure what they perceive as a form of punishment for the sake of their appearance.

"I won't sacrifice comfort for slimness."
"If you feel good, you look good. If you are uncomfortable, it shows. A girdle makes you uncomfortable."
"If you choose your clothes correctly, you don't have to be thin to look nice."

Liberalized attitudes toward sex reinforce the trend—making the overt sexuality of the uncontrolled female body more acceptable. Career-oriented women reject many traditional attitudes about clothing and appearance. Some consider girdles a symbol of male chauvinism.

In our youth-oriented society, these attitudes have, in a very short time, turned the wearing of a girdle into a sign of acceptance of chauvinistic attitudes, age, and/or loss of muscle tone. Dichter reports that these attitudes put even the confirmed wearer on the defensive, and make many would-be wearers fearful of the hypocrisy of trying to make themselves appear what they are not.

Milton Brand, of Brand, Gruber and Company, summarizes: "In the last 15 years, casualness has replaced formalism, comfort has become an objective, rather than a by-product, in clothes for all ages. Many younger women never even started to wear girdles, many who did for years have stopped, and even older women have decreased their use."

Husbands don't like girdles. A man wants his wife to "feel like a woman," and when their husbands accept them "as they are," wives find opinions of others less important. In interviewing, Dichter found that men considered a girdle a shield or barrier, something they must fight through. Something stiff, rigid, and unyielding on a woman's body feels unnatural and anti-erotic to them.

"A girdle on a woman definitely turns me off. I like to feel a woman's behind. A girdle is just too cumbersome. It seems to delay things. It is like a brick wall."
"A girdle is not free, natural. A natural look for a woman means a lot of things moving—parts which wiggle, like on her rear end."
"A chick with a girdle just isn't free. She isn't into the natural feeling, she's just not with it. . . . There has to be something wrong with her."

Women do not want to admit that they are out of shape. Dichter found that to many women, wearing a girdle is a psychological blow, an admission of failure:

"If I have to wear a girdle, that tells me I am getting old, that I'm aging. Taking off your girdle is like having to take out your false teeth."
"There has always been a stigma attached to wearing a girdle. If you wore a girdle, you were fat."

Wearing a girdle to correct faults simply exchanges one problem for another. In smoothing a fanny or a tummy, you create a bulge at the waist or thigh, and strong girdle control creates a "mono-buttock" look. Brand and Dichter found that the concept of "bulge" was the most negative idea of all with regard to shape.

Girdles are viewed as dull. There is nothing exciting about buying or wearing a girdle; the word itself is unappealing. One interviewee indicated, "in all clothes you want quality, fit, comfort and, if possible, a little pizazz." Dichter's research concluded that, "in a world of color, girdles have been presented in an aseptic, therapeutic manner." Brand concluded that, "Conventional girdles are perceived to be antiseptic, almost prescription, devices. An amazing number of women feel that this most intimate of all garments is the least feminine garment available."

Women are not aware of the full range of lightweight controlling garments available today. Perhaps because of a lack of communication from the industry to the consumer, the word *girdle* still connotes something bulky, lumpy, uncomfortable, constricting—the antithesis of the kind of clothing women like to wear today. Brand found that in rejecting girdles women were rejecting this image of yesterday's products, that they were unaware of the comfort and performance potential of many of today's products. Dichter concluded that, "unexpectedly, our findings indicate a major factor in the declining market is lack of promotion, absence of attempts to bring new life and excitement into the field."

A totally negative buying experience provides the final discouragement. Many departments in which girdles are sold are isolated, away from the flow of customer traffic, making the products seem "disdained." Brand found that women had a distinct impression that retail outlets were "hiding" control garment merchandise, making the shopping experience difficult. Garments are badly displayed on undersized rigid, "corpse-like" forms which cause fabric folds, making the girdles look more constricting than they are. Sales people are often considered inadequate—unable to advise, and unaware of product characteristics. No effort is made to coordinate cross-sell between under and outer garments. Dichter also found that the saleswomen are often so unattractive they reinforce the tired, old image.

"An 80-year old matron who didn't understand and couldn't care less about my figure."
"She was bulging out all over the top of her girdle, and I didn't want to look as bad as her."

Brand concluded: "It is our strong belief that the combination of inadequate manufacturer communication and minimal retail assistance has played as much of a role in the decline of the girdle market as has any social phenomenon."

The Market for Control Garments

The "Wearers"

Those who have always worn girdles in public, whether they are slim or heavy, probably will continue to do so. Mostly over 45 and of conventional attitudes, they believe it proper and "moral" to wear a girdle. They indicate, however, that they will keep looking for new, less bulky garments which promise greater comfort with true control.

The "Occasional Wearers"

Some consider themselves basically "wearers," who want control but only wear such a garment for "dress-up" occasions. Others consider themselves "non-wearers," although they may actually wear control just as often. The latter never consider the lightweight garments they do wear as "girdles."

These women represent a big potential market for control garments, and, as demonstrated by panelist reactions, a market that is relatively easy to reach. They indicate they would like more comfortable, feminine garments with lighter control.

The "Non-wearers"

Some women don't wear any kind of controlling garment and can't ever see themselves doing so. It should be noted, however, that when these non-wearers were shown soft, unstructured all-in-ones, they were pleasantly surprised, and their reactions were positive.

Motivations to Wear Control Garments

From the research, the reasons why so many women wear control garments infrequently or not at all seem clear. Understanding what motivates women to wear such garments when they do, however, is of key importance. Following are the most important reasons given by interviewees:

1. Under certain clothes, especially revealing ones, they create sleeker lines, eliminate bulges. A flat tummy was the most common objective. Even the most liberated women were conscious of their sexual role in marriage and wanted to look pretty for their husbands.
2. For many they are "morale builders," giving self-confidence—a psychological as well as a physical sense of well-being. It was found that many women, both slim and heavy, thought a body garment "gets it together," eliminates "looseness" and "flabbiness." One woman commented: "I hate the need for a girdle, but I feel more comfortable with one, because without it I look sloppy."
3. They give support and reduce fatigue.
4. They improve posture.
5. They satisfy good grooming requirements for dress-up occasions.
6. They serve as a gentle reminder against over-eating.

7. Some women gain weight in the winter and will wear some light control for their "winter figures."
8. They provide extra warmth in the winter.

Focal Topics

1. What are the relative advantages and disadvantages of using focus group interviews as opposed to other methods of gathering research data?
2. Based upon the research reported here, what conclusions can you draw about the future of the market for control garments?
3. What specific recommendations would you make to control garment marketers in terms of:
   a. Product design
   b. Product names
   c. Communications strategies
   d. Sales personnel selection and training
4. What other types of research should be undertaken at this time?

Appendix

The Three Studies, the Methods, and the Investigators

"The Role of Controlling Garments in 1975"

A DuPont Marketing Research Study

In this study, 126 women in the Philadelphia area were interviewed in thirteen group discussions, each lasting two hours. Interviews were conducted from August to November of 1974. Sixty-nine percent of interviewees were between the ages of fourteen and forty-four, and 75 percent earned between $10,000 and $20,000.

"Breaking the Girdle Barrier"

A Motivational Research Study by Ernest Dichter Associates International, Ltd.

In interviewing seventy-five people, Dichter conducted twenty-five individual, in-depth interviews; four group sessions with women (thirty-one total); and two group sessions with men (nineteen total).

Analysis of four previous focus groups conducted for DuPont was also included.

Dr. Ernest Dichter is recognized here and abroad as a leading exponent and practitioner of motivational research. He is a member of the American Psychological Association and the American Marketing Association and is the author of numerous books and articles on psychology and consumer motivation for business and advertising.

His independent Institute for Motivational Research (Ernest Dichter Associates) was established in 1946 and now operates from Croton-on-Hudson, New York.

"Understanding and Revitalizing the Market for Control Undergarments"

A study by Brand, Gruber and Company, Marketing Consultants.
In this study, seventy-five people were interviewed in nine group sessions. The interviews were designed to test interviewees' concepts about control undergarments.

Milton Brand is President of Brand, Gruber and Company, and its subsidiary, General Interviewing Surveys, both in Southfield, Michigan, a suburb of Detroit. Since 1960, these firms have provided marketing and product planning, consulting, and research services to an industrial clientele that covers the entire country.

Mr. Brand is active in the American Management Association and is involved in teaching several of its continuing courses. He has, for the last seventeen years, been an American Management Association seminar leader and guest speaker. He has appeared as guest speaker before many professional organizations and industrial associations throughout the country and abroad. He is also a member of the American Marketing Association (President, Detroit Chapter, 1972–1973) and several smaller professional groups.

Case 18

Consumer Medical Attitudes (A)*

In planning and designing this research project, a number of practical concerns—such as implications and strategies for which the data might be used and methodological concerns for achieving the highest validity and reliability consistent with the resources available for the study—were considered.

Objectives of the Study

The purpose of this study is to assess attitudes and behavior of consumers concerning health care and physician services, with special attention to consumer support for possible solutions to the medical malpractice problem. More specifically, the objectives of this study are:

1. to describe criteria used by patients to select and evaluate health care by physicians,
2. to identify persons likely to bring a malpractice suit in specified situations, and

*This case has been adapted from Roger D. Blackwell and W. Wayne Talarzyk, *Consumer Attitudes toward Health Care and Medical Malpractice* (Columbus, Ohio: Grid, Inc., 1977). The adaptation was made with the permission of Grid, Inc. The research reported in the case was conducted under a grant from the Malpractice Research Fund of the Ohio State Medical Association. Results from the research are presented in Consumer Medical Attitudes (B).

3. to determine levels of support for alternative approaches for dealing with the malpractice study.

Research Methodology

Telephone Sample

This study was conducted using a telephone questionnaire administered to a random sample of 1,500 adult residents in Ohio. The telephone format was selected after consideration of both mail and personal interviews, which it was felt would provide less reliable data in this particular study than would telephone interviews. The sample was drawn with the assistance of the Chicago-based Reuben Donnelly Company, which maintains telephone directories from all cities of the United States. It provided a computer-generated random sample of telephone numbers in Ohio cities and rural areas.

A sample of 1,500 is reliable and provides a reasonable base for making inferences about the Ohio adult population. However, all samples have some limitations. For example, persons who were not at home when calls were made or who do not have telephones could be under-represented in this study. To minimize these problems, three callbacks were attempted at various time periods.

The interviewing for this study was completed by Dwight Spencer Associates from WATS line facilities in Columbus, Ohio, using skilled and continuously monitored interviewers.

Design and Pretest of Questionnaire

The questionnaire used in this study was developed from prior studies on medical care and physician services as well as standardized forms used for securing demographic and attitudinal data. A preliminary form of the questionnaire was administered by telephone to twenty respondents in the Columbus area; it was further tested through a focus group interview in which male and female consumers discussed each question and possible responses on the questionnaire.

After the telephone pretest, the focus group interview, and consultation with the Ohio State Medical Association staff, numerous changes were made in order to clarify some questions unlikely to provide useful information in their original form. Very few difficulties were encountered in the administration of the final questionnaire. Even though it was lengthy—it took an average of nineteen minutes for completion—it was of sufficient interest and clarity that few terminations were encountered. The Appendix contains the complete questionnaire.

Focal Topics

1. In what ways do you believe the questionnaire in the research project could have been improved?
2. Evaluate the research methodology used in this study. What changes would you recommend in sample design, pretesting, and ways of gathering the data?
3. What methods of analysis would you recommend for evaluating the data acquired via this questionnaire?
4. Discuss ways in which the results of this research could be communicated to interested parties such as consumers, physicians, medical associations, legislative groups, the media, and so forth.

Appendix

Medical Practices Survey Form*

Hello. My name is _____ .
I am affiliated with _____
and we are working on a research project concerned with medical practices. I have a number of questions that we are asking many people in Ohio, and we will

(CC) appreciate your opinion being included.

(5) 1. First, do you have a family doctor? That is, one you would go to most of the time when you are sick? Yes 1   No 2

(6–7) 2. Approximately how many times were you, your spouse, and children living at home treated during the past twelve months by a physician? ☐ ☐ (write in number.)

(8–9) 2a. How many days were you or members of your family in a hospital during the past twelve months? ☐ ☐

3. If you or members of your family were treated by more than one type of physician or specialist, how many times were you treated by each doctor during the past twelve months?

                                                        Number of Treatments
(10–11) 1. Family Practice   _____
(12–13) 2. Surgeon   _____
(14–15) 3. OB-Gyn   _____
(16–17) 4. Ophthalmologist   _____
(18–19) 5. Pediatrician   _____
(20–21) 6. Internist   _____
(22–23) 7. Emergency Room   _____
(24–25) 8. Other MD (Specify _____)   _____
(26–27) 9. Other non-MD (Specify _____)   _____

(28–29)   Total number of treatments   _____

(30) 4. Thinking about your primary doctor or family doctor, can you think back and tell me how you happened to choose that doctor? (Record all reasons mentioned.) Were there any other reasons? (Check all reasons mentioned.)

1. Recommended by friend or relative   _____

---

*Interviewer is to read orally all words except answer headings and instructions to interviewer.

    2. Recommended by another physician   _____

    3. Looked in yellow pages of directory   _____

    4. Recommended by hospital   _____

    5. Met the doctor socially or heard of him as civic leader   _____

    6. Treated as member of hospital staff (emergency, etc.)   _____

    7. Required physician (clinics, insurance, etc.)   _____

    8. Can't remember, always been our doctor, etc.   _____

    9. Other (Specify) _____   _____

(31)   5. Of those reasons, which one would be the most important for your choice?_____(1–9)

    6. Here's an imaginary question. Suppose your present doctor were to move away suddenly and you had to choose a new one. I have a list of characteristics of doctors that people sometimes use to evaluate a doctor. I would like for you to rate each characteristic on a scale of 1 to 5 according to its importance to you personally. If something is very important to you, you should rate it as a 1; if it is somewhat important, you should rate it a 2; if it is neutral in importance, rate it 3; if it is somewhat unimportant, rate it a 4; and if it is very unimportant, rate it a 5.

(32)   1. The doctor's office is near you.   1 2 3 4 5

(33)   2. The doctor has access to the hospital you want.   1 2 3 4 5

(34)   3. The doctor has a good personality and appearance.   1 2 3 4 5

(35)   4. How much the doctor charges.   1 2 3 4 5

(36)   5. The doctor is willing to talk with you about your illness.   1 2 3 4 5

(37)   6. The doctor has many years of experience.   1 2 3 4 5

(38)   7. The doctor has never been sued for malpractice.   1 2 3 4 5

(39)   8. The doctor is recommended by other doctors.   1 2 3 4 5

(40)   9. The doctor has evening or weekend office hours.   1 2 3 4 5

(41)   10. The doctor is recommended by your friends.   1 2 3 4 5

(42)   11. How long it takes to get an appointment.   1 2 3 4 5

(43)   7. What is your feeling about the quality of health care given by your doctor? Would you describe it as:

1. Excellent_____ 2. Good_____

3. Average_____ 4. Poor_____ or 5. Very Poor_____

(44)   8. What is your feeling about the quality of health care given by doctors in general?
1. Excellent_____ 2. Good_____

3. Average_____ 4. Poor_____ or 5. Very Poor_____

(45)   9. What is your feeling about the charges you pay your doctor? Are they:

1. Entirely too high for the services provided you?   _____

2. Too high for the services provided you?   _____

3. Reasonable for the services provided you?   _____

4. Low considering the services provided you?   _____

(46)   10. In recent years, the amount that doctors pay for malpractice insurance has increased drastically. In a few words, what do you personally believe is the cause of increased costs of malpractice insurance?

_____

_____

_____

1. Doctors at fault.   _____

2. Lawyers at fault.   _____

3. Insurance companies at fault.   _____

4. The government or laws are at fault.   _____

5. Juries and/or judges are giving too much.   _____

11. Several ways of handling the malpractice problem have been proposed. We would like to describe some of these methods and ask you to rate your support for them on a 1 to 5 scale. If you would be strongly for this method, rate it 1. If you would be somewhat for the method, rate it a 2. If you are neutral, a 3. Somewhat against it, a 4; and strongly against it, a 5.

(47)   1. A law that lowered the proportion of the settlement that lawyers could receive for malpractice suits. 1 2 3 4 5

(48)   2. A requirement that patients agree to arbitration of malpractice claims (the patient and the doctor would appoint skilled
arbitrators to settle malpractice claims).   1   2   3   4   5

(49)   3. A state agency, something like the workmen's compensation
bureau, which would collect malpractice insurance premiums from all physicians and decide what benefits would be
given all patients with malpractice claims.   1   2   3   4   5

(50)   4. A state law which limited the amounts that could be collected by patients with malpractice claims.   1   2   3   4   5

(51)   5. A peer group review system in which a group of physicians
reviewed malpractice claims and decided which ones should
be taken to trial.   1   2   3   4   5

(52)   6. A release signed before a person is accepted as a patient
agreeing not to sue for malpractice.   1   2   3   4   5

(53)   7. More time spent by your physician in explaining the risks or
potential problems of your operation or medicine even
though the charge for the doctor's services would be higher
than now.   1   2   3   4   5

(54)   8. A state law which requires insurance companies to reduce
malpractice rates to doctors in return for correspond-
ingly higher rates on health insurance to the general
public.   1   2   3   4   5

(55)   9. Countersuits by physicians against patients and their attorneys who sue for malpractice with no basis for the malpractice suit.   1   2   3   4   5

(56–58) 12. Of the malpractice suits that are brought against physicians,
what percentage would you say are instances in which the doctor was negligent? ☐ ☐ ☐ %

(59–61) 13. Of the malpractice settlement, what percentage of the money
do you believe goes to the lawyer? ☐ ☐ ☐ %

(62)   14. Let's assume that your doctor was unable to determine a cure
for you, and you thought your doctor might be at fault. Would
you be very likely to bring a malpractice suit, somewhat likely,
undecided, somewhat unlikely, or very unlikely to bring a malpractice suit?

    1. Very likely   _____   4. Somewhat unlikely _____

    2. Somewhat likely   _____   5. Very unlikely   _____

    3. Undecided   _____

(63)   15. Let's assume that you developed a serious medical problem in which you thought your physician might be at fault. Would you be very likely to bring a malpractice suit, somewhat likely, undecided, somewhat unlikely, or very unlikely to bring a malpractice suit.

    1. Very likely   _____   4. Somewhat unlikely _____

    2. Somewhat likely   _____   5. Very unlikely   _____

    3. Undecided   _____

(64)   16. Let's assume that your spouse or your parent died and you thought your physician might be at fault. Would you be very likely to bring a malpractice suit, somewhat likely, undecided, somewhat unlikely, or very unlikely to bring a malpractice suit?

    1. Very likely   _____   4. Somewhat unlikely _____

    2. Somewhat likely   _____   5. Very unlikely   _____

    3. Undecided   _____

(65)   17. Have you ever personally brought a malpractice suit against a physician?

    1. Yes _____ (please continue)

    2. No _____ (skip to question 24)

(66)   18. What happened to your suit? What is the current status?

    1. Dismissed with a settlement to you   _____

    2. Dismissed without a settlement to you   _____

    3. Brought to trial with a judgment to you   _____

    4. Brought to trial with no judgment to you   _____

    5. Case currently pending   _____

(67)   19. What was the specialty of the physician who was sued?

    1. Family practice   _____

    2. Surgeon   _____

    3. OB-Gyn   _____

    4. Ophthalmologist   _____

    5. Pediatrician   _____

    6. Other (specify _____)   _____

(68)   20. In a few words, can you tell me what caused you to decide to pursue a malpractice suit against the physician?

_____

_____

_____

    1. Self influences   _____

    2. Family influences   _____

    3. Physician influences   _____

    4. Other medical personnel (nurses, etc.)   _____

    5. Attorney influences   _____

    6. Other influences   _____

    7. Other reasons   _____

(69–71) 21. Of the amount that was paid to you, what percentage went to the attorney? ☐☐☐

(72)   22. If you had to decide again to pursue the malpractice suit, would you be very likely to do it again, somewhat likely, undecided, somewhat unlikely, or very unlikely to bring the malpractice suit if you were able to do it over?

    1. Very likely   _____   4. Somewhat unlikely _____

    2. Somewhat likely   _____   5. Very unlikely   _____

    3. Undecided   _____

(73)   23. If you were to need medical treatment again, would you be very likely to go to the same physician, somewhat likely, undecided, somewhat unlikely, or very unlikely to go to the same physician again?

    1. Very likely   _____   4. Somewhat unlikely _____

    2. Somewhat likely   _____   5. Very unlikely   _____

    3. Undecided   _____

24. Now, I would like to read some statements that some people agree with and some do not agree with. We would like to know if you strongly agree, somewhat agree, are neutral, somewhat disagree, or strongly disagree with each statement. There are no right or wrong answers. We are simply interested in your opinion about each statement.

(CC) (1–4)
Same as
Card 1

		SA	A	N	D	SD
(5)	1. I generally have a physical checkup at least once a year.	1	2	3	4	5
(6)	2. I generally approve of abortion if a woman wants one.	1	2	3	4	5
(7)	3. I have a great deal of confidence in my doctor.	1	2	3	4	5
(8)	4. About half of the physicians in Ohio are not really competent to practice medicine.	1	2	3	4	5
(9)	5. If I had a terminal illness, I would not want my physician to tell me.	1	2	3	4	5
(10)	6. Most doctors are overpaid.	1	2	3	4	5
(11)	7. I wish there were brochures which explained things to me when a doctor treats me.	1	2	3	4	5
(12)	8. I often watch TV programs that discuss health problems.	1	2	3	4	5
(13)	9. In most malpractice suits, the physician is actually negligent or in the wrong.	1	2	3	4	5
(14)	10. My physician adequately explains my medical problems to me.	1	2	3	4	5
(15)	11. Most physicians are ethical and responsible persons.	1	2	3	4	5
(16)	12. Most physicians are more concerned about making money than the welfare of their patients.	1	2	3	4	5
(17)	13. Most physicians in Ohio are not very competent.	1	2	3	4	5
(18)	14. It is wrong for a doctor to go on strike for any reason.	1	2	3	4	5
(19)	15. I usually read the nutrition information on food packages.	1	2	3	4	5
(20)	16. In most malpractice suits, the physician is not really to blame.	1	2	3	4	5

(21) 17. I believe that a very ill person
      should be allowed to die when
      there is no chance of
      recovering again.   1   2   3   4   5

(22) 18. I generally do exercises (like
      push-ups or sit-ups or jogging) at
      least twice a week.   1   2   3   4   5

(23) 19. I am careful about what I eat.   1   2   3   4   5

(24) 20. I usually have a good tan
      every year.   1   2   3   4   5

(25) 21. I frequently play tennis or
      other sports where I can get a
      lot of exercise.   1   2   3   4   5

(26) 22. I weigh about what my doctor
      says I should.   1   2   3   4   5

(27) 23. I usually go on a weight
      control diet at least twice
      a year.   1   2   3   4   5

(28) 24. It seems that I am sick a lot
      more than my friends are.   1   2   3   4   5

Finally, we have just a few questions to make sure we
have all types of opinions represented in our survey.

(29) 25. With what religion or denomination, if any, do you
      identify?

      1. Catholic   _____   6. Other Protestant

      2. Baptist   _____   (specify   )   _____

      3. Methodist   _____   7. Jewish   _____

      4. Lutheran   _____   8. Other (specify   ) _____

      5. Presbyterian   _____   9. None   _____

(30) 26. Would you consider your political views to be:

      1. Very liberal   _____

      2. Somewhat liberal   _____

      3. Middle of the road   _____

      4. Somewhat conservative   _____

      5. Very conservative   _____

(31) 27. Please stop me when I come to the category that describes your age.

    1. Under 25 ＿＿＿＿　4. 45 to 54 ＿＿＿＿

    2. 25 to 34 ＿＿＿＿　5. 55 to 64 ＿＿＿＿

    3. 35 to 44 ＿＿＿＿　6. 65 & older ＿＿＿＿

(32) 28. What is the last year of school you have completed? (check appropriate category below)

    1. Did not attend ＿＿＿＿

    2. Elementary or grammar school ＿＿＿＿

    3. Went to high school or trade school for less than 4 years ＿＿＿＿

    4. Graduated from high school or trade school ＿＿＿＿

    5. Some college, junior college, or technical school ＿＿＿＿

    6. Graduated from college ＿＿＿＿

    7. Some post-graduate work ＿＿＿＿

    8. Have post-graduate degree ＿＿＿＿

(33) 29. Is your residence in: (check appropriate category below)

    1. A rural area ＿＿＿＿

    2. A small town ＿＿＿＿

    3. An urban area ＿＿＿＿

    4. A suburban area ＿＿＿＿

(34) 30. Counting your spouse and children as well as yourself, how many persons in your family are living at home now?

    ＿＿＿ 1, ＿＿＿ 2, ＿＿＿3, ＿＿＿ 4, ＿＿＿ 5, ＿＿＿ 6, ＿＿＿ 7, ＿＿＿ 8, ＿＿＿ 9 or more

(35) 31. Finally, as I read a number of income categories, please stop me when I come to the one that describes your household's total income last year (before taxes).

    1. Less than $3,000 ＿＿＿　4. $10,000 to $14,999 ＿＿＿

    2. $3,000 to $7,999 ＿＿＿　5. $15,000 to $19,999 ＿＿＿

    3. $8,000 to $9,999 ＿＿＿　6. $20,000 to $24,999 ＿＿＿

    7. $25,000 to $34,999 _____   9. $50,000 or more   _____

    8. $35,000 to $49,999 _____

(36) 32. Record sex of respondent:

    1. Male _____   2. Female _____

Part Four
Planning Components of the Marketing Program

Case 19
Baskin-Robbins 31 Ice Cream Stores (A)

In December 1976, Baskin-Robbins celebrated its thirty-first birthday. This organization, a nationwide manufacturer and distributor of high-quality ice cream through franchised outlets, represents one of the outstanding marketing success stories in North America.

When the firm reached 500 stores in 1967, the original partners merged with United Brands. In 1973 United Brands sold Baskin-Robbins to J. Lyons Company of London, owners of Tetley Tea, for $37 million, plus another $8 million paid to a separate group of stockholders.

Today there are over 2,000 stores, serving over 800 cities in every major market from coast to coast in Europe and Asia. In recent years a new store has opened approximately every three days.

The company illustrates how promotional philosophy is a direct cause in successful marketing. Baskin-Robbins is unique in that its philosophy has been more closely related to products and product distribution than to formal mass-communication efforts. From the outset the company has exhibited both sensitivity and flexibility in promotional activities and has relied heavily on in-store promotions for mass exposure.

The overall nature of Baskin-Robbins today can best be illustrated by the description given in Exhibit 19–1, which was written by Professor Warren Schmidt, UCLA Graduate School of Business Administration and a special consultant to Baskin-Robbins.

Background Orientation

Company Development

In 1945 the trend in ice cream marketing was to prepackaged, self-service sales primarily in supermarkets. It was in this year that Burton Baskin and Irvine Robbins entered the ice cream business. Sparkling, attractive stores would feature only hand-packed ice cream of the highest quality and, because of more costly ingredients, higher priced than the supermarket ice cream product. Prior to that time the corner drugstore with its soda fountain service and strategic location had dominated retail ice cream distribution.

The supermarkets based their appeal on price and shopping convenience and ignored ice cream sodas, sundaes, cones, hand-packing, and all forms of personal service. When Baskin-Robbins entered the field, the basic marketing premise was to make the product and the stores so attractive to the public that the buyer would seek out and purchase the unique product—even though it meant extra effort. An essential ingredient in establishing demand was the creation of an unprecedented variety of unusual ice cream flavors. The initial marketing efforts were carried out by stores in Pasadena and Glendale, California. In these outlets the marketing theory was put to test. These stores were an immediate success. They proved the public was flavor conscious. The buyer was happy to shop for top quality ice cream in immaculate stores that featured personalized service.

A Uniform Identification

In 1948 Baskin-Robbins made a significant marketing decision that was to shape the total company image. It selected Carson-Roberts Inc. as its advertising agency. Then in embryonic stage, Carson-Roberts is today a division of Ogilvy & Mather, the eighth largest advertising agency in the world. Among the other Horatio Alger companies guided by Carson-Roberts is Mattel Toys. A close rapport between client and agency has resulted in what agency principal Ralph Carson refers to as total involvement in advertising-merchandising efforts.

Baskin-Robbins had sought out the agency to create advertisements for the *Los Angeles Times*. The total budget was $500. At the time the ice cream stores had two separate identities; some of the stores were known as *Snowbird Ice Cream Stores*, and the remainder were called *Burton's Ice Cream Stores*. Both sets of stores sold identical products and held the same basic philosophy.

Carson-Roberts's recommendation—unorthodox considering that their primary purpose was to create and place advertisements—was *not to run any advertisements.* The agency counseled that a new name was needed, to effect a uniform identification. The dual image of *Snowbird and Burton's* was to be consolidated under the trade name "Baskin-Robbins." To aid customer brand recognition, the numeral 31 was added (other classic examples of numeric trademarks are Heinz 57 Varieties and Union 76 oil products). Trademark design and truck-trademark identification were also recommended. The agency felt that the marketing theory was sound and that uniform identification would aid in promotion.

The image consolidation was successful. Within two years, an advertising budget of $5,000 had been established for a radio campaign in the Los Angeles market. The ensuing years brought a media mixture of local spot radio and local newspaper display advertising. At the writing of this case study, Baskin-Robbins had shifted the emphasis from newspaper to television and magazines, although newspaper display advertising and radio are used at the local level.

Marketing Information

Chairman of the board, Irvine Robbins has stated the firm's philosophy: "We don't sell ice cream, we sell fun." From the outset, Baskin-Robbins has marketed its brand of "fun" in a very creative manner.

Creating and Naming

Baskin-Robbins is pledged to the highest possible quality, and it has received Gold Medal Awards periodically at state and county fairs in competitive judging over a number of years. The company features the most complete assortment of ice cream products available anywhere in America and has been listed in the *Guinness Book of Records* as marketing a world record 600-plus flavors. As can be seen from the partial list of Baskin-Robbins flavors in Exhibit 19–2, every effort is made to tempt the public appetite with exotically created and named flavors. Vanilla, for example, becomes *Pennant Winning Vanilla* when combined with *Umpire Style Razzberries* and *Nutty Cashews* in *Baseball Nut Ice Cream.*

With a reputation for being a master at the game, Baskin-Robbins applies a timely twist of events of the day in naming and creating products. *Beatnut* was introduced in the early 1960s to catch the flavor of the "Beatniks," and *Astro-nut* honored the first astronaut put into orbit. A zany concoction of almonds, cherries, toffee, and caramel called *Would You Believe?* was created to tie in with the phrase made popular by Don Adams, the bumbling star of the television show, *Get Smart.* As skirts went up, *Mod Mini-Mint* ice cream was created to show approval of the trend in women's fashions.

Well-known characters and television shows brought more flavors such as *Charley Brownie, Jolly Green Mint, Bewitched, My Three Sons' All American Flavor Chocolate Mint,* and *Jack Lemmon Ice Cream.*

To celebrate the bicentennial, Baskin-Robbins introduced such flavors as *Yankee Doodle Strudel* (with cherries and strudel crumbs), *Valley Forge Fudge* (chocolate fudge ice cream with brownie pieces), *Concord Grape,* and *Minute Man Mint* (green peppermint ice cream with peppermint candy and marshmallow ribbons).

Performance Record

Americans have traditionally led the world in ice cream consumption (the annual consumption rate, now at 30 pints of ice cream per year per person, is still growing). Baskin-Robbins has contributed to this growth in consumption, especially in recent years. In 1962 the firm sold ice cream enough to fill 50 million cones; by 1975 annual sales exceeded the equivalent of 800 million cones. During 1976 the chain sold about 28 million gallons of ice cream, worth almost $75 million in gross sales and revenues.

Custom-made Products

Custom-made ice cream desserts are an important part of Baskin-Robbins's product line. Standard or special-order custom-made desserts of ice cream or ice cream combined with cakes are made in the stores. Franchisees and their employees are trained to make approximately twenty standard items, which they display in a specially designed ice cream dessert display case. Many franchisees merchandise special items of their own creation. High-profit products that lend themselves well to advertising and promotional opportunities, especially during holiday seasons, ice cream desserts comprise approximately 12 percent of the average store's business. Illustrations of such products are shown in Exhibit 19–3, taken from a franchise bulletin. Exhibit 19–4 shows some of the items on display for immediate sale in the case.

Special Merchandising

Baskin-Robbins utilizes many different types of special merchandising efforts for its products. As shown in Exhibit 19–5, *Gift of Joy* gift certificates, redeemable at any Baskin-Robbins 31 Ice Cream Stores, are available for easy giving. Seasonal promotions include such products as beach balls, book covers, and other items given with various purchases. Exhibit 19–5 also shows an example of a similar special for an ice cream scoop with every three-pound (half-gallon) carton of ice cream. Also featured in Exhibit 19–5 are two additional examples of special merchandising—one supporting Baskin-Robbins's offer of sample tastes and the other introducing PDQ (personalized decorations quickly).

Promotional Strategy

National Advertising

The first national advertising campaign, paid for jointly by Baskin-Robbins and franchised operators, took place in May–June 1970. Using a tongue-in-cheek concept, the company introduced their Top Secret 32d Flavor with full-color ads in *Life* and *Look* magazines and in the Sunday supplements of selected newspapers throughout the country.

National advertising was supported by a promotion at the store level featuring television star Jonathan Winters as the president of B.R.U.C.E. (Baskin-Robbins United Closet Eaters), "a society dedicated to eating the Top Secret 32d Flavor in a closet or other secret places." Membership cards carrying Jonathan Winters's photo and signature were distributed in stores and through publicity and promotional channels. Stickers, window posters, and point-of-scale display material supported the campaign, as did local newspaper ads, radio spots, and publicity releases. National publicity was obtained with a B.R.U.C.E. press party given by Winters.

Since 1970 Baskin-Robbins has made regular use of national advertising. It has advertised during television coverage of the Rose Parade and on such network programs as *The Waltons, Little House on the Prairie, The Jeffersons, Wonderful World of Disney, Tom Sawyer Special, Bionic Woman, Donnie and Marie,* and others. Latest television advertising features a thirty-second spot with the theme "Get That 31derful Feeling."

As part of its national promotion campaign, Baskin-Robbins regularly uses its ice cream as prizes to contestants and participants on television quiz and game shows. Some of the shows involving Baskin-Robbins include *The Price is Right, Hot Seat, Let's Make a Deal, The Gong Show,* and *Wheel of Fortune.*

Baskin-Robbins has selected women 18 to 49 years of age with children as its target market for television communications. This market segment is perceived to represent the firm's best customers.

Reseller Support Activities

Kits of in-store displays, special promotions, and tie-ins with national advertising are provided to each franchisee every month. Local franchisees are also encouraged to place advertisements in their local advertising media. Baskin-Robbins supplies support materials which include newspaper mats, radio scripts and jingle transcriptions, layout and copy suggestions, and publicity releases.

Each store also has a Birthday Club for all children. Each child registered is offered an ice cream on his or her birthday each year until the age of thirteen. The redemption card, which is sent to the home shortly before the child's birthday, also features a message just for Mom about ice cream desserts.

Publicity and Merchandising

Since its beginning, Baskin-Robbins's management has been publicity oriented, and its activities and merchandising in this area have been numerous. Several of the more eventful publicity and merchandising events are described below.

Here Comes the Fudge One of the most successful promotions Baskin-Robbins has had was a tie-in with the television show *Laugh-in* for a *Here Comes the Fudge Ice Cream* flavor. Before the flavor was introduced in the stores, it was served at a Chamber of Commerce luncheon for over 700 guests in "Beautiful Downtown Burbank," honoring the show's cast, producers, and crew. Resulting publicity swept the country, and when the flavor went on sale it zoomed to a top seller in the first few weeks. Stickers, printed pullover shirts, special window posters, counter display cards, and advertising mats were added to the regular merchandising support material. The campaign was so successful that it was extended for a month, and the flavor was so popular that it has periodically been returned to the flavor list by popular demand.

Lunar Cheesecake When the Apollo 11 astronauts landed on the moon, Baskin-Robbins had *Lunar Cheesecake Ice Cream* in all of the stores within hours after the landing. This entailed considerable planning and timing. The product, all merchandising, and publicity material were produced in advance, delivered to the stores, and held until the men landed on the moon. Warning was issued to stores that should any disaster befall the return flight, all products and signs should be pulled immediately from the stores. This promotion received wide national coverage in the press and on radio. UPI, food editors, radio commentators, and columnists publicized the promotion.

Herbie Goes to Monte Carlo. In another campaign, Baskin-Robbins and Walt Disney joined promotional efforts around the Disney movie, *Herbie Goes to Monte Carlo*. For the tie-in campaign, Baskin-

Robbins created a new flavor, *Monte Carlo Stripe*, a fruit-flavored ice cream combining orange-pineapple and peach flavorings with a red raspberry ribbon. A thirty-second television commercial, four radio commercials, a series of print advertisements, and a variety of point-of-purchase materials were developed to promote the ice cream flavor and a special Monte Carlo Sweepstakes. An example of a print advertisement for this campaign is presented in Exhibit 19–6.

Other Tie-ins. Baskin-Robbins also urges local stores to develop individual tie-in promotions. Exhibit 19–7 displays information about some successful local promotions between banks and Baskin-Robbins stores.

Focal Topics

1. Evaluate Baskin-Robbins's marketing strategy. Do you recommend any changes?
2. What effectiveness do you attribute to the firm's publicity efforts?
3. What should be the established objectives for the advertising and promotion of Baskin-Robbins ice cream?
4. What media strategy, message strategy, and creative strategy do you recommend for future Baskin-Robbins advertising?

Exhibit 19–1
A Description of Baskin-Robbins

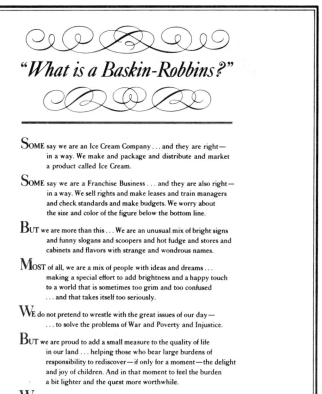

"*What is a Baskin-Robbins?*"

SOME say we are an Ice Cream Company . . . and they are right—
in a way. We make and package and distribute and market
a product called Ice Cream.

SOME say we are a Franchise Business . . . and they are also right—
in a way. We sell rights and make leases and train managers
and check standards and make budgets. We worry about
the size and color of the figure below the bottom line.

BUT we are more than this . . . We are an unusual mix of bright signs
and funny slogans and scoopers and hot fudge and stores and
cabinets and flavors with strange and wondrous names.

MOST of all, we are a mix of people with ideas and dreams . . .
making a special effort to add brightness and a happy touch
to a world that is sometimes too grim and too confused
. . . and that takes itself too seriously.

WE do not pretend to wrestle with the great issues of our day—
. . . to solve the problems of War and Poverty and Injustice.

BUT we are proud to add a small measure to the quality of life
in our land . . . helping those who bear large burdens of
responsibility to rediscover—if only for a moment—the delight
and joy of children. And in that moment to feel the burden
a bit lighter and the quest more worthwhile.

WE try not to take ourselves too seriously . . . to carry out our daily
tasks with buoyancy and a chuckle.

BUT in the moments of our greatest pride we think of ourselves
as those who contribute in a special way to our fellow humans
— helping to nourish that quality of childlike enjoyment
which is perhaps the most precious and hopeful part
of our humanity.

WARREN H. SCHMIDT

Exhibit 19–2
A Partial List of Baskin-Robbins Flavors

100 & 31 FLAVORS

(And more are being created each month)

APRICOT BRANDY SHERBET	CHOCOLATE MARSHMALLOW RIBBON	ORANGE SHERBET
APRICOT MARMALADE	CHOCOLATE MINT	OREGON BLACKBERRY
APRICOT-ORANGE ICE	CHOCOLATE RIBBON	PARIS PARFAIT
APPLE PIE	CHOPPED CHOCOLATE	FRESH PEACH
APPLE STRUDEL	FRESH COCONUT	PEACH CHIFFON
FRESH BANANA	COCONUT ALMOND FUDGE	PEACHES MELBA
BANANA ALMOND FUDGE	COCONUT STRAWBERRY	PEACHES 'N CREAM
BANANA BERRY	COCO 'N FUDGE	PEANUT BUTTER 'N JELLY
BANANA COCONUT	CRANBERRY SHERBET	PEPPERMINT
BANANA DAIQUIRI ICE	CREME DE CARAMEL	PEPPERMINT FUDGE RIBBON
BANANA MARSHMALLOW	CREME DE MENTHE	PINEAPPLE CHEESECAKE
BANANA ROCKY ROAD	DAIQUIRI ICE	PINEAPPLE ICE
BANANAS 'N STRAWBERRY	DAIQUIRI ALMOND ICE	PINEAPPLE NUT
BASEBALL NUT	DATE KRUNCH	PINEAPPLE UPSIDE DOWN CAKE
BAVARIAN CHOCOLATE MINT	DEVILS FOOD CAKE	PINK GRAPEFRUIT ICE
BLACK RASPBERRY	EGG NOG	PISTACHIO ALMOND
BLACK WALNUT	ENGLISH TOFFEE	PISTACHIO ALMOND FUDGE
BLUEBERRY CHEESECAKE	ESPRESSO	PLUM NUTS
BLUEBERRY MARSHMALLOW	FRENCH VANILLA	PRALINES 'N CREAM
BLUEBERRIES 'N CREAM	FUDGE BROWNIE	PUMPKIN PIE
BOYSENBERRY CHEESECAKE	GERMAN CHOCOLATE CAKE	RAINBOW SHERBET
BOYSENBERRIES 'N CREAM	GOOSEBERRY SHERBET	RASPBERRIES 'N CREAM
BOYSENBERRY SHERBET	GRAHAM CRACKER	RASPBERRY SHERBET
BITTERSWEET CHOCOLATE	GRAPE ICE	RED APPLE JACK ICE
BURGUNDY CHERRY	HERE COMES THE FUDGE	RED, WHITE & BLUEBERRY
SPARKLING BURGUNDY ICE	JAMOCA	R.S.V.P.
BUTTER PECAN	JAMOCA ALMOND FUDGE	ROCKY ROAD
CAFÉ OLÉ	JACK LEMMON	RUM RAISIN
CARAMEL ALMOND CRUNCH	LEMON CHIFFON	SARSAPARILLA
CARAMEL BRITTLE	LEMON CUSTARD	SPUMONI
CARAMEL ROCKY ROAD	LEMON SHERBET	SHIBUI GINGER
CARAMEL WALNUT	LEMON LIME SHERBET	FRESH STRAWBERRY
CHAMPAGNE GRAPE ICE	LEMON PEEL SHERBET	STRAWBERRY CHEESECAKE
CHERRY CHEESECAKE	LICORICE	STRAWBERRY DAIQUIRI ICE
CHERRY PIE	LIME ICE	STRAWBERRY ICE
CHERRIES ROMANOFF	MACADAMIA NUT	STRAWBERRY RHUBARB SHERBET
CHERRY VANILLA	MANDARIN CHOCOLATE SHERBET	STRAWBERRY SHORTCAKE
CHARLEY BROWNIE	MANGO SHERBET	TANGANILLA
CHOCOLATE	MINT ON MINT	TANGERINE SHERBET
CHOCOLATE ALMOND	NEW ENGLAND MAPLE NUT	TIN ROOF
CHOCOLATE CHEESECAKE	NUTCRACKER SWEET	VANILLA
CHOCOLATE CHIP	NUTS TO YOU	WATERMELON ICE
CHOCOLATE ECLAIR	NUTTY COCONUT	32ND FLAVOR
CHOCOLATE FUDGE	ORANGE CUSTARD	

© 1972 BASKIN-ROBBINS, INC.   PRINTED IN U.S.A.

Exhibit 19–3
Illustrations of Holiday, Custom-Made Products

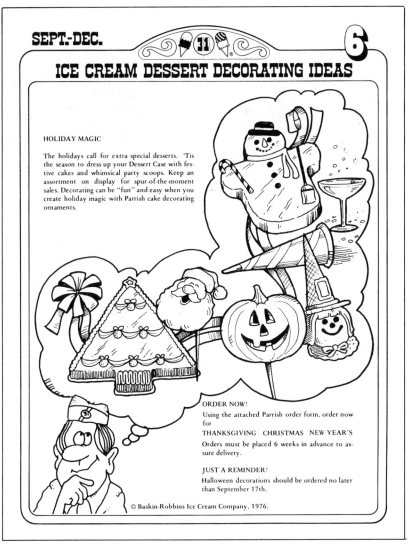

Exhibit 19-4
Specially Designed Ice Cream Dessert Display Case

Exhibit 19–5
Examples of Advertisements Supporting Special Merchandising

Exhibit 19–6
Sample Print Advertisement of the Monte Carlo Sweepstakes

Exhibit 19–7
Information about Local Tie-in Promotional Campaigns

Case 20

Baskin-Robbins 31 Ice Cream Stores (B)

There is little question that the aggressive selling efforts of local franchised operators, in addition to the various promotion and publicity programs described in Baskin-Robbins 31 Ice Cream Stores (A), have combined to form an effective demand stimulation effort. An important key to continued success is the assurance of a well-trained, fully informed, franchised owner who will cooperatively support the total marketing efforts of Baskin-Robbins.

Franchising Operations

When the marketing concepts employed in the original stores met with such positive acceptance, Baskin-Robbins was ready to enter into a new phase of the business—franchising. Another dimension was added in the person of the franchised store owner. A successful specialty ice cream business requires constant supervision and attention best furnished by an individual operator with a personal interest. Therefore, the Baskin-Robbins stores were created for franchised store owners, not as a chain of company-owned outlets.

The Baskin-Robbins franchise program was outlined in the *Harvard Business Review* as follows:

An example of a rapidly growing and highly successful franchise operation is the California-based Baskin-Robbins "31" Flavor ice cream stores.... These unique stores, offering a wide assortment of high-quality ice cream products, are owned and operated by individual businessmen, many without previous ice cream or dairy experience. Actually, the nature of the franchise arrangement does not require operators to be experienced in this line, for the essentials are all planned by Baskin-Robbins—including advertising, promotion, store layout and fixtures, portion control, and other operating factors. Even a training program for store personnel is included, which is administered by the store owner. Each store receives advice from regional supervisors, who are competent, well-trained specialists. No one store, of course, could afford this level of assistance.[1]

Management Guides

Baskin-Robbins has published a three-volume set of *Management Guides* for the use of franchisees and management personnel. These are available to all areas for distribution to franchisees. So far as is known, no other franchise company has ever produced such an in-depth, comprehensive coverage of every phase of the store's operation in manual form. Each volume is contained in a loose-leaf binder, so that revisions and additions may be inserted. Each set is packaged in a holder, as shown in Exhibit 20–1.

New franchisees are given a month's training before taking over the operation of their stores. Training is held in the national training center. The guides, which contain a wealth of information, techniques, and tools all contributed by participants in the Baskin-Robbins Program, are an integral part of the training program.

Each volume of the set of management guides is briefly described by the company as follows:

1. *Employee Training Manual.* Since competent, efficiently trained employees are so essential to the success of your business, we consider this one of the most important volumes in your set. You'll find tested techniques and concepts which work in a Baskin-Robbins Ice Cream store—and which, if followed, will aid your success.
2. *Desserts Manual.* A good ice cream dessert business caters to customers' needs and provides a substantial increased profit for your store. Here in this volume, you will find proven recipes for making and decorating every dessert item. Each step is carefully explained and illustrated. Pages are made of washable, durable plastic-like material, and the easel-type cover will make this volume an invaluable reference and training aid. [A sample page from this volume is shown in Exhibit 20–2.]

---

[1]Alton F. Doody and William R. Davidson, "Growing Strength in Small Retailing," *Harvard Business Review*, July–August 1964, p. 71.

3. *Operations Manual.* Franchisees must be cognizant of the various operational aspects of a Baskin-Robbins store. *All* the particulars of products and supplies, financial management, equipment and store maintenance, selling techniques, advertising, merchandising, and public relations are included in this volume. A handy tab system and table of contents helps direct franchisers to the appropriate section.

    Products and Supplies. Product knowledge and methods of handling and serving are a must in order to deal creatively with your customers. They result in increasing sales and impart an image of competency. This section covers every item you sell—in detail. Graphic illustrations are included. All fountain recipes are given and there is a complete division on supplies, and how to order and receive merchandise.

    Financial Management. A good understanding of the financial control of your business is essential. This section explains in a clear, simplified manner the financial management of a Baskin-Robbins store. The part on analyzing financial statements will give you numerous ideas for controlling expenses. The new computerized accounting system is covered and there is even a division on setting up an efficient record-keeping system in your store.

    Equipment and Store Maintenance. In order to create an ideal environment which will be attractive to customers and employees alike, the store must be clean and in good repair. The section on equipment and store maintenance provides background and preventative maintenance information on all equipment and leasehold improvements. Proven methods and procedures for virtually all jobs regarding physical and mechanical maintenance are set forth. Included are the Work Schedule Guides, which will offer you a tool for accomplishing your maintenance goals on a systemized basis.

    Selling Techniques. Mastering selling techniques and taking advantage of all opportunities is the trademark of a truly successful merchant. This requires learning and training—anyone can be taught to sell. Many tools and ideas for teaching your frontline—employees—are included in this segment. Opinions and ideas which successful salesmen have used for generations are reflected upon. Time proven ideas and concepts along with new tested plans of action and examples, as they relate to a Baskin-Robbins store, are set forth.

    Advertising/Merchandising. This segment was designed to give you good, solid *factual* knowledge on Advertising/Merchandising, along with examples of promotions, ad mats, radio copy, television materials and direct mail pieces available to you. These aids are coded and may be ordered through your accommodation stock. New ads, promotions and ideas will be coming to you for insertion.

Training does not end with the four-week, formal program. Periodic day-long seminars are held in the field for the continuing education of district representatives and franchisees.

Local Advertising Kits

As indicated in Baskin-Robbins 31 Ice Cream Stores (A), kits of in-store displays and materials for special promotions are provided to local stores each month. To further encourage franchisees to place advertisements in their local media, Baskin-Robbins supplies advertising aids that include newspaper mats, radio scripts and jingle transcriptions, layout and copy suggestions, and publicity releases. An example of an advertising mat supporting a special promotion is shown in Exhibit 20–3.

Action Planner

Every three months, each store receives from its district representative a Marketing & Operations Action Planner, including a variety of materials helpful to the individual franchisee in understanding, planning, and executing operations for the time period. For example, the franchisee receives detailed information describing upcoming promotional activities for the period. Exhibit 20–4 illustrates the cover of the planner for January–March 1977. An action planning calendar, featuring reminders to franchisees and key dates for promotions, is also provided each month (see Exhibit 20–5). Some of the other items in the planning kits are information flyers for employees (to be posted on bulletin boards), suggestions and outlines for meetings with employees, updated insertions for the *Management Guides*, and other important communications from Baskin-Robbins.

Filmed Training Programs

In order to make the almost constant and time-consuming activity of training new employees easier for franchisees, Baskin-Robbins has developed a series of filmed training programs. In tests, these training programs effectively communicated the basic training procedures to new employees—especially the younger ones, who have been conditioned practically since birth to respond to visual educational aids. The training programs currently available include "Scooping & Cone Wrapping," "Handpacking," "Ice Cream Production & Quality Assurance," "Welcome to Baskin-Robbins," and "Fountain Treats, Part I, Fountain Items, Part II." Additional programs planned for later completion include "Small Equipment Maintenance and Sanitation," "Cash Handling," "Suggestive Selling," and "Customer Relations."

Focal Topics

1. Using the information given in the case, evaluate the *Management Guides*. What other types of information and instructions would be helpful to franchisees and employees?
2. Evaluate the types of advertising and promotional materials supplied to the franchisees. Should any other materials be provided?
3. Do you feel that the amount and types of communication between Baskin-Robbins and the individual stores are sufficient? How should communication be changed?
4. What is your evaluation of the new filmed training programs? In what other ways might this form of communication be used by Baskin-Robbins?

Exhibit 20–1
Picture of Management Guides

Exhibit 20–2
Sample Insert from the Management Guide

Materials Needed: *Assemble before starting*

1   PIE SHELL HOLDER (foam)
1   KNIFE
1   ICE CREAM SPADE
1   SPATULA (large)
1   5-inch square DRY ICE (optional)

Ingredients Needed:

1   9″ frozen GRAHAM CRACKER PIE SHELL
10 ounces HOT FUDGE (at room temperature)
        (4 ounces in bottom of shell, 6 ounces on
        top of ICE CREAM)
24 ounces JAMOCA ALMOND FUDGE ICE
        CREAM
1   can REAL CREAM TOPPING
        (see directions for use on Page 29b)
        ROASTED ALMOND BITS

MUD PIE

1. Take one of the foam protectors from graham cracker pie shell box. Cut into two sections.
2. Place frozen pie shell in one section of foam holder.
3. Place pie shell in foam holder on scale, add 4 ounces of Hot Fudge. Remove from scale, spread Fudge in bottom (not sides) of pie shell with clean dry spatula. Freeze 30 minutes.
4. New Chiffon Technique -- produces a higher, chiffon-textured pie.

    Using the spade, skim the surface of the Jamoca Almond Fudge, lift off a thin sheet of Ice Cream, lay it on the layer of Hot Fudge. Lay, in an overlapping pattern, additional thin sheets of Ice Cream, until 24 ounces of Ice Cream, slightly mounded in the center, is in the shell.

    Using a clean dry spatula, gently press the Ice Cream into the shell until the Ice Cream is just below the edge of the pan and is slightly mounded in the center.
5. Top with a piece of dry ice. Freeze 30 minutes. (If dry ice is not used, freeze 2 hours.)

6. Place pie on scale, add 6 ounces of Hot Fudge. With spatula (do not dip spatula in water) spread Fudge evenly over surface of the mounded Ice Cream.
7. Place pie in a 4-inch deep pie box. Top with dry ice, close box. Freeze 30 minutes. (If dry ice is not used, freeze 2 hours.)
8. Take a fresh can of Real Cream Topping and following directions on can (see procedure on Page 29b) make a rosette on a waxed paper square to be sure can is dispensing cream properly.)
9. To make rosettes, position Real Cream can over pie, 3/4-inch in from edge, press lever--start in center of rosette, and in a clockwise movement, build rosette to a height of about 1-inch. Continue adding rosettes, each abutting the one just made, until a wreath of rosettes (about 12) circle the edge of the pie. Then add one in the center.
10. Sprinkle roasted almond bits on the rosettes only, not on the exposed Hot Fudge.
11. Immediately, place finished pie in its box in the freezer, not the Dessert case. Freeze 2 hours, or until rosettes are thoroughly frozen.

SERVES 6 to 8

Ice Cream Desserts, Section C, Page 29a

Exhibit 20–3
Sample of Advertising Copy Mat

It's a hula dance on your tongue! Exotic mango,
papaya and poah berry islands swim in a sea of
fruity white ice cream. Whipped Fruit a la Hawaiian
means more fruit chunks than ever. It's a 31derful
fruit-lovers paradise!

Exhibit 20–4
Sample Cover from Store Owner's Marketing & Operations
Action Planner

Exhibit 20–5
Sample of Action Planning Calendar

Case 21
Gistner Funeral Home

Phil Gistner had just returned from the annual convention of his state's association of funeral directors and was reviewing some of his notes from the management sessions:

Death is not as commonplace as it once was. Millions of Americans have never experienced the loss, by death, of someone close to them. Millions of Americans have never been to a funeral, or have even seen a funeral procession, except one which was televised. Millions of Americans have never seen a dead body except on TV, in a movie, on a battlefield, or on a highway. Even where people have been directly involved in the arrangements of a funeral service there is often confusion or doubt about the role of the funeral director and the cost for his services.

Often the place of the casket in the over-all funeral service is unclear or undefined. Historically, the funeral director has been a provider of goods and some services. A casket was purchased and all other services provided "free." Today, on the average, the merchandise amounts to only about 20 percent of the total cost of a funeral service.

The casket is not the funeral service, nor is the funeral service the casket. The failure of some funeral directors to accept this fact and explain it to those they serve is in some ways responsible for much of the concern over funeral practices and prices today.

Pricing structures for funeral services at the Gistner Funeral Home had always been based upon a multiple times the wholesale cost of the casket, and Phil was wondering if maybe the time had come to change to a different method of pricing. He was concerned, though, about how customers, the other funeral homes in the area, and his father would react to any such changes.

Background Information

The Gistner Funeral Home was founded in 1906 by George Gistner, Sr., in a small town on the West Coast. George Sr. ran the business with the help of his wife and son until his death in 1947. At that time the funeral home was conducting an average of 75 funeral services a year. Phil joined his father, George Jr., in the operation of business in 1965, at which time the firm was doing about 100 services per year.

Two other funeral homes were operating in the area, one about the same size as Gistner and the other conducting an average of 60 services a year. Both of these homes utilized a pricing system similar to Gistner's, with the price of a funeral service based upon a multiple of the funeral home's cost for the casket. Prices were difficult to compare, since each funeral home represented several different manufacturers of caskets and carried a wide range of casket styles and qualities. Few customers made any attempt to check a competitor's price due to the nature and timing of the purchase decision.

Financial Operations for 1977[1]

In 1977 Gistner Funeral Home conducted 160 services at an average price of $1210. The average wholesale cost of merchandise sold was $330, broken down into $220 for the casket and $110 for the vault. The costs of the casket and vault were multiplied by an average of 4.5 and 2.0, respectively, to arrive at selling price. Average variable expenses per funeral were $60. Other relevant financial information for 1977 included: total fixed expenses ($94,000); inventory ($8,000); accounts receivable ($20,000); and fixed assets at market value ($130,000). These figures were relatively consistent with those of the preceding three years. Average national operating expenses for funeral firms are shown in percentages in Exhibit 21-1.

---

[1]The figures in this section have been simplified and adjusted somewhat for ease of calculation and analysis and are, therefore, not representative for the typical funeral home.

Historical Development of Pricing[2]

The pricing policies of the typical funeral firm evolved by historical accident. Funeral directors in the United States were originally casket builders and sellers. Frequently, they were furniture dealers or cabinet makers who began to sell caskets because of their carpentry skills. By 1850 some casket builders had begun to add some services, such as restorative art and livery. Basically, though, they were sellers of caskets until around 1900, when the modern concept of the funeral director became fairly well developed. The funeral director was still judged, however, by the quality of caskets he sold and the breadth of casket selections he offered.

The pricing system used by early funeral directors was obtained by taking three times the cost of the casket. One-third was for the cost of the casket, one-third for the extra services offered by the funeral director, and one-third for overhead and profit. Although the multiplier has changed, even today funeral directors frequently use a multiple pricing system.

Changing Role of the Funeral Director

In the earlier part of this century, when the church, the family, and the neighborhood were all tightly knit groups, they helped the surviving family members adjust to changes in their lives and relationships brought about by a death. All that was required of funeral directors was an adequate casket and a few simple arrangements.

Today, funeral directors serve the living, and their professional reputation rests upon the ability to assist the survivors in this transition process. They are counselors upon whom the survivor must rely.

To operate successfully within the changing environment, a funeral director must provide comfortable facilities, develop sound technical skill for the restorative process and sanitary control, have legal know-how to cut through government and insurance red tape, and possess the psychological knowledge to instill confidence in his judgment during the adjustment process. The Appendix to this case gives additional background on factors involved in operating a funeral home.

---

[2]For a detailed review of the funeral service field, see Roger D. Blackwell, "Price Levels of Funerals: An Analysis of the Effects of Entry Regulation in a Differentiated Oligopoly," unpublished PhD dissertation, Northwestern University, 1966.

Alternative Pricing Methods

In reviewing alternative pricing systems, Phil compiled the following information on the three widely used methods.[3]

Unit Pricing

In unit pricing, one price covers all the costs of the funeral except cash advances and optional extras. This method, the most widely used at the present time, is frequently based upon some multiple times the funeral director's cost of the casket. Some funeral homes vary the value of the multiple, using a higher multiple for lower cost caskets than for more expensive ones. Other funeral directors actually compute their overhead structure and add this to a reasonable markup on a given casket to arrive at the total price unit. The unit price usually includes such items and services as:

1. removal of remains to mortuary,
2. complete preparation and dressing of remains,
3. securing of necessary certificates and permits,
4. use of mortuary facilities,
5. assistance of the mortuary staff,
6. transportation of the remains to the cemetery,
7. fixed amount of additional transportation to cemetery,
8. acknowledgment cards and memorial register, and
9. casket selection.

Complete Itemized Pricing

Complete itemized pricing goes to the other extreme, adding a separate price for each element of the funeral service. Certain states have passed legislation requiring all funeral homes to use this pricing method, thinking that if consumers know what they are paying for, they will be better able to select exactly what they need and want.

This system provides a separate price for each of the following:

1. removal of remains,
2. embalming,
3. dressing, casketing, and cosmetizing,
4. use of chapel,
5. use of other mortuary facilities and equipment,
6. staff assistance,
7. funeral coach,
8. additional vehicles,

---

[3]Portions of these descriptions are adapted from a study done by the Batesville Casket Company entitled "Funeral Directors' Pricing Methods, a Comprehensive National Survey," 1968.

9. casket,
10. memorial register, and
11. acknowledgment cards.

The list then continues with all other items that are considered extras in other pricing methods.

Professional Pricing

The professional pricing system, sometimes called the functional approach, involves charging a separate fee for the professional services of the funeral director rather than just including them with the merchandise he or she sells. Funeral directors charge for their services in the same manner as doctors or lawyers. The casket is then sold separately with a normal markup.

Two to five separate categories may be used with this method. Together they cover the cost of the funeral except any cash advances or optional extras. Various categories that may be used in different combinations are:

1. professional services,
2. preparation for burial,
3. use of facilities and equipment,
4. motor vehicles, and
5. cost of the casket.

Possible Need for Change

Based on a national sample of 1,060 respondents, a recent marketing research study found that the majority of consumers would prefer to have more information concerning funeral prices.[4] When offered a choice of the three common methods of pricing funerals, 33.3 percent stated a preference for unit pricing, 16.5 percent preferred professional pricing, and 50.2 percent voiced a preference for itemized pricing. These responses seem consistent with current consumer concepts which have led to public demand for more information on which consumers can make decisions.

In August 1975 the Federal Trade Commission issued a series of proposed rules for the funeral industry, including a specific approach to price disclosures. While it may be some time before a final decision is made regarding the rules proposed by the federal government, certain states have already enacted legislation which requires funeral

---

[4]From Roger D. Blackwell and W. Wayne Talarzyk, *American Attitudes toward Death and Funeral Service* (Evanston, Illinois: The Casket Manufacturers Association, 1974).

directors to disclose more price information in their dealings with consumers.

The specific language of the FTC proposal regarding the price list is as follows:

In connection with the sale or offering for sale of funeral services and/or merchandise to the public, in or affecting commerce as "commerce" is defined in the Federal Trade Commission Act, it is an unfair or deceptive act or practice for any funeral service industry member: To fail to furnish to each customer who inquires in person about the arrangement, purchase, and/or prices of funeral goods or services, prior to any agreement on such arrangement or selection by the customer or to any customer who by telephone or letter requests written price information, a printed or typewritten price list, which the customer may retain, containing the prices (either the retail charge or the price per hour, mile or other unit of computation) for at least each of the following items:

(i)   Transfer of remains to funeral home.
(ii) Embalming.
(iii) Use of facilities for viewing.
(iv) Use of facilities for funeral service.
(v)   Casket (a notation that a separate casket price list will be provided before any sales presentation for caskets is made).
(vi) Hearse.
(vii) Limousine.
(viii) Services of funeral director and staff.
(ix) Outer interment receptacles (if outer interment receptacles are sold, a notation that a separate outer interment receptacle price list will be provided before any sales presentation for such items is made).[5]

Focal Topics

1. What is the economic logic behind the unit pricing system?
2. What are the basic advantages and disadvantages of each pricing system?
3. Do you think customers really understand the pricing systems of funeral homes?
4. How would you go about determining the price charged for a director's professional services and facilities?
5. What are the possible advantages to Gistner in switching to a professional pricing system?

---

[5]Extracted from the *Federal Register*, Vol. 40, No. 169, Friday, August 29, 1975, p. 39903.

Exhibit 21–1
Component Breakdown of the Funeral Director's Operations

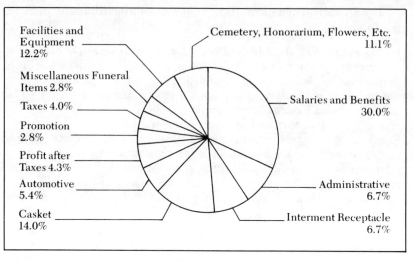

Source: "A Factual Guide to Funeral Costs," published in the public interest by The Ohio Funeral Directors Association.

Appendix

Various Factors Involved in Operating a Funeral Home[6]

The costs of a funeral are predominantly for services and facilities offered by the funeral director and his staff. As a licensed funeral director, he has met the qualifications to serve the needs of the survivor. These needs may include:

... immediate availability of a professionally trained person when death occurs.
... facilities to care for the deceased.
... an appropriate place to receive friends.
... persons to supervise details.
... a listener who understands emotions.
... a time to mourn between death and final disposition of body.
... a meaningful ceremony honoring the deceased.

In order to serve these needs, the funeral director must maintain continuous staffing of the funeral home, adequate funeral home facilities, and cover other general operating expenses demanded of a service oriented business. A complete description of these and other cost areas follows.

Property

Land for buildings and parking must be large enough to meet the peak demand of visitations and of the funeral service. Owning such property—in a convenient and accessible location where the public can be properly served—constitutes one of the major, ongoing costs of funeral home operation.

Facilities

A funeral home is tastefully furnished to provide a homelike atmosphere, and easily adaptable to visitation and to the funeral service. Facilities must be adequate to accommodate more than one family at a time.

---

[6]Excerpted from "A Factual Guide to Funeral Costs," published in the public interest by The Ohio Funeral Directors Association.

Automotive Equipment

Funeral directors must provide adequate automotive equipment to properly perform services for the survivors. Owning and maintaining this equipment, much of which is specially designed, is costly.

Selection Room

Special facilities house the wide variety of merchandise (caskets, vaults and clothing) made available by the funeral home for burial purposes. Providing this service requires considerable space and investment in inventory.

A Professional Staff

Salaries and benefits make up the largest part of the funeral expense. Personnel are chosen carefully so that families will receive professional and efficient service. To attract qualified personnel, funeral homes must compete with salaries paid by other professions, business and industry.

Educational Requirements

Funeral directors and embalmers today are required under state law to meet certain college academic standards and pass state board examinations before they may practice funeral directing and embalming under state-approved licensure requirements. This highly specialized training prepares the funeral director to offer expert professional service to bereaved families, and salaries must be paid for services performed.

Documents and Death Benefits

A number of documents that the funeral director is prepared to process must be completed with every death. Not only does he follow through on these matters; he also counsels and assists survivors on procedure(s) to follow for various financial benefits.

Counseling Skill

Another tangible factor included in funeral costs is that of counseling. The funeral director helps families to better accept death, grief and bereavement. The ability to take a traumatic situation and mold it into a meaningful and impressive service of remembrance for the surviving family is an important part of our social structure and of personal health, both mental and emotional. That's why the funeral director's knowledge and experience are so helpful to those who mourn.

24-Hour Service

The funeral home is open for service continuously. This means the telephone must be attended, and personnel must be available to assist those who have experienced a death—regardless of the day or hour.

Taxes and Insurance

The funeral director is like every other businessman; he operates a taxable enterprise, so he must pay his share of all taxes. The funeral director's insurance premiums are sizable because he must offer protection to the many people he serves.

Community Involvement

Families prefer that the funeral director they call be a respectable, civic-spirited, well-known member of his community. To maintain his position of confidence, the funeral director takes part in many functions at the business, civic and religious levels.

Cost of Living

According to the consumer price index using 1967 as the base year, funeral service costs have increased, as of 1977, 156.3% for adult funerals, while the cost of living on all other items has increased 181.5%.

The funeral director's after-tax profit is 4.3%, not a high rate of return—below the average, in fact, for service-related businesses. [The chart shown in Exhibit 21–1 further illustrates the breakdown of the funeral director's operation as per findings of a survey conducted by the National Funeral Directors Association with funeral directors nationwide.]

Case 22
Hill Industrial Supply*

Mr. Dick Kay, General Manager of Hill Industrial Supply, has become increasingly concerned about Hill's rate of growth. After a 15-year period of solid increases, reflecting the economic expansion of its southern California trading area, Hill's sales slumped—a downturn thought to be due primarily to a decline in the Los Angeles area aerospace contracts and persistent price competition. Actually, Hill's shipment volume had increased slightly.

The industrial supply business, consisting largely of derived demand, is subject to any variation in the level of industrial activity. The local trade association collects business activity reports monthly, which are read with great interest by all suppliers. These reports showed that all business was down. Monthly trade association meetings were rife with discussions of major aerospace contracts, plant relocations, slow collections, increasing imports of low-priced Japanese and European tools, large orders won or lost, and more, a new approach to selling called *systems selling*.

*Modified for inclusion in this text with the permission of David McConaughy, University of Southern California, author of the original case.

Hill's Selling Methods

Like most industrial distributors, Hill employs outside salesmen who call on large accounts and solicit business from their purchasing department with the aid of a catalog. Hill prides itself on the quality of its catalog. The most comprehensive in Hill's history, it lists about three hundred lines of tools and supplies. While Hill only stocks the main items in about fifty lines, it has access through factory warehouses or other wholesalers to every item in the catalog. The breadth of the catalog gives Hill's six salesmen an opportunity to sell a high proportion of a customer's tool and supply needs, thus increasing the average sale amount and enabling Hill to be a primary supplier for all its customers' industrial supply requirements.

Hill's selling methods fall into four types, depending upon the customer, the quantity of the order, and the urgency of the need. These types of selling methods are illustrated in Exhibit 22–1.

Hill's outside salesmen are typical of those in the industry and are well described by a composite published by the National Industrial Distributors Association. The average outside salesman makes 6 calls each working day, handles about 125 active accounts and contacts from 10 to 13 individuals at each account. He sells about $300,000 worth of products annually, has been with his present firm 12 years and is 43 years old. The average salesman has attended college and more than one manufacturer's training school. Hill's salesmen are paid a salary that ranges from $400 to $700 per month plus a sales commission of from 1½ percent to 5 percent, depending on the profit margin Hill is able to get on the items sold.

In addition to the outside salesmen, Hill has six inside salesmen who take telephone orders. Routine purchases and price quotes are frequently made by telephone and Hill emphasizes the efficiency of its inside salesmen. Hill also has a small counter-sales area where rush orders can be picked up and walk-in customers served.

Systems Selling

Systems selling appears to be a widely discussed but narrowly understood concept of supply and purchasing. Essentially, it involves contractual agreements between a distributor and user for the total supply of agreed-upon lines of tools and supplies at a predetermined price. The agreement assures a user of a ready source of the tools and supplies it uses, since the distributor agrees to always carry stock. And because of agreed-upon prices and discounts, costs associated with getting bids and quotes and purchasing routines and requirements are substantially reduced. By working closely with customers under the systems selling concept, distributors hope to reduce, if not eliminate, inventories of tools and supplies and traditional purchasing paperwork for customers.

Systems selling appears most similar in concept to requirements contracts, but it is more comprehensive in that it includes all purchases of industrial supplies regardless of the quantity used. Typically, requirements contracts are used only for high-volume items where bidding results in very low prices.

Many alternatives in pricing and coverage are possible under proposed systems selling but two major distinguishing advantages are: (1) a switch from multiple source purchasing to a single source for supplies and (2) the elimination of a traditional purchase requisition and purchase order for each transaction. One case reported in the trade press resulted in cost savings in maintenance, repair, and operation supplies as follows:

TANGIBLE SAVINGS FOR A CUSTOMER USING SYSTEMS SELLING:

85% reduction in present $95,000 inventory
    $\times$ 15% annual carrying cost   = $14,250

Annual volume of $230,000 $\times$ 5% guaranteed
    reduction in total cost of supplies   = $11,500

SAVINGS OF UNDETERMINED VALUE:

Reduction of floor space of 1800 sq. ft.
Elimination of 2300 purchase orders per year
Elimination of 2100 invoices per year
Elimination of 1500 stock record cards

Another potential savings of systems selling is the elimination of sales commissions on purchases under a systems selling plan, since once the arrangements are set up, orders are placed by phone or mail.

In spite of the apparently attractive savings, many firms were expected to resist the changes in the financial controls and purchase authorization that would be required. Also, the purchasing executives of large customers are generally reluctant to use a single source. Multiple sources are often regarded as good insurance against disruption from strikes, fires, and stock-outs and as a guarantee that the benefits of competition on service and price continue to exist. Many distributors stock only some of the items they catalog; to be successful, systems selling requires that increased stocks be carried.

Executive Pondering

A combination of concern about the downturn in sales, its implications for Hill's growth, and the cyclical business pattern led Mr. Kay to give a great deal of thought to systems selling. Mr. Kay was not sure how much of his existing business might be converted into systems selling or what type of purchasing agreements would be replaced with systems selling. A recent trade study had collected information on buyer attitudes, shown in Exhibit 22–2, which caused him to wonder if systems selling would work at all.

Mr. Kay knew that his customers often purchased from larger competitors and sometimes from local hardware stores. He also was curious about what brands they were buying. To answer these questions, he selected a sample of 100 industrial firms from the *California Manufacturer's Register* and had one of the telephone salesmen call the purchasing departments and ask (without identifying himself) what brand of cutting tools they currently were purchasing and from what company. Many buyers did not have strong brand preference or at least brand recall, and many were reluctant to identify sources of supply. At the end of the calls, forty-five more or less usable responses were obtained, as reported in Exhibit 22–3.

Since systems selling was relatively new, articles in trade publications stressed the need for a study of costs and a firm proposal to prospective customers. The general recommendations were that the distributors take the offensive in making the necessary arrangements.

Mr. Kay was also concerned about the questions and objections that might come up in negotiating systems selling with a prospective account. He wondered how successful Hill might be in pioneering such an approach in its highly competitive market, especially if competitive imitation, if not retaliation, occurred as it had in past years.

To assist him in his evaluations, Mr. Kay collected data from the accounting department on the fixed and variable costs of doing business and other statistics on actual orders. This information is included, along with income statements for 1968 and 1969, in Exhibits 22–4 through 22–6.

Focal Topics

1. Should Hill Industrial Supply offer a systems selling program to its customers at the present time? Why or why not?
2. What do you anticipate the competitive response will be if Hill introduces systems selling? If Hill does not introduce it?
3. If the decision is made to introduce systems selling, how should the concept be marketed?

Exhibit 22–1
Basic Types of Selling Methods Utilized by Hill

1. "Requirements contracts" where the price and terms for items to be sold are agreed upon for supplying a firm's total requirements, usually over a 1-year period. Written bids and letter agreements become the principal selling instruments and quite often prices are very low due to stiff competition. Most requirement contracts specify the expected usage for the items but often the actual purchase volume is much lower than projections.

2. "Bid and buy" or "quote and buy" for larger orders not subject to requirements contracts. This approach covers the bulk of Hill's business and requests for quotes are a substantial part of the telephone call volume to inside salesmen. While price lists and discount sheets are supplied to major customers along with catalogs, price competition is a fact of life and many suppliers are offering additional discounts, especially if they get some encouragement about getting the order.

3. Orders purchased at prevailing published prices and discounts because of the small quantity purchased or the emergency nature of the purchase. Smaller customers tend to buy at prevailing prices because they do not have a strong bargaining position. Rush orders are usually placed with the first supply house that can make immediate delivery from stock. Price in this circumstance is secondary, but because of the high cost of processing rush orders for one or two items and making a special delivery, many supply houses, including Hill, view rush orders as a goodwill activity rather than as a profit-making transaction.

4. Counter sales, where small customers in the immediate area buy their needs and pick ups can be delivered. Although technically wholesale, counter sales are very similar to retail hardware sales, and several of Hill's competitors are large hardware stores. Unlike some larger industrial distributors, Hill does not enforce a minimum purchase amount at either the counter or telephone sale. Many counter sales are quite small, but by limiting credit terms and keeping a running invoice for regular small customers, some of the selling expense is minimized. Again, goodwill is emphasized as some of the smaller customers are expected to become major customers someday.

Exhibit 22–2
Buyer Attitudes Concerning Industrial Purchases

How buyers view dividing business among suppliers*

"Good Business"	50%
"Keeps Suppliers Honest"	40
"Good"	10
"Time Consuming"	5
"Unnecessary"	5
"Unwise"	1

"In purchasing tools and supplies how important are the following?"

	Very Important	Somewhat Important	Not Too Important
Low Price	16%	49%	35%
Quick Delivery Time	93	7	—
Regular Sales Calls	18	31	51
Technical Advice	22	47	31
Well-Known Brand	49	46	7

Why firms trade with particular suppliers

Service	80%
Delivery	70
Stock	50
Price	50
Salesmen	10
Miscellaneous	25

Why firms do not trade with particular suppliers

Product Quality	75%
Product Line	65
Inventory	55
Delivery	50
Order Board	35
Salesmen	35
Prices	30
Miscellaneous	30

Importance of distance between buyer and seller

Very Important	10%
Somewhat Important	60
Not Important	30

*Categories sum to over 100 percent because of multiple responses.

Exhibit 22–3
Cutting Tools and Supplies Brands Mentioned (N = 45)

Brands	Number of Mentions	Carried by Hill
Cleveland	8	
Union	6	
Butterfield	6	
Starrett	6	x
National	5	
Sossner	5	
Ace	4	x
Besley	4	
Chicago Latrobe	4	
Whitman & Barnes	3	x
Carbaloy	3	
Greenfield	3	x
Morse	3	x
Illinois	3	
New York	2	
Kennametal	2	
Proto	2	x
Brown & Sharpe	2	x
Vermont	1	
Millers Falls	1	
Momax	1	
Courmet	1	
Quinco	1	
L & F	1	
Holo Krome	1	x
Carborundum	1	
Niagara	1	
Putnam	1	x
Hardinge	1	x
No Preference	4	
Did Not Know	4	

Exhibit 22–4
Analysis Data from the Accounting Department

Order Analysis, March 1979 (Sample N = 100)

	Lines/Order	Orders	Percentage
	1	47	50.5
	2	13	14.0
	3	11	11.8
	4	8	8.6
	5	14	15.1
Total	252	93	100.0
Average Lines/Order	252/93 = 2.7		

Dollar Sales Volume Analysis, March 1979 (Sample N = 100)

Order Size	Orders Number	Percentage	Dollars	Total Sales Percentage	Average Sales/Order
$ 0-$10	24	25.8	$ 146.93	3.1	$ 6.80
$11-$20	18	19.4	287.06	6.0	15.95
$21-$30	12	12.9	300.55	6.3	25.00
$31-$50	12	12.9	469.59	9.8	39.00
$50-$75	7	7.5	422.33	8.8	60.00
>$75	20	21.5	3,170.62	66.0	158.40
	93	100.0	$4,797.08	100.0	$ 51.50

Analysis of Order Processing and Delivery Cost

Duties

Answering phone	$ .25
Checking catalog for item	.20
Checking stock for item	.50
Writing order	1.25
Checking order	.10
Posting (filing)	.20
Billing	.50
Total	$ 3.00/order

Delivery Truck and Driver $1000.00/month

$$\frac{\$1000/month}{22\ days/month} = \$45\ day/30\ deliveries/day = \$1.50/delivery$$

Exhibit 22-5
Hill Supply's Income Data for 1968 and 1969

	1968		1969	
Sales	$2,011,201	100.0%	$1,888,650	100.0%
Cost of Goods	1,573,776	78.3	1,492,834	79.0
Gross Margin	$ 437,425	21.7%	$ 395,816	21.0%
Expenses:				
Selling	$ 126,206	6.3	$ 118,582	6.3%
Occupancy	7,800	.4	7,800	.4
Warehouse	20,679	1.0	21,752	1.2
Office	113,197	5.6	103,303	1.2
General Administration	86,783	4.3	89,912	4.8
Net Operating Profit	$ 82,760	4.1	$ 54,467	2.9
Other Income	13,010	.6	7,284	.4
Taxes	25,250	1.3	15,566	.8
Net Profit	$ 70,520	3.5%	$ 46,185	2.4%

Exhibit 22–6
Hill Supply's Fixed and Variable Costs for 1968 and 1969

	1968		1969	
	Fixed	Variable	Fixed	Variable
Selling:				
Salaries	$ 34,970		$33,116	
Commissions		$55,549		$55,079
Selling Expenses		6,107		8,821
Travel Expenses	17,000	818	12,176	1,462
Advertising	10,726		5,897	
Miscellaneous		1,036		2,031
Total	$ 62,696	$63,510	$51,189	$67,393
Warehouse:				
Salaries	$ 17,086		$18,454	
Trucking	976		2,160	
Equipment	231		197	
Supplies		$ 1,768		$ 891
Miscellaneous		616		50
Total	$ 18,293	$ 2,384	$20,811	$ 941
Office:				
Salaries	$ 94,838		$83,726	
Equipment	2,788		2,796	
Supplies		$ 6,218		$ 7,604
Credit and Collection	512	920	519	453
Data Processing	1,755		1,794	
Miscellaneous	1,143	5,023	1,143	5,268
Total	$101,036	$12,161	$89,978	$13,325
General Administration:				
Salaries	$ 20,908		$20,908	
Fringe and Bonus		$11,091		$12,783
Expenses		4,109		4,987
Taxes and Licenses	21,433		22,397	
Utilities		14,229		15,301
Miscellaneous	8,182	6,831	7,427	6,109
Total	$ 50,523	$36,260	$50,732	$39,180

Case 23
City National Bank and Trust Company (C)

Research conducted by City National Bank and Trust Company (CNB) indicated that customers of all Columbus banks had two basic complaints about service: first, banks were not open during convenient hours, and second, once inside the bank they had to wait in long lines to complete their transactions. These two complaints were registered by a wide socioeconomic cross section of the banking public.

It was obvious to management that a definite and significant service differential could be achieved if these two problems could be solved for present and potential bank customers. The marketing department was assigned the task of evaluating all possible service alternatives to determine if, in fact, there were economically justifiable changes that could be made to provide longer banking hours and shorter lines.

Expanding Branch Operating Hours

The alternative of expanding operating hours was evaluated in light of the fact that branch personnel were presently working an average forty-hour week without being open on the weekend. Therefore, if the branches were to stay open longer, it would require a second shift, or split shift, or overtime for the present shift. It was estimated that this alternative would require a minimum of six people to staff each of the branch offices (twenty-nine branches) and eight people to staff the central file at the computer center for account balance information. Evaluation indicated that return on investment based on additional business that could be expected if the branch hours were extended would be low (less than 10 percent before taxes). Therefore, another alternative was considered.

Automated Banking Facilities

During 1969–1970 several manufacturers were experimenting with automatic banking machines which were designed to provide customers with all routine banking services. These automated tellers could dispense cash, transfer money, accept bills for payment, and accept all types of deposits. Although little was known about these machines, they appeared to offer a significant alternative for the branch staffing problem.

Evaluation of all available equipment soon to be introduced indicated that one small company in Dallas, Texas, appeared to have the competitive edge. The company had successfully tested an automated teller machine that would provide all the basic services that customers needed, and it would operate on a twenty-four hour a day, seven days a week basis.

Several questions had to be answered before the final decision was made to use either personnel or automated equipment or both to provide extended banking services for customers. First, the company supplying the automated equipment was very small and under-capitalized. Second, even if the company could supply the equipment, would customers use it or would they demand personal banking services? No bank in the United States had installed automated banking equipment for general customer use. Therefore, there were no realistic or reliable marketing statistics relating to customer acceptance.

Recommendation and Decision

Based on the present consumer acceptance and use of automated equipment, such as vending machines, automated post offices, automated car washes, and so on, it was decided that customers would soon see the benefits of automated banking facilities. It was calculated that if 15 percent or more of the present customers used the automated equipment, the investment could be justified from a return on investment point of view. Also, based on the fact that the automated equipment would provide around-the-clock service to all customers, it was considered more beneficial to provide automated cash dispensing machines at the outset and then add or switch to more complete service machines as they become available.

Systems Descriptions

In 1971 City National Bank installed automatic banking machines in all of its branch offices. The new service, called Bank24, was promoted heavily as the new convenient way to complete routine banking transactions. An example of the newspaper advertising for these cash dispensing machines is shown in Exhibit 23–1. At the same time, the bank issued 200,000 special cards to its customers so that they could have access to the automatic banking equipment. In addition, all new customers received a Bank24 card which became a basic part of the bank's total service package. A descriptive brochure used to inform consumers about the system is shown in Exhibit 23–2.

Focal Topics

1. Do you agree with the decision to provide automated banking facilities as opposed to staffed branch offices?
2. How do you think various consumer segments will respond to the Bank24 system?
3. What role does the Bank24 system play as both a supplement and complement to CNB's total marketing program?

Exhibit 23–1
Newspaper Advertising for Cash 'n Carry Machines

100,000
of your neighbors aren't worried about running out of cash over the Memorial Day weekend.

You wouldn't be worried either, if you had a BankAmericard. Because all a City National customer has to do to get cash this weekend is take his BankAmericard to his nearest City National office (anytime, day or night) and . . .

slip it into the Cash 'n Carry money machine located outside the bank . . .

punch his private identification number . . .

punch another button that tells the machine whether he wants $25 or $50 . . .

and, in less than 30 seconds, he has his cash.

The money comes out of his City National Checking account, just like a regular check (and costs no more). Or, if he doesn't have a checking account, the money is charged as a cash advance to his BankAmericard.

City National Bank
and Trust Company
Member FDIC

100,000 neighbors can't be wrong— what are you waiting for?

Ask City National for a BankAmericard of your own. Then you'll be able to get cash when you need it . . . day, night, weekends, holidays.

I want one!

Name _____

Address _____

City _____ State _____ Zip _____

I already have a City National Checking Account.

My checking account number is _____

I want a City National Checking Account, too!

That way, using my BankAmericard to get money from the Cash 'n Carry machine costs no more than writing a check, and appears along with my checks on my bank statement each month.

Enclosed is an initial deposit of $_____ ($25 minimum).

MAIL TO: Mr. John Russell, City National Bank, 100 East Broad St., Columbus, Ohio 43215

Exhibit 23-2
Descriptive Brochure for Bank24 System

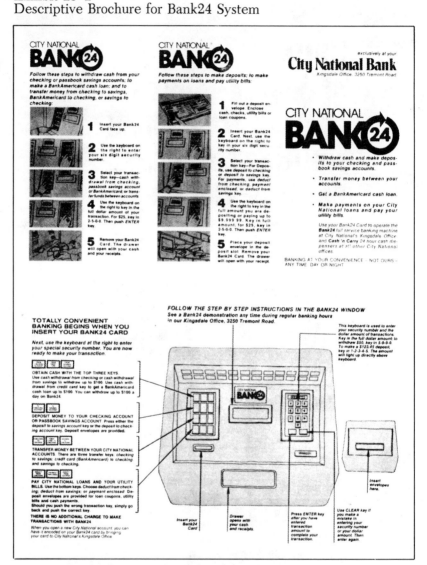

Case 24
Wolverine Brass Works

Wolverine Brass Works, a division of The Citation Companies, sells plumbers' brass goods to over twenty thousand quality-conscious builders and contractors. The firm is the only company in its field to sell directly and exclusively to plumbing contractors and other professionals. Its products cannot be bought at retail; nor does the company market through distributors.

The Citation Companies

Individual divisions of The Citation Companies are engaged in various activities related to the home. Its largest operation, Wolverine Brass Works, markets a complete plumbing products line including over two thousand stock items.

Another division, H. B. Sherman, is one of the top two makers of nationally sold lawn sprinklers, hose nozzles, and related accessories. The company sells through manufacturer's representatives. Retail customers include leading hardware chains and co-ops, mass merchandisers, and garden supply outlets.

Handy Things Manufacturing Company, another consumer division, is one of the nation's largest manufacturers of Christmas tree stands. The company also manufactures household utensils such as potato ricers, kitchen tongs, and fruit presses and a line of housewares including towel racks, soap dishes, and clothes line reels.

In the area of builders' hardware, The Newell Manufacturing division markets pneumatic door closers, door latches, and accessories to retail outlets, mill supply houses, and storm door manufacturers. The firm recently introduced a "WeatherAll," do-it-yourself plastic storm window kit in the retail market.

Glynn-Johnson, another builders' hardware division, specializes in architect-specified products for commercial and industrial construction. Its high styled products, designed to appeal to architects and designers, include overhead door holders, invisible door latches, door catches, bumpers, and special builder's hardware items. The company sells to jobbers through commissioned sales representatives; its retail marketing is insignificant.

Exhibit 24–1 presents a five-year summary of The Citation Companies' operating and financial statistics. A summary of sales and earnings by line of business is shown in Exhibit 24–2.

Wolverine Brass Works

Wolverine Brass Works is over eighty years old. Its line of faucets, tubular traps, bronze valves, compression stops, and related specialty items is among the broadest in the industry. Some companies may produce more of a single item, but no competitor serves the plumber's needs with as wide a variety of supplies. Wolverine employs seventy-five full-time salesmen and selected sales agents who sell to 20,000 contractors in all parts of the country.

The fact that Wolverine Brass Works is the only company in its field to market directly and exclusively to plumbing contractors and other professionals attracts loyal customers. This is one of the firm's principal reasons for staying with this form of distribution. In management's opinion, plumbers' loyalty means reliable sales, an advantage that outweighs the potential sales which might be realized by competing with others in the retail market.

A computerized order entry system enables the company to move with unusual speed, efficiency, accuracy, and low cost. The goal is to fill orders within twenty-four to thirty-six hours of receipt. This goal is designed not only to win customer satisfaction but also to aid production scheduling, inventory control, and trouble shooting in various areas. Management believes its order entry system is a key to profitability and a major reason for success with such a diversified product line and so many individual customers.

The division also makes service fixtures for hospitals and scientific laboratories, including foot-operated and gooseneck faucets, service turrets for controlling and transmitting gases, needle valves, and gas shut-off valves. These products are sold to laboratory furniture manufacturers and scientific apparatus jobbers.

Wolverine Brass sales historically have been stable despite the varying pace of new home construction because, management conjectures, a high percentage of its products are used for remodeling or replacement of plumbing fixtures in existing homes.

Product Areas

Wolverine Brass products are designed and manufactured to assure quality, quick installation, and minimum service. The firm's product offering is divided into six basic areas:

(1) Faucets, including necessary accessories, for sinks, showers and tubs, lavatories, laundry, and lawn;
(2) valves of all types, including gate, ball, globe, check, relief, and regulating, and valve repair kits;
(3) water closet and tank accessories;
(4) tubular and cast drainage products;
(5) supplies, such as flexible and rigid supply lines and supply valves, tubes, and connections; and
(6) miscellaneous plumbing products, including waste disposals, sump pumps, sinks, nuts, bolts, screws, washers, gaskets, and plumbers' supplies and tools.

Advertising

Consistent with its distribution strategy, Wolverine Brass directs its advertising to contractors. Exhibit 24–3 shows two typical advertisements used in trade publications. The firm also utilizes a series of mailings from the "Wolverine Brass Tacks Department" to inform customers of new products and services. Exhibit 24–4 gives two examples of such mailings. Advertising specialties such as memo pads, key chains, and coin holders are widely distributed to supplement other advertising efforts.

Current Plans

Wolverine Brass Works sells most heavily to plumbing contractors engaged in repair/remodeling work and builders of custom homes, where quality and service are usually as important or more important than price. As part of the program implemented to attain a stronger position in the larger brass market—especially in speculative multi- and single-family dwellings—Wolverine introduced the competitively priced Encore line of faucets in 1977, planning to add other inexpensive brass products to its line in 1978, keeping cost down by designing simpler products, and still retaining some premium features.

Robert J. MacIntyre, President of Wolverine Brass Works, states:

Wolverine's most important objective, far and away, has been additional strength in the competitively priced field. Our successful introduction of the Encore faucet lines now moves us in that direction. Furthermore, sales of higher priced lines have continued to move ahead, indicating that we're not sacrificing profits in one direction to gain them in another. I should also emphasize that there is a substantial difference between competitive pricing of quality products, which is our program, and the marketing of cheap merchandise on which price is everything and quality means nothing. We'll stay away from that field.

Focal Topics

1. Discuss the relative advantages of marketing exclusively through plumbing contractors and other professionals as compared to alternative forms of distribution.
2. Evaluate Wolverine's product and advertising strategies.
3. What marketing recommendations would you make to Wolverine's management? Be specific in terms of distribution, product strategy, pricing, and advertising.

Exhibit 24-1
Five-Year Summary of the Citation Companies' Financial Statistics

	1977	1976	1975	1974	1973
Operating Results					
Total revenues	$48,669,260	$44,253,409	$37,002,707	$41,873,770	$44,075,095
Operating expenses	43,335,606	40,090,670	35,124,554	38,622,585	40,135,622
Operating income	5,333,654	4,162,739	1,878,153	3,251,185	3,939,473
Interest expense	749,864	703,342	831,337	1,170,384	985,611
Write-off of goodwill	—	—	1,589,417	—	—
Income (loss) before income taxes	4,583,790	3,459,397	(542,601)	2,080,801	2,953,862
Income taxes	2,090,000	1,283,000	549,000	995,000	1,487,000
Net income (loss)	2,493,790	2,176,397	(1,091,601)	1,085,801	1,466,862
Depreciation and amortization of property and equipment	1,239,427	1,043,163	1,006,310	1,036,681	972,700
Capital expenditures, including leased equipment under capital leases	2,011,481	1,561,033	667,824	672,850	1,204,753
Balance Sheet Data					
Current assets	20,889,584	19,871,228	17,874,314	19,931,542	22,652,294
Net property and equipment and leased equipment	9,996,649	9,590,973	9,099,074	9,456,959	9,841,803
Total assets	32,409,320	30,748,981	28,492,722	32,553,215	35,736,855
Current liabilities	7,102,469	7,332,253	5,654,090	7,001,019	11,774,589
Long-term debt, including obligations under capital leases	7,467,607	7,452,500	8,506,500	9,624,422	8,769,809
Stockholders' equity	16,930,691	15,111,908	13,506,593	15,181,306	14,507,460
Working capital	13,797,115	12,538,975	12,220,224	12,930,523	10,877,705

Exhibit 24–1 (continued)

Ratio analysis

Return on sales	5.1	4.9	(3.0)	2.6	3.3
Revenues per $ of assets	1.50	1.43	1.30	1.29	1.23
Assets per $ of equity	1.91	2.03	2.11	2.14	2.46
Return on assets	7.7	7.1	(3.8)	3.3	4.1
Return on average equity	15.6	15.2	—	7.3	10.5
Current assets to current liabilities	2.9 to 1	2.7 to 1	3.2 to 1	2.8 to 1	1.9 to 1
Debt to equity	.44	.49	.63	.63	.60

Per Share

Net income (loss)[a]	1.63	1.44	(.71)	.71	.95
Dividends[a]	.43	.34	.32	.26	.25
Payout percentage	26%	23%	—	38%	26%
Stockholders' equity[b]	11.30	11.08	11.35	12.53	11.97
Average shares outstanding[a]	1,532,788	1,516,319	1,530,751	1,539,355	1,542,226

Notes: (a) Restated for stock dividends in 1976 and 1977.
(b) Based on actual number of shares outstanding at the end of each year.

Exhibit 24–2
Sales and Earnings by Line of Business

Year	Plumbing Products	Consumer Hardware	Builders' Hardware	Other*
	%	%	%	%
1977 Net Sales	56.9	30.4	12.7	—
1977 Earnings	49.3	36.1	12.9	1.7
1976 Net Sales	54.3	29.9	14.4	1.4
1976 Earnings	52.8	32.3	16.2	(1.3)
1975 Net Sales	54.7	28.7	15.3	1.3
1975 Earnings	53.4	28.3	21.5	(3.2)
1974 Net Sales	53.7	29.7	14.2	2.4
1974 Earnings	52.9	39.4	13.0	(5.3)
1973 Net Sales	48.9	26.4	15.6	9.1
1973 Earnings	68.2	29.9	6.1	(4.2)

*Mobile Home Products discontinued in 1976

Exhibit 24–3
Typical Trade Advertisements for Wolverine Brass

At Wolverine Brass, it's a total effort in behalf of the Plumbing Contractor

Every year we look for new ways to serve our customers

For more than 70 years, our products have been sold exclusively through the Plumbing Contractor, a distribution policy which reflects a company attitude of support for the role of the Plumbing Contractor. Wolverine Brass helps to strengthen the Plumbing Contractor's "complete service" to customers by enabling him to stock and install, with confidence, a recognized quality line of products no other market source can offer.

Wolverine Brass
Concealed Fixtures

WB WOLVERINE BRASS

WOLVERINE BRASS WORKS
Grand Rapids, Michigan 49502

PRODUCTS THAT GIVE AN EXTRA MEASURE OF VALUE

When a Plumbing Contractor has something to say to us, we get the message...

through 75 on-the-spot full-time representatives

Wolverine Brass products are sold directly to Plumbing Contractors. The full-time WB man in each marketing area establishes company-to-Contractor communication. He's a customer-oriented man who keeps us sensitive to product and service requirements.

Valves for homes
and institutions

WB WOLVERINE BRASS

WOLVERINE BRASS WORKS
Grand Rapids, Michigan 49502

PRODUCTS THAT GIVE AN EXTRA MEASURE OF VALUE

Exhibit 24–4
Sample Wolverine Brass Tacks Department Mailings

*From the Wolverine
Brass Tacks Department:*

LAVATORY CENTER SET

This new twist for the bathroom ends dripping once and for all. The polished ceramic seats in its Finale cartridge "slice" off water instead of "pinching" it, turn water flow from full-off to full-on with an easy one-quarter twist. Won't drip, won't wear, won't corrode. Eliminate the need for bibb washers and conventional packing. You can install it and forget it.

One-piece center set design has integral cast brass body, spout and threaded shanks. Available with crystal-clear acrylic handles (a special N.A.S. acrylic that resists household chemicals) or chrome plated metal handles. Pop-up drain optional.

*From the Wolverine
Brass Tacks Department:*

NEW AQUA-FLO WATER FILTER for removing rust and sediment or unpleasant tastes and odors

Here's a new profit maker for you that *keeps on* making profits. One you can quickly and easily install. And give your customers positive removal of rust and sediment or taste and odor from household water. The new Wolverine Aqua-Flo Water Filter has replaceable filter elements for removing either rust and sediment or taste and odor. Elements last from one to six months, depending on conditions, and can be easily replaced by the homeowner (and bought from you, of course). The perfect answer for clearing up discolored, sediment-laden water from private systems. For removing offensive tastes and odors from chemically treated municipal systems, as well. And for making continuous profits for you.

Case 25
DuPont (B)*

The concept of integrating inner and outerwear merchandise is still considered provocative and radical by many retailers. It is certainly not the way things have always been done.

Resistance, however, may be more a political problem than a marketing one for many control garment retailers. The idea has long been accepted in other areas of retailing. In furniture departments, for example, sterile rows of similar furniture pieces have been replaced in many stores by integrated arrangements whose area is completely decorated with accessories from many departments to create a total room look. The stimulus to sales of all items by such integration no longer needs proving in the departments where it has been tried.

The need for this clear visualization of the concept is even greater in fashion than in furniture. Women who already know that rooms must have a coordinated look must be taught how the concept works in apparel. The "lost market" for women's control undergarments may be recapturable. It is possible that given the right garments and incentives, women may become customers again.

---

*This case is an edited version of "A Strategy for Selling 'Control' Garments," a report prepared by DuPont for retailing organizations. It is based on the research studies discussed in this text as DuPont (A).

The Retailing Strategy

The strategy—here called "Outerwear Enhancers"—is based on the concept of coordinating apparel from the skin out, a total system for buying clothes. It is designed to reposition control undergarments in the customer's mind, showing what they can do for the body as well as what they can do for the finished fashion look. Such a different philosophy naturally requires substantial changes in a retail store's department design, marketing, and personnel training.

Selling a look, not a garment is the overall philosophy of "Outerwear Enhancers." The control garment should relate to a woman's clothes, not to her body. Dressing should be a system, with all outerwear coordinated with compatible underwear to make the finished look work.

Integrated Department Layout

The traditional intimate apparel department set-up will no longer work, since it has been shown that women in the target market avoid this department. If they happen in, usually looking for robes or sleepwear, they find the displays dull and the merchandise outdated. They tend to ignore altogether the section for "bottom" garments.

The traditional separate intimate apparel department must be abandoned. Instead, related merchandise must be sold together, in integrated departments. To buy a total look, a woman must be able to try and buy all the pieces at the same time. To one degree or another, innerwear must be integrated with outerwear in departmental organization. This is the most wrenching change suggested by the new strategy, for it requires close cooperation among all involved departments and management personnel, but it is essential for success. Some possible ways to achieve the desired integration are described below.

The Optimum Plan Optimally, every outerwear department would contain an appropriate undergarment section and system selling would prevail, with sales people oriented to sell innerwear-outerwear outfits.

The Mini-Boutique A modification of the optimum plan is a mini-boutique of undergarments in every major ready-to-wear department, with a sample inventory of related, popular garments available for trying on and powerful displays to illustrate the concept.

The "Hub" Department Received with great enthusiasm in the suburban store it was designed for, this idea places one undergarment department at the hub of encircling ready-to-wear departments. All departments are contiguous, but each retains its historic identity. Exhibits 25–1 and 25–2 illustrate some possible layouts for this type of department.

Cross-Department Displays Instead of actual undergarments available in ready-to-wear departments, reciprocal displays in both departments would carry the message. This method depends on displays of great persuasiveness and prominence—such as side-by-side manikins or paired photographs—to illustrate the concept.

A Walk-through "Fashion Magazine" An exciting version of the cross-department display mounts three-dimensional, full-sized photographic blow-ups on department walls or room dividers. These displays, changed frequently to show new styles, would be traffic-pullers in themselves.

Focal Topics

1. Evaluate the relative advantages and disadvantages, as perceived by the consumer and the retailer, of the five possible ways to achieve the desired integration of innerwear and outerwear.
2. What other ways can you suggest to effectively market control garments?
3. Based on your responses to 1 and 2, which strategy for marketing control garments do you recommend most highly? Why?
4. What suggestions would you have for the implementation of your recommended marketing strategy in terms of
   a. display of merchandise
   b. advertising strategy
   c. type of sales personnel and their training

Exhibit 25–1
Possible Layout for the Hub Department

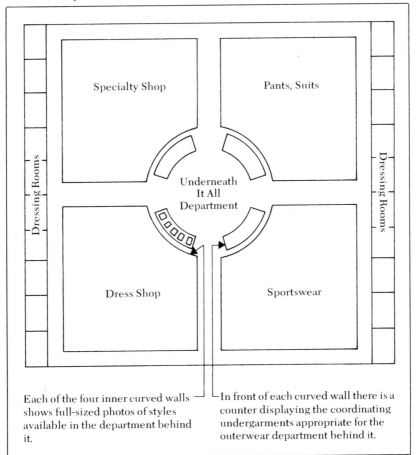

Each of the four inner curved walls shows full-sized photos of styles available in the department behind it.

In front of each curved wall there is a counter displaying the coordinating undergarments appropriate for the outerwear department behind it.

Exhibit 25-2
Another View of the Hub Department Layout

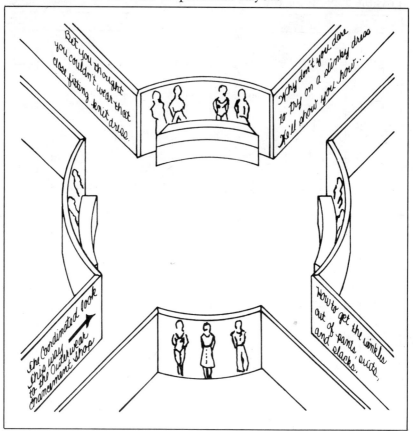

Part Five
The Expanding Role of Marketing in Society

Case 26
Franklin County Children Services

During the summer of 1976 it became increasingly apparent that Franklin County Children Services (FCCS) had a need that was not being satisfied: enough homes for special needs foster and adoptive children. At the same time a general agency thrust to have long-term foster placements settled into adoptive homes came into being. FCCS had a crucial need for parents to provide either temporary or permanent care for black, biracial, and handicapped children, white children over the age of eight, and teenagers. Siblings of three or more also needed foster or adoptive parents.

Early in October the foundation was laid for the *Tie A Yellow Ribbon* campaign. FCCS staff had decided it was time to create a fervor in the community. It was deemed necessary to communicate to the community that "these are *your* children in need of homes. You can help lick this problem by being part of the solution."

History and Services of FCCS

Eleven years after the passage of the Ohio Children's Home Law in 1866, Franklin County voters supported construction of a children's home. In 1945 the Child Welfare Services Act made possible modernization of the county's services to children. The Franklin County Child Welfare Board was established under this law and was authorized to provide a wide-ranging program to allow youngsters to grow up in a family setting. No longer was there help only for orphaned children.

In 1945 voters also approved a $1,250,000 bond issue for construction of a new child-care center, since the seventy-one-year-old structure was by then inadequate. In 1951, eighty-five youngsters moved into the nine ranch-style cottages of Franklin Village. This facility, with its eighty-five wooded acres, is still in operation and can provide a temporary home for up to 150 children.

The Child Welfare Board became Franklin County Children Services by legislative action in 1969. FCCS was designated as the primary agency responsible for the county's dependent and neglected young—the children whose parents are unable or unwilling to give them proper care. By 1976 the agency had a staff of over five hundred, working through Franklin Village, thirteen office locations, and five group homes throughout the county.

FCCS is committed to strengthening home life so that every youngster may have a happy and secure childhood with his or her own family. When there is no parent willing or able to provide adequate care, however, separation is necessary. Separation is costly and, more important, traumatic for the children involved. The agency, therefore, does everything possible to keep families together.

Exhibit 26–1 presents some of the representative types of situations in which FCCS carries out its responsibilities. A specific listing of the agency's services follows:

1. Makes investigations concerning any child who may be in need of protection or care.
2. Counsels families with problems to prevent family breakdown and placement of children.
3. Accepts custody of children from the Court of Domestic Relations.
4. Maintains neighborhood offices to bring services closer to those it serves.
5. Certifies and supervises foster homes and places children in them.
6. Operates Franklin Village and several neighborhood group homes for the care of children.
7. Is developing a residential treatment program for emotionally disturbed adolescents.
8. Assists unmarried parents in making suitable plans.
9. Provides adoption services.
10. Makes certain that physically handicapped children receive proper care.
11. Acts on reports of child abuse.
12. Provides homemakers to maintain the family routine in times of stress.
13. Works with unruly youngsters and their parents in an effort to keep children out of the juvenile justice system.

The Campaign

The *Tie a Yellow Ribbon* campaign was designed to recruit forty homes in Franklin County. Nearly three hundred children—many of whom currently resided in short term foster care homes or institutions—were in need of temporary or permanent placement. A secondary goal of the campaign was to alert the community to a dire problem—insufficient homes for its homeless children. By increasing public awareness, FCCS hoped to raise the level of the public's understanding of foster care and adoption.

April 18, 1977, was the kickoff day for the countywide, ten-day campaign. A parade, complete with decorated cars, floats, marching bands and children's groups, made its way through the downtown area and wound up at a civic park. At the park a ceremonial tree planting took place to signify every child's need for roots, permanence, and a place to belong. Mrs. America of 1977, Ruth Johnson, took part in all of the kickoff events.

After the tree was planted, scores of yellow ribbons were tied to its branches in keeping with the campaign theme, "Tie a Yellow Ribbon If You Want Me." Popularized in song by Tony Orlando and Dawn, the yellow ribbon story dated back to a folk tale about a boy who ran away from home and sent a message to his parents to decorate a tree if they wanted him to return.

Promotional Support

Franklin County Children Services utilized the media, speaking engagements, and personal efforts by present foster parents to support the campaign. Proclamations by political figures, billboards and taxi advertising, door-to-door visits, and other activities were also used to make the community aware of the campaign. Volunteers and FCCS personnel participated in many ways; they stuffed leaflets in grocery bags, staffed informational booths in shopping centers, distributed posters, spoke to civil and religious clubs and organizations, and even knocked on doors. All residents of the community were asked to wear yellow ribbons and to tie them to trees, mailboxes, car antennas, lamp posts, and door knobs to show that children were wanted.

A number of promotional materials were used to advertise the *Tie a Yellow Ribbon* campaign. Some examples include:

Bumper Stickers One thousand two hundred twenty-five bumper stickers costing $224 were distributed.
Bus Signs Two hundred seventy-four bus signs were printed at a cost of $125. Transportation workers installed them at a cost of

$274 to cover labor involved in installing and withdrawing them.
Taxi Signs Twenty cabs carried signs at no cost. The cost of printing the signs was $80.
Advertising Flyers One hundred thousand flyers, printed at a cost of $998, were distributed throughout the community in a variety of business and public locations. Most were stuffed in grocery store bags. Both sides of this 5½ by 8½ inch flyer are shown in Exhibit 26–2.
T-shirts One hundred T-shirts valued at $350 (donated by a local shirt imprinting firm) were worn by staff and volunteers during public appearance phases of the campaign.
Church Flyers Samples of possible statements about the campaign which could be printed in bulletins, programs, and newsletters were mailed to 750 ministers throughout the county.

Media Support

Six weeks prior to the April 18 kickoff a press conference was held to obtain commitment for media support during the ten-day campaign. Six radio stations, all three television stations, and both newspapers covered some aspect of the campaign kickoff. In addition, ten suburban newspapers and sixteen company newsletters publicized the *Tie a Yellow Ribbon* campaign. Eight public affairs programs were presented on either radio or television either immediately prior to or during the campaign. Community services staff determined that this was FCCS's most highly publicized campaign or sales promotion of its kind.

Focal Topics

1. What is the real product being offered and the consumer need being satisfied by Franklin County Children Services?
2. Indicate how you would measure the effectiveness of the *Tie a Yellow Ribbon* campaign.
3. Discuss other ways in which the campaign could have been promoted to the community. Be specific in terms of media and appeals.
4. Based upon your analysis of the case, what specific marketing recommendations would you make to Franklin County Children Services to recruit foster care and adoption homes?

Exhibit 26–1
Illustrative Cases Served by Franklin County Children Services

---

Case

The family consists of the mother and father, who were divorced in 1970. The three children, ages six, ten, and eleven, are under the mother's custody.

Problem: The mother was admitted to the Columbus State Hospital for extensive residential psychiatric care (her second admission). The father lives in a one-room apartment, is unemployed, and has a drinking problem.

Plan: The children were placed in FCCS's receiving center when their mother was hospitalized. They are now in a foster home until the mother is able to resume care of the children.

Case

The family consists of the parents and their seven children, ages ten to twenty-one.

Problem: The upper middle class parents had trouble setting limits for their children. Their sixteen-year-old-son had particular trouble adjusting to this leniency. He often cut school, ran away from home, or stayed out all night. His school psychologist felt that the child was not delinquent but that he stayed away from home because his emotional needs were not being met. FCCS was asked to attend a court hearing when the teenager was charged with auto theft.

Plan: The probation officer felt that the boy stole the cars so he wouldn't have to return home. He was temporarily committed to FCCS and is now at Franklin Village. His adjustment has been excellent; he seems to respond to the highly structured life at the Village and is doing well in school. His parents are undergoing counseling, and the boy will soon return home.

Case

The family consists of an immature twenty-year-old woman, her twenty-one-year-old husband, and their three-month-old daughter.

Problem: Neither parent was emotionally prepared to care for a baby. They didn't want to be bothered. The husband didn't want a baby anyway. The case came to FCCS's attention when a neighbor reported that the infant was being neglected and left at home alone for hours at a time.

Plan: After obtaining temporary commitment, the agency tried to work with the family to prepare them to care for their baby. After a year both parents decided they did not want the child and signed permanent surrender papers. The little girl has now been adopted by a warm, loving family that thinks she's the most wonderful child in the world.

Exhibit 26–2
Front Side of Flyer for the Campaign

Tie a Yellow Ribbon...
...if you want me.

FOSTER CARE-ADOPTION

THE FOSTER CHILD "ME"

I am a child who needs a home and family temporarily.
My own family has problems, and they need time to work
things out. Then we can be together again.

But meanwhile, I need the love and security that only
you can give me as a foster parent.

I may be an infant, a black preschooler, or a teenager.
Or perhaps an emotionally or physically handicapped
child. Or a child with a brother and sister who want
to stay with me.

IF YOU WANT ME...you should:

      *be between 22 and 60 years old
      *be married at least one year
      *have a stable income
      *have extra room in your home and in your heart

You will be reimbursed for my care.

For more information, call the Foster Care Recruitment
Department at Franklin County Children Services.
                  276-9061

Exhibit 26–2 (continued)
Back Side of Flyer for the Campaign

<u>THE ADOPTIVE CHILD "ME"</u>

I'm a youngster who needs a permanent home. A family
I can call my own. Someone to grow with and to show
me the way to a healthy, happy adulthood.

My own family has problems, and is unable or unwilling
to care for me. In some cases, they love me enough to
give me up...so that another family can provide the
love and care I need.

I may be a black or biracial child of any age, an older
white child above the age of eight or the member of a
brother and sister group that wants to share our lives
with the same family. Or I may be a handicapped child
...either physically or emotionally.

IF YOU WANT ME...you should:

      *be married, single, widowed or divorced
      *be at least 21 years of age and within the
       normal age range of parenting
      *be a Franklin County resident
      *be in good health
      *if married, have been so at least two years
      *have a stable income

For more information, call the Adoption Department at
Franklin County Children Services.

276-9061

Franklin County Children Services

1951 Gantz Rd., Grove City, Ohio 43123/276-9061

This agency partially financed by Title XX funds.

Case 27

Campus Crusade for Christ International

After a period of careful evaluation, officials of Campus Crusade for Christ decided in early 1973 to undertake an international Christian ministry dedicated to using the specialized skills of members to help meet the spiritual, physical, and social needs of people in countries where they serve. The project, named The *Agape* Movement, called for 100,000 vocationally trained Christians to serve abroad, where their skills could be utilized and their aggressive evangelism and discipleship practiced. As planning for the project progressed, organizers developed a strategy designed to (1) recruit needed personnel most efficiently, (2) present the program to the cooperating leaders most convincingly, and (3) meet the needs of the individuals in each country involved most effectively.

Background Information

History

Campus Crusade began as an interdenominational student Christian movement on the campus of the University of California at Los Angeles in the fall of 1951, when Bill Bright and his wife, Vonette, leased a house near the campus and began to tell students about Jesus Christ. A twenty-four-hour chain of prayer was organized, and teams of students were trained to take the gospel into fraternities, sororities, and residence halls. Approximately two hundred fifty students, including many campus leaders and most of the starting eleven on the UCLA football team—then national championship winners—committed their lives to Christ during that first year.

Soon, laymen began to ask for the same training that staff and students were receiving. Soon the organization reached laymen, high school students, and military personnel throughout the world. With a staff of approximately six thousand, Campus Crusade for Christ now has an active ministry on hundreds of U.S. campuses and in ninety-seven countries and protectorates of the world.

Campus Crusade does not represent a particular denomination or solicit membership in the usual sense of the word. Serving as an evangelistic arm of the church, it is staffed by volunteer members who raise their own financial support. All operating funds are derived from voluntary donations.

Objective

From its beginning, Campus Crusade has embraced the historical Christian position that to change a world one must first effect a change in the hearts, minds, and lives of its people. Racism, violence, crime, immorality, and other problems, according to this point of view, have grown out of man's self-centeredness and separation from God. This separation is the result of sin; matters will not change unless man accepts the free gift of love and forgiveness offered by Jesus Christ.

Therefore, the basic purpose of the movement is to change the world through "spiritual revolution" in obedience to Christ's command that His message of love and forgiveness be taken to all corners of the earth. Campus Crusade's goal is to help fulfill this Great Commission in this generation. Specifically, Campus Crusade is committed to a target timetable of helping to reach the entire world with the claims of Jesus Christ by 1980.

The Four Spiritual Laws

The Christian message must be presented in such a way that it provides workable answers for the concerns that are uppermost in people's minds. In addition, it must state clearly how an individual can receive Christ into his life. The *Four Spiritual Laws* booklet, as illustrated in Exhibit 27–1, was prepared with these needs in mind. Millions of copies in many translations are used each year as a basic tool for communicating the Christian message. Other materials, which amplify and expand upon this presentation, are also available.

Training

Campus Crusade emphasizes the role of the church and as a cooperative arm seeks to work closely with Christian organizations and churches of all denominations. As men and women are won to Christ, they are taught to experience the abundant Christian life and to share it with others. The many thousands associated with the movement are trained in the foundations of the Christian faith and are encouraged, individually and collectively, to share their faith with others. Special training is also given for this latter purpose so that the Christian message can be presented in an effective manner.

Individual Ministries

Campus Ministry

Campus Crusade for Christ staff members serve on hundreds of strategic campuses across the nation and in more than half of the major countries of the world. They have the privilege of sharing Christ daily with students, thousands of whom come to know Him personally. These students arc trained to live and share the Christian life through personal witnessing, College Life meetings, musical and athletic programs, team meetings in fraternities, sororities, and dormitories, Leadership Training Classes, action groups, and conferences.

Lay Ministry

The Lay Ministry, working in cooperation with thousands of local churches, has developed the Lay Institute for Evangelism, a program that trains lay men and women and students how to experience and share the abundant life. They learn how they can experience God's power in daily situations through the Holy Spirit and become involved in a strategy to help fulfill the Great Commission in our time. This Institute is available in media form also, utilizing the latest teaching techniques of films, slides, tapes, and structured note-taking outlines.

The Lay Ministry has also developed the Way of Life Plan, a plan for building a growing church through training and equipping church members in evangelism and discipleship. A church accomplishes its purpose in the world by developing a movement of spiritual multiplication through evangelism and discipleship. As this movement develops, an environment in the church can lead to: (1) a place for every church member to function; (2) increasing levels of commitment for each individual; and (3) a filtering process to find potential leaders as disciples of others. Through involvement in this plan, all church members will experience a more consistent "way of life" walk with Christ, and will be sharing Christ wherever they go—as a "way of life."

High School Ministry

The High School Ministry has a mission field—17 million high school students—the future leaders of America. Its message is that Jesus Christ is the only one who can meet their needs and enable them to experience an abundant life. The ministry cooperates with local churches in implementing a program that includes the following:

1. Developing a Christ-centered movement on the high school campus through evangelizing and discipling key students.
2. Conducting conferences geared to youth for evangelizing and training them to share their faith with others, and teaching principles of discipleship.
3. Recognizing the high school culture's uniqueness and learning how to best relate Christ to that culture.

Military Ministry

The Military Ministry was created in 1965 to assist chaplains in bringing the good news of Jesus Christ to military personnel and their families. This ministry has the unique privilege of working with chaplains in a community often ignored by civilians.

Working in close cooperation with chaplains, the Military Ministry helps to present to service personnel and their dependents the claims of Jesus Christ through personal witnessing and mass evangelistic programs. These men and women are then trained and discipled, becoming "ambassadors for Christ" through their assignments to various military installations.

Neither a military background nor a college degree is necessary for serving with the Military Ministry, but a deep desire to reach military men and women for Christ is essential. Training in this Ministry is a continuing process, including: Institute of Biblical Studies, New Staff Training, Management Training Seminars, and Field Training. This ministry is involved with enlisted men, officers, reserves, National Guardsmen, dependents, and retired personnel.

"P.S." Ministry

The "P.S." Ministry has the objective of presenting every prison inmate in North America with the claims of Jesus Christ. Campus Crusade for Christ staff members are trained to work as para-chaplains in cooperation with prison chaplains. They provide those who respond to the gospel message with a personal understanding of the basic scriptural principles of the Christian life. Special training in Biblical counseling is given to all "P.S." staff members. "P.S." also offers programs to help cushion a parolee's reentry into society. Through a network of social/spiritual fellowship groups, the parolee and his or her family receive continued encouragement to grow in their Christian experience and to become fruitful witnesses for Christ.

International Ministries

The scope of the International Ministries is to help reach every segment of a nation's society for Christ, with special emphasis given to students. Students in many countries already determine political climate and leadership. They can have an impact on more segments of their society than can any other group. The International Ministries operate on the principle that the national can do the most effective job of reaching his own people. Accordingly, dedicated Christian leaders are recruited and trained in each country, and they in turn recruit and train others to evangelize their own countries. In addition, a number of international representatives from the United States assist the national staff overseas. Already established in ninety-seven nations on six continents, the International Ministries are trusting God for expansion into all 210 countries and protectorates of the world by 1980.

Special Ministries

Indians, blacks, Mexican-Americans, and members of other ethnic groups can be most effective in reaching their own people with the claims of Christ. Thus, the following strategic outreaches have been initiated to communicate His claims to every segment of society. The Ethnic Student Ministry seeks to introduce students from various ethnic backgrounds to Jesus Christ and train them to share Christ with others. The Black Campus Ministry works with the Campus Ministry to implement a strategy to win and train black students for Jesus Christ. The Minorities Lay Ministry implements a strategy to communicate God's love and forgiveness to members of minority groups in the United States. The Black Lay Ministry, a special branch, seeks to win and train black lay men and women for Jesus Christ.

The International Student Ministry is helping to reach 124,000 international students in the United States for Christ. Among these students are the future leaders of every nation in the world. It is the prayerful strategy of this ministry that each one will have an opportunity to hear the truth about Jesus Christ during his visit to the United

States, and that those who receive Him will return to their own countries as discipled multipliers for Him.

Campus Crusade for Christ's Athletes in Action weight lifting, basketball, wrestling, and track teams tour the country each season, competing against major college and university teams and compiling respectable records. At every contest, Athletes in Action team members share the gospel of Jesus Christ with spectators. They have spoken to millions in person and on radio and television.

Presenting the gospel of Jesus Christ through music is the purpose of the Campus Crusade for Christ music groups. They are: The New Folk, touring U.S. college and university campuses; the Forerunners, touring European campuses; The Armageddon Experience, performing in U.S. high schools; The Crossroads, touring Asian campuses; and The Great Commission Company, performing in churches, challenging laymen, students, and pastors in the United States with the world-wide strategy of Campus Crusade for Christ.

World-famous illusionist and magician Andre Kole tours college and university campuses throughout the world, speaking about the reality of Jesus Christ during each performance. Thousands of people have been introduced to Christ through his ministry.

Use of Mass Media

Campus Crusade for Christ utilizes many ways to communicate the Christian message, the most important of which is face-to-face conversation. Mass media techniques, however, are becoming increasingly important. The mass media ministry serves the field staff through films, literature, radio, television, and other audiovisual materials.

The publications department creates and produces two evangelistic magazines and a monthly magazine informing students, laymen, and pastors how God is using Campus Crusade, churches, and other Christian organizations throughout the world as well as encouraging the reader to help fulfill the Great Commission and giving him practical helps to do so.

In 1975 the audiovisual department developed a concept designed to train large numbers of people in how to be filled with the Holy Spirit and how to be effective witnesses. Called mediated training, it utilizes slides, 16mm films, cassette tapes, soundtracks, and programmed learning workbooks to communicate the organization's message. The package—constructed so that 80 percent of the audience will retain 80 percent of the material—was used to train more than three hundred thousand workers in hundreds of cities around the country during 1976.

The audiovisual department also produces films, filmstrips, slide shows, reel and cassette tapes, overhead projectors and other electronic equipment to help reach men and women for Jesus Christ, build them in their faith, and challenge them to be available to God.

The Agape Movement

While the United States has only 6 percent of the world's population, it possesses more than half of the world's trained Christian workers and an estimated three-fourths of the world's Christian wealth. Campus Crusade has operationalized the *Agape* Movement to utilize this manpower and money to the maximum to help spread the Christian message around the world.

The *Agape* Movement is designed to be staffed by 100,000 volunteers equipped with vocational experience as well as the training, ability, and desire to share their faith in Jesus Christ with others. The objective is to reach the total person, supplying physical, social, and spiritual needs. With the approval of individual governments, the movement assists communities in all parts of the world.

The first *Agape* candidates were assigned to the field in February 1974. Presently, the *Agape* staff consists of approximately two hundred persons in office and field assignments. Teams of agricultural, educational, administrative, and medical *Agape* missionaries serve in eleven countries throughout six continents.

Participation Requirements

Participants in the *Agape* Movement must have a college degree or special vocational experience, be at least twenty-one years old, and be willing to accept a two- to three-year overseas assignment. The applicant must have been a Christian for one year or more and may be single or married without dependent children between the ages of three and eighteen, except by special permission. No language skills or teaching background is necessary for application to the *Agape* Movement. Those accepted attend Campus Crusade staff training and receive additional training in crosscultural communications, language, culture, and history. Upon reaching their assignment, trainees take an intensive four- to six-week advanced language course.

Recruiting Program

An extensive recruiting program for the *Agape* Movement has been developed in the form of specialized informational brochures and advertisements. Initial communications involved a brochure detailing the plan, mailed to 190,000 pastors, educational directors, and college placement offices. Nine Christian periodicals and educational journals ran advertisements for Christian personnel to "Help Change the World" through the *Agape* Movement. An example of one of the early advertisements is shown in Exhibit 27–2.

Current advertising is run through Campus Crusade for Christ publications. Exhibits 27–3 and 27–4 are being used in *Worldwide Challenge*. In addition, slide and film presentations are made in churches throughout the United States and at special Campus Crusade meetings. A series of specialized brochures are used when presentations or mailings are made to professional or skilled groups. A selection of these brochures is shown in Exhibit 27–5.

World Thrust

World Thrust—a series of dynamic regional conferences conducted in approximately thirty urban areas across the United States and Canada—not only brings together churches, laymen, pastors, and mission agencies; it has also proved an effective recruitment tool. The conference strategy uses a variety of creative audiovisual communication vehicles to mobilize Christian laymen in world evangelizing.

Focal Topics

1. What is the real product being offered by Campus Crusade for Christ?
2. Evaluate the overall Campus Crusade program from the point of view of its strategy in reaching various market segments.
3. How can the *Agape* Movement best be marketed to potential volunteers?
4. How might the *Agape* Movement be marketed so that the services it has to offer meet the needs of potential recipients (including countries and individuals within each country)?

Exhibit 27–1
The Four Spiritual Laws

four spiritual laws?

LAW ONE

GOD LOVES YOU, AND HAS A WONDERFUL PLAN FOR YOUR LIFE.

Just as there are physical laws that govern the physical universe, so are there spiritual laws which govern your relationship with God.

(References contained in this booklet should be read in context from the Bible wherever possible.)

GOD'S LOVE

"For God so loved the world, that He gave His only begotten Son, that whoever believes in Him should not perish, but have eternal life" (John 3:16).

GOD'S PLAN

(Christ speaking) "I came that they might have life, and might have it abundantly" (that it might be full and meaningful) (John 10:10).

Why is it that most people are not experiencing the abundant life?

Because
LAW TWO

MAN IS SINFUL AND SEPARATED FROM GOD, THUS HE CANNOT KNOW AND EXPERIENCE GOD'S LOVE AND PLAN FOR HIS LIFE.

MAN IS SINFUL

"For all have sinned and fall short of the glory of God" (Romans 3:23).

Man was created to have fellowship with God; but, because of his own stubborn self-will, he chose to go his own independent way and fellowship with God was broken. This self-will, characterized by an attitude of active rebellion or passive indifference, is an evidence of what the Bible calls sin.

MAN IS SEPARATED

"For the wages of sin is death" (spiritual separation from God) (Romans 6:23).

God is holy and man is sinful. A great chasm separates the two. Man is continually trying to reach God and the abundant life through his own efforts: good life, ethics, philosophy, etc.

The Third Law gives us the only answer to this dilemma . . .

LAW THREE

JESUS CHRIST IS GOD'S ONLY PROVISION FOR MAN'S SIN. THROUGH HIM YOU CAN KNOW AND EXPERIENCE GOD'S LOVE AND PLAN FOR YOUR LIFE.

HE DIED IN OUR PLACE

"But God demonstrates His own love toward us, in that while we were yet sinners, Christ died for us" (Romans 5:8).

HE ROSE FROM THE DEAD

"Christ died for our sins . . . He was buried . . . He was raised on the third day according to the Scriptures . . . He appeared to Cephas, then to the twelve. After that He appeared to more than five hundred . . ." (I Corinthians 15:3-6).

HE IS THE ONLY WAY

"Jesus said to him, 'I am the way, and the truth, and the life; no one comes to the Father, but through Me'" (John 14:6).

God has bridged the chasm which separates us from Him by sending His Son, Jesus Christ, to die on the cross in our place.

It is not enough just to know these three laws . . .

LAW FOUR

WE MUST INDIVIDUALLY RECEIVE JESUS CHRIST AS SAVIOR AND LORD; THEN WE CAN KNOW AND EXPERIENCE GOD'S LOVE AND PLAN FOR OUR LIVES.

WE MUST RECEIVE CHRIST

"But as many as received Him, to them He gave the right to become children of God, even to those who believe in His name" (John 1:12).

WE RECEIVE CHRIST THROUGH FAITH

"For by grace you have been saved through faith; and that not of yourselves, it is the gift of God; not as a result of works, that no one should boast" (Ephesians 2: 8,9).

WE RECEIVE CHRIST BY PERSONAL INVITATION

(Christ is speaking): "Behold, I stand at the door and knock; if any one hears My voice and opens the door, I will come in to him" (Revelation 3:20).

Receiving Christ involves turning to God from self, trusting Christ to come into our lives, to forgive our sins and to make us what He wants us to be. It is not enough to give intellectual assent to His claims or to have an emotional experience.

These two circles represent two kinds of lives:

SELF-CONTROLLED LIFE
E—Ego or finite self on the throne
†—Christ outside the life
•—Interests controlled by self, often resulting in discord and frustration

CHRIST-CONTROLLED LIFE
†—Christ on the throne of the life
E—Ego—self dethroned
•—Interests under control of infinite God, resulting in harmony with God's plan

Which circle represents your life?
Which circle would you like to have represent your life?

The following explains how you can receive Christ:

YOU CAN RECEIVE CHRIST RIGHT NOW THROUGH PRAYER
(Prayer is talking with God)

God knows your heart and is not so concerned with your words as He is with the attitude of your heart. The following is a suggested prayer:

"Lord Jesus, I need You. I open the door of my life and receive You as my Savior and Lord. Thank You for forgiving my sins. Take control of the throne of my life. Make me the kind of person You want me to be."

Does this prayer express the desire of your heart?

If it does, pray this prayer right now, and Christ will come into your life, as He promised.

HOW TO KNOW THAT CHRIST IS IN YOUR LIFE

Did you receive Christ into your life? According to His promise in Revelation 3:20, where is Christ right now in relation to you? Christ said that He would come into your life. Would He mislead you? On what authority do you know that God has answered your prayer? (The trustworthiness of God Himself and His Word.)

THE BIBLE PROMISES ETERNAL LIFE TO ALL WHO RECEIVE CHRIST

"And the witness is this, that God has given us eternal life, and this life is in His Son. He who has the Son has the life; he who does not have the Son of God does not have the life. These things I have written to you who believe in the name of the Son of God, in order that you may know that you have eternal life" (I John 5:11-13).

Thank God often that Christ is in your life and that He will never leave you (Hebrews 13:5). You can know that the living Christ indwells you, and that you have eternal life, from the very moment you invite Him in on the basis of His promise. He will not deceive you. What about feelings?

Exhibit 27–2
Early Advertisement for the Agape Movement

Exhibit 27–3
Example of Current Advertisement

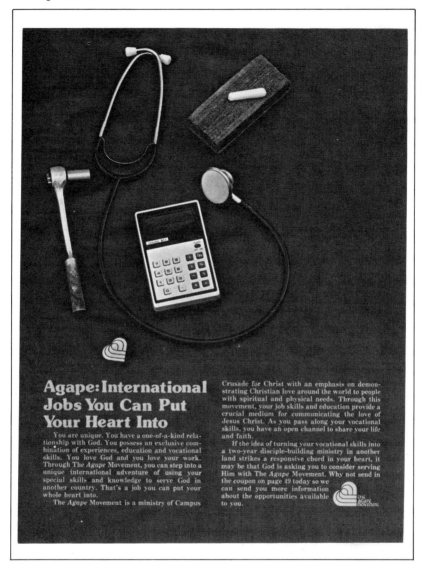

Agape:International Jobs You Can Put Your Heart Into

You are unique. You have a one-of-a-kind relationship with God. You possess an exclusive combination of experiences, education and vocational skills. You love God and you love your work. Through The *Agape* Movement, you can step into a unique international adventure of using your special skills and knowledge to serve God in another country. That's a job you can put your whole heart into.

The *Agape* Movement is a ministry of Campus Crusade for Christ with an emphasis on demonstrating Christian love around the world to people with spiritual and physical needs. Through this movement, your job skills and education provide a crucial medium for communicating the love of Jesus Christ. As you pass along your vocational skills, you have an open channel to share your life and faith.

If the idea of turning your vocational skills into a two-year disciple-building ministry in another land strikes a responsive chord in your heart, it may be that God is asking you to consider serving Him with The *Agape* Movement. Why not send in the coupon on page 49 today so we can send you more information about the opportunities available to you.

Exhibit 27–4
Example of Current Advertisement

Exhibit 27–5
Selection of Specialized Recruitment Brochures

Case 28
Consumer Medical Attitudes (B)*

This report is based upon a comprehensive research project designed to measure attitudes towards health care in general and medical malpractice issues in particular. The research involved telephone interviews with 1,500 Ohio residents selected randomly.

Every state's environment for health care is unique in some ways, and the results in Ohio are not necessarily applicable to another state. Nevertheless, Ohio is to a degree a microcosm of the entire United States. Thus, it is believed that the findings in this study provide thought-provoking information about the problems of health care and malpractice on a broad geographic scale.

The Changing Environment for Health Care

In 1962 President John F. Kennedy enunciated four rights of the American consumer:
1. the right to safety,
2. the right to be informed,

*This case has been adapted from Roger D. Blackwell and W. Wayne Talarzyk, *Consumer Attitudes toward Health Care and Medical Malpractice* (Columbia, Ohio: Grid, Inc., 1977). The adaptation was made with the permission of Grid, Inc. The research reported in the case was conducted under a grant from the Malpractice Research Fund of the Ohio State Medical Association.

3. the right to choose, and
4. the right to be heard.

These consumer rights, affirmed by every administration since then, serve as a foundation for more aggressive attitudes and expanded activities on the part of consumers.

This report describes a study based on the consumer's right to be heard about a topic of highest concern—medical care. Contemporary consumers want their attitudes and opinions to be heard and this study, hopefully, provides them that opportunity. Unfortunately, many of their comments and concerns are being presented in the courtroom today and some consumers may feel that this strategy is the only way to be heard, to get their questions answered, to finally get someone in society to take them seriously. This study attempts to understand what consumers are saying about their physicians, about health care in general, and especially about malpractice.

The health care environment is characterized by a discontinuity unparalleled in any period of American history. As a consequence of rapid and dislocative change, a different set of planning premises is necessary to provide an acceptable level of health care. This report makes available a thorough review of the consumer's viewpoint for all persons who must plan health care programs.

The environment for health care includes four major elements: technological systems; cultural and life-style systems; economic systems; and political, legal, and regulatory systems shown in Exhibit 28–1. Physicians must consider each element of the environment when planning the way a practice should be conducted to maximize consumer satisfaction with health care.

Technological Systems

Technological systems create the potential for satisfying consumers' needs for health care. Interdisciplinary applications of research in areas such as chemistry, electrical engineering, physics, and the behavioral sciences increase the potential of medicine. Such advances in these systems have a great impact on the practice of medicine and on consumer perceptions of medicine as well.

The American approval of scientific research and technological progress, toward which a great amount of resources are devoted, leads to a faith in medicine and in physicians' capabilities to solve any health problem. And continued improvement in medical technology may result in even higher consumer expectations for physician capabilities. When consumer expectations outpace the ability of medical technology to solve health problems, dissatisfaction is inevitable, and malpractice litigation may result.

Cultural and Life-style Systems

Life-styles—patterns of activities, interests, and opinions of individuals or groups of individuals in a society—are influenced by demographic and economic influences but are basically a function of the values or cultural norms transmitted to individuals in a society.

Individuals are not born with a set of values about what is right and wrong, good and bad, or desirable and undesirable. Their expectations are learned as the result of interactions with certain institutions —primarily the family, religion, and school—and significant lifetime experiences. Because patients, especially younger ones, have experienced and are experiencing different institutional influences, medicine is now practiced in a changed environment.

New cultural attitudes and life-styles of medical service consumers are the understandable and predictable consequences of changes that have occurred in the family, religious groups, and schools. While young consumers will probably grow more conservative as they become older, their values and attitudes about life in general appear likely to remain qualitatively different from those of previous generations. The specific attitudes of this group toward medical services is therefore of particular importance in understanding the future environment for health care.

Economic and Demographic Systems

Economic and demographic influences are critical to understanding or "dimensioning" the environment for any type of consumer product or service, including health care. They may operate either as a positive or negative influence on medical services and may be related in certain segments of the population.

During the past decade millions of Americans have enjoyed steadily increasing earnings, although there have been setbacks in individual years. This increase in affluence resulted in the shift of millions of families from lower earning levels to the middle income brackets.

Several implications may be drawn from the income changes that have occurred. One pertains to the social problem created by pockets of poverty in the midst of affluence. When low-income families find themselves the minority rather than the majority, many observers would argue, the frustration of the outnumbered poor is accentuated.

The fastest growing segment of the population during the past decade—the 15 to 24 age group—grew approximately three times faster than the total population. As that group continues to age, however, the fastest expansion among all age categories in this decade will be in the 25 to 34 age group. More than half the total U.S.

population increase between 1970 and 1980 will be accounted for by these young people, who are launching employment careers, getting married, setting up households, and having their first child—for whom these are years of intense economic interest.

Another important dimension of the economic and demographic environment is the greater participation by women in the labor force. Today, almost 45 percent of wives are employed outside the home. As women attain more employment rights and their wages improve, more economic and political power shifts to women.

Consumers are becoming better educated. In 1960 there were only 8.2 million college graduates in the United States, but by 1980 there will be more than 19 million. Today over 60 percent of adults above age 25 are high school graduates whereas in the 1960s the majority of adult Americans had not graduated from high school.

Higher education is likely to mean greater sophistication in a wide range of consumer decisions. Consumers are likely to be more demanding in the areas of service, quality, warranties, information, and so forth. Moreover, they will be supported in their demands by a multitude of consumer protection agencies which have evolved in recent years and which, studies disclose, proliferate with increasing levels of education.

Political, Legal and Regulatory Systems

Political, legal, and regulatory systems for both the general and health care environments are proliferating at every level. Increased interest in national health programs has become apparent with several pending pieces of legislation designed to provide national solutions to health care problems. The range of federal and state programs and regulatory forces affecting medical care is nearly limitless, and in recent years some of these have been directed toward the specific problem of malpractice. Several states have enacted malpractice legislation, and the National Conference of Commissioners on Uniform State Laws is working to establish a uniform medical malpractice act for all state governments.

Research Results

This section describes the basic attitudes and behavior of respondents relating to medical care and health issues. For specific details on how each question was asked, the reader is referred to the Appendix of Case 18, "Consumer Medical Attitudes (A)."

Reasons for Selection of Physician

Respondents were asked to indicate the most important reason they had for choosing their primary or family doctor. Exhibit 28–2 lists the frequency with which various reasons were given. It discloses that recommendation by friends or relatives (40.6 percent) and recommendation by other physicians (14.5 percent) are cited as the most important factors. Convenience of location (6.5 percent) is the third most frequently mentioned reason.

Importance of Physician Characteristics

As another measure of the importance of various physician characteristics, respondents were asked to rate eleven attributes on a five-point scale; a 1 indicated that the attribute was very important and a 5 indicated that it was very unimportant. Exhibit 28–3 reports the percentage of respondents using each evaluation point on the five-point scale across all eleven attributes. The mean importance (average rating) for each of the physician characteristics is also given in this exhibit.

The most important physician characteristic as rated by patients is the willingness of the doctor to talk to the patient about the illness. The second most important characteristic is how long it takes to get an appointment, followed in importance by access of the doctor to the hospital desired by the patient.

The least important physician characteristic of those listed (which are all relatively important, however) is the recommendation of friends. This indicates that while friends are the initial source of information about physicians, the actual performance of the physician is the key element in continued patient satisfaction. The perception that the doctor has never been sued for malpractice and the fees that the doctor charges are also of lesser importance in evaluating a physician than the other given characteristics.

Quality of Health Care

People in Ohio have a high opinion of the quality of health care provided by their own doctors. Their evaluation of the quality of health care given by doctors in general, however, is somewhat lower. As shown in Exhibit 28–4, 52.5 percent of the respondents rated their own doctors as providing excellent health care, and an additional 34.9 percent rated the care given by their personal doctor as good. Only 12.8 percent evaluated the quality of health care given by doctors in general as excellent.

Physician Charges

The majority of respondents (70.5 percent) feel that the charges which they pay their physicians are reasonable for the services provided. See Exhibit 28–5.

Health and Medical Statements

To gain a better understanding of a variety of topics dealing with physicians, personal health and appearance factors, medical communications, and other related subjects, respondents were asked to indicate their agreement or disagreement with a series of AIO statements—statements used by researchers to examine a person's activities, interests and opinions. The ranges of responses to this set of statements and the mean agreement (average response) to each statement are presented in Exhibit 28–6.

Using the research technique involving AIO statements, physicians again receive high evaluations. Over 90 percent of respondents have a great deal of confidence in their doctor and feel that most physicians are ethical and responsible persons. Respondents were split in terms of their agreement or disagreement with the statement "most doctors are overpaid," and almost 20 percent agree that most physicians are more concerned about making money than about the welfare of their patients.

Respondents were asked if physicians are really to blame in most malpractice suits. Exhibit 28–6 reveals that a much higher proportion of respondents agree (44.0 percent) that doctors are not to blame than disagree (14.8 percent) with the statement. However, 40.9 percent are neutral about this topic, indicating that a high proportion of the population has little information that would enable a judgment about this topic.

In terms of appearance and health activities, almost 40 percent of the respondents said that they generally do exercises at least twice a week, and 37 percent frequently participate in sports where they can get a lot of exercise. Some 68 percent of the respondents agree that they are careful about what they eat, and 64 percent say they weigh about what their doctors say they should. About 75 percent of the respondents generally have a physical checkup at least once a year. Some of the levels of agreement with these statements can be expected to be overstated due to the respondents' desire to give socially acceptable responses; however, it still may be concluded that there is a high degree of involvement and interest in health and appearance activities.

When asked about medical communications, 86 percent agree with the statement, "My physician adequately explains my medical problems to me," while 8 percent disagree. Over 75 percent express agreement with the statement, "I wish there were brochures which explained things to me when a doctor treats me."

Exhibit 28–6 also reports results concerning medical topics of current interest such as abortion, nutrition information, and euthanasia. There is substantial agreement (70 percent) that a very ill person should be allowed to die when there is no chance of recovery, high interest in nutritional information on food packages, and polarity of opinion about abortion.

General Beliefs about Malpractice

When asked about their personal beliefs as to the causes of the increased costs of malpractice insurance, respondents reported a variety of ideas, as shown in Exhibit 28–7. Almost 41 percent indicated reasons such as "People want something for nothing" or "People are greedy." About 21 percent felt that doctors were at fault, and almost 20 percent cited lawyers as being at fault.

Likelihood of Bringing Malpractice Suits

Respondents were presented three separate scenarios and asked to indicate how likely they would be to bring a malpractice suit under the condition described. The three scenarios, the ranges of responses to the likelihood question, and the mean likelihood are presented in Exhibit 28–8.

Under the scenario of a physician being at fault in the case of inability to determine a cure, only about 4 percent of the respondents indicated that they would be very likely or somewhat likely to bring a malpractice suit, while almost 83 percent reported that they would be unlikely or very unlikely to bring a suit. About 13 percent were undecided.

Some 27 percent said they would be likely to file a malpractice suit if they developed a serious medical problem thought to be the fault of the physician. With this scenario, 29 percent were undecided as to what their actions would be, and almost 44 percent reported that they would be unlikely to sue.

For the scenario involving the death of a spouse or parent, almost 31 percent indicated the likelihood of bringing a malpractice suit against a physician thought to be at fault. Some 30 percent were undecided, and almost 40 percent reported that they would be unlikely to file a suit.

Levels of Support for Solutions to the Malpractice Problem

The issue of how to handle the malpractice problem was explored by asking respondents to indicate the degree of support they would give to each of nine alternative ways of dealing with the malpractice problem. Ranges of support and the mean level of support for each alternative are given in Exhibit 28–9.

Segmentation Analysis of Persons Most Likely to Bring Malpractice Suits

To identify those individuals or groups of persons most likely to bring malpractice suits, the dependent variable (likelihood of bringing a malpractice suit) was measured with three levels of intensity based upon the three scenarios described in questions 14, 15, and 16 of the survey questionnaire. The overall results for the total sample are reported in Exhibit 28–8. This section analyzes the likelihood of bringing a malpractice suit on the basis of three sets of independent variables—patterns of medical treatment, socioeconomic characteristics of patients, and selected attitudinal (AIO) statements.

Medical Pattern Variables

The importance of the patient-doctor relationship in predicting intentions for malpractice action is clearly demonstrated in this study. Exhibit 28–10 indicates that persons who have a family doctor are far less likely to indicate they would bring a malpractice suit than those who do not have a family doctor. This relationship is true for all three scenarios.

Persons who have not visited a doctor in the last twelve months (for self or a member of the family) are also more likely to state they will bring a malpractice suit than are those who have visited a doctor. No clear patterns emerge, however, concerning the relationship between malpractice suit intentions and the frequency of visits to a doctor or the frequency of days spent in hospitals.

Socioeconomic Variables

Data on the relationship between likelihood of bringing a malpractice suit and socioeconomic variables (summarized in Exhibit 28–11) disclose a number of very significant relationships.

Sex Males are somewhat more likely than females to bring malpractice suits under all three scenarios.

Age A general trend indicates that as age increases the likelihood of bringing a malpractice suit decreases. This relationship holds for all three scenarios.

A relatively high proportion of young persons (under age 25 and in the 25 to 34 age group) indicate that they would be likely to bring a malpractice suit. Under scenario C, for example, 52.4 percent of the respondents under age 25 indicate they would be likely to bring a malpractice suit, compared to only 16.8 percent of those age 65 and over. This may signal increased problems for the medical profession in coming years unless these attitudes change. This implication is of special importance since this age group constitutes one of the fastest-growing segments of the population in the near term.

Education Some variation in malpractice suit attitudes exists between educational groups. Under scenario A, those most likely to bring a malpractice suit have completed some high school or are high school graduates. Under scenarios B and C, those most likely to bring malpractice suits have slightly more education than those likely to bring suits under scenario A.

Income Some variation in malpractice suit attitudes exists between income groups, although the differences are not pronounced. Under scenario A, the persons stating that they would be likely to bring a malpractice suit are in the $8,000 to $14,999 income group. Under scenario C, 35.2 percent of those earning $15,000 to $19,999 implied that they would file suit, while only 21.2 percent of the group earning less than $8,000 would.

Family Size Family size does not appear to be a very useful variable in predicting likelihood of malpractice suits. Under scenario A, there is no clear pattern. With scenarios B and C, families with three or four members seem somewhat more likely to bring suits.

Political Views Under the low intensity problem (scenario A), very liberal and very conservative persons are most likely to bring a malpractice suit. In the middle-intensity scenario B, the somewhat liberal and the very conservative are more likely to bring a suit, and under scenario C, the most likely persons are those who are somewhat liberal. These patterns are somewhat confusing in their complexity, but they do imply that persons with middle-of-the-road political views are the least likely to bring a malpractice suit under all three scenarios.

Place of Residence Only minor variations exist in attitudes toward malpractice suits by place of residence, with the exception that people in urban areas are the most likely to file malpractice suits under all three scenarios.

Religious Identification Minor variations exist among religious groups in their attitudes toward bringing malpractice suits. Once again, such observations must take into consideration the small sample size of some of the religious groups. In general, however, those with no denominational affiliation are the most likely to file under all three scenarios.

Medical and Health Attitude Variables

Segments of the population are increasingly being identified in research studies on the basis of attitudinal (AIO) statements rather than demographic or other variables. These statements may be more valuable in a diagnostic sense, because they may indicate more directly the beliefs or feelings associated with certain patterns of behavior and interest. Some of the relationships between selected AIO statements and the stated likelihood of bringing a malpractice suit (described in Exhibit 28–12) provide revealing insights.

As might be expected, those respondents who indicated that they have a great deal of confidence in their doctors also reported a much lower likelihood of bringing a malpractice suit under each of the scenarios. Respondents agreeing with the statements "About half of the physicians in Ohio are not really competent to practice medicine" and "In most malpractice suits, the physician is actually negligent or in the wrong" indicated much greater likelihood of filing a malpractice suit for each of the scenarios. Those who agree that doctors are overpaid also have a greater likelihood of filing a malpractice suit.

Respondents who agree that "My physician adequately explains my medical problems to me" are less likely to file a malpractice suit than those who disagree with the statement. The likelihood of bringing malpractice suits was greater for those respondents who agreed with the statement, "I wish there were brochures which explained things to me when a doctor treats me."

In general, those who agree that they exercise and weigh about what their doctors suggest are more likely to bring malpractice suits than those who are overweight and do not exercise. Respondents who agree with the statement "It seems that I am sick a lot more than my friends are" are more likely to bring malpractice suits under scenarios A and B than those who disagree with the statement. Individuals who agree with the statement "If I had a terminal illness, I would not want my physician to tell me" are more likely to file a malpractice suit under all three scenarios.

Focal Topics

1. Discuss the various ways in which marketing concepts and principles can be used in the delivery of health care services.
2. Based upon this research, what recommendations would you give to individual physicians in terms of better serving their patients?

3. What recommendations can you draw from this research for state and federal legislative groups concerned about medical services and malpractice?
4. To supplement the results of this study, what other types of analyses should be done on the data?
5. What other types of research do you think should be undertaken?

Exhibit 28–1
The Environment for Health Care Delivery

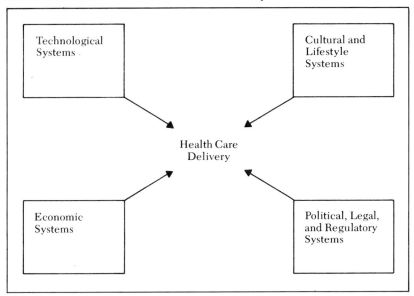

Exhibit 28–2
Reasons Cited as Most Important One for Having
Chosen a Physician

Reasons for Having Chosen a Physician*	Respondents Citing Reason as Most Important One
Recommended by friend or relative	40.6%
Recommended by another physician	14.5
Looked in yellow pages or directory	1.7
Recommended by hospital	1.1
Met the doctor socially or heard of him as a civic leader	3.3
Treated as member of hospital (emergency, etc.)	1.2
Required physician (clinics, insurance, etc.)	.7
Convenient location	6.5
Other reasons	4.5
Can't remember, always been our doctor, etc.	6.1
No response	19.8
	100.0%

*The question asked: Thinking about your primary doctor or family doctor, what was the most important reason for choosing that doctor?

Exhibit 28–3
Rated Importance of Characteristics of Physicians (Total Sample)

Characteristic	Rated Importance					Mean Importance*
	Very Important	Somewhat Important	Neutral Importance	Somewhat Unimportant	Very Unimportant	
The doctor's office is near you.	40.9%	19.6%	21.7%	9.1%	8.6%	2.25
The doctor has access to the hospital you want.	64.4	19.4	8.9	3.8	3.5	1.63
The doctor has a good personality and appearance.	42.3	27.4	16.5	7.8	6.0	2.08
How much the doctor charges.	33.1	24.6	24.2	10.3	7.7	2.35
The doctor is willing to talk with you about your illness.	93.7	4.9	.8	.3	.2	1.08
The doctor has many years of experience.	38.9	25.9	21.8	8.4	4.9	2.14
The doctor has never been sued for malpractice.	33.5	15.5	24.5	11.7	14.8	2.59
The doctor is recommended by other doctors.	58.2	25.3	10.5	3.9	2.1	1.66
The doctor has evening or weekend office hours.	34.7	24.7	20.9	11.6	8.0	2.33
The doctor is recommended by your friends.	23.9	27.3	23.1	13.1	12.5	2.63
How long it takes to get an appointment.	62.2	27.0	7.3	2.1	1.4	1.54

*The lower the number, the more important the characteristic.

Exhibit 28–4
Evaluation of Quality of Health Care (Total Sample)

Question	Excellent	Good	Average	Poor	Very Poor	No Response
What is your feeling about the quality of health care given by your doctor?	52.5%	34.9%	9.5%	.9%	.4%	1.9%
What is your feeling about the quality of health care given by doctors in general?	12.8	45.9	32.1	4.0	1.2	4.0

Exhibit 28–5
What Is Your Feeling about the Charges You Pay Your Doctor?

Entirely too high for the services provided you	4.5%
Too high for the services provided you	21.7
Reasonable for the services provided you	70.5
Low considering the services provided you	2.2
No opinion	1.1

Exhibit 28-6
Levels of Agreement with Health and Medical Statements
(Total Sample)

Statements	Level of Agreement					Mean Agreement*
	Strongly Agree (1)	Somewhat Agree (2)	Neutral (3)	Somewhat Disagree (4)	Strongly Disagree (5)	
Doctor Related Statements						
I have a great deal of confidence in my doctor.	71.5%	19.3%	5.8%	2.1%	.9%	1.41
About half of the physicians in Ohio are not really competent to practice medicine.	4.0	9.2	29.5	26.7	30.3	3.70
Most doctors are overpaid.	16.7	22.9	23.3	22.3	14.5	2.95
In most malpractice suits, the physician is actually negligent or in the wrong.	2.9	7.9	38.0	30.4	20.2	3.57
Most physicians are ethical and responsible persons.	56.5	34.3	6.5	1.7	.7	1.55
Most physicians are more concerned about making money than the welfare of their patients.	5.7	14.1	19.5	33.4	27.1	3.62
Most physicians in Ohio are not very competent.	2.1	4.6	21.2	33.1	38.3	4.02
It is wrong for a doctor to go on strike for any reason.	49.2	13.9	15.3	12.2	8.9	2.17
In most malpractice suits, the physician is not really to blame.	18.1	25.9	40.9	11.2	3.6	2.56
Medical Communications Statements						
I wish there were brochures which explained things to me when a doctor treats me.	52.2%	24.4%	8.9%	8.1%	6.3%	1.92
I often watch TV programs that discuss health problems.	32.7	27.5	10.1	13.2	16.3	2.53
My physician adequately explains my medical problems to me.	61.5	24.6	5.4	5.4	2.8	1.63
If I had a terminal illness, I would not want my physician to tell me.	6.0	3.1	7.9	11.9	71.1	4.39

General Statements

I generally approve of abortion if a woman wants one.	27.4%	14.1%	15.5%	8.6%	34.2%	3.08
I usually read the nutrition information on food packages.	37.3	27.7	8.7	11.1	15.3	2.39
I believe that a very ill person should be allowed to die when there is no chance of recovering again.	54.3	15.7	17.1	4.1	8.7	1.97

Appearance and Health Statements

I generally have a physical checkup at least once a year.	56.0%	19.7%	4.2%	8.9%	11.2%	2.00
I generally do exercises (like push-ups or sit-ups or jogging) at least twice a week.	21.7	17.4	5.8	14.9	40.1	3.34
I am careful about what I eat.	37.1	31.3	9.9	12.1	9.6	2.26
I usually have a good tan each year.	22.9	19.3	12.9	16.2	28.3	3.08
I frequently play tennis or other sports where I can get a lot of exercise.	19.9	17.1	7.9	16.3	38.7	3.37
I weigh about what my doctor says I should.	39.0	25.4	6.0	15.6	13.8	2.40
I usually go on a weight control diet at least twice a year.	22.7	12.7	5.9	15.5	43.0	3.43
It seems that I am sick a lot more than my friends are.	4.1	5.4	4.1	18.5	67.9	4.41

*The lower the number, the more agreement with the statement.

Exhibit 28-7
Beliefs as to Causes of Increased Costs of Malpractice Insurance

Causes of Increased Costs of Malpractice Insurance*	Percentage of Respondents Believing Each to Be a Cause
Doctors at fault	21.3%†
Lawyers at fault.	19.7
Insurance companies at fault.	11.7
The government or laws are at fault.	8.4
Juries and judges are giving too much.	11.3
People want something for nothing/greedy.	40.7
Other responses.	6.3
No response.	12.7

*The question asked: In recent years, the amount that doctors pay for malpractice insurance has increased drastically. In a few words, what do you personally believe is the cause of increased costs of malpractice insurance?

†Percentages total more than 100 percent because of multiple responses.

Exhibit 28–8
Stated Likelihood of Bringing Malpractice Suit under Alternative
Scenarios (Total Sample)

	Stated Likelihood of Bringing Malpractice Suit					
Alternative Scenarios	Very Likely (1)	Somewhat Likely (2)	Undecided (3)	Somewhat Unlikely (4)	Very Unlikely (5)	Mean Likelihood*
Let's assume that your doctor was unable to determine a cure for you, and you thought your doctor might be at fault. Would you be very likely to bring a malpractice suit, somewhat likely, undecided, somewhat unlikely, or very unlikely to bring a malpractice suit?	1.0%	3.3%	12.6%	16.6%	66.1%	4.44
Let's assume that you developed a serious medical problem in which you thought your physician might be at fault. Would you be very likely to bring a malpractice suit, somewhat likely, undecided, somewhat unlikely, or very unlikely to bring a malpractice suit?	7.1	20.0	29.0	17.0	26.7	3.36
Let's assume that your spouse or your parent died and you thought your physician might be at fault. Would you be very likely to bring a malpractice suit, somewhat likely, undecided, somewhat unlikely, or very unlikely to bring a malpractice suit?	11.2	19.4	29.9	16.3	23.2	3.21

*The lower the number, the greater that stated likelihood of bringing a malpractice suit.

Exhibit 28–9
Levels of Support for Alternative Ways of Handling the Malpractice Problem (Total Sample)

Ways of Handling Malpractice Problem	Levels of Support for Alternative Ways					Mean Support*
	Strongly For (1)	Somewhat For (2)	Neutral (3)	Somewhat Against (4)	Strongly Against (5)	
A law that lowered the proportion of the settlement that lawyers could receive for malpractice suits.	50.8%	20.7%	20.0%	4.6%	3.7%	1.90
A requirement that patients agree to arbitration of malpractice claims (the patient and the doctor would appoint skilled arbitrators to settle malpractice claims).	37.6	29.5	23.5	5.2	4.0	2.08
A state agency, something like the Workmen's Compensation Bureau, which would collect malpractice insurance premiums from all physicians and decide what benefits would be given all patients with malpractice claims.	17.1	21.5	29.5	11.3	20.3	2.96
A state law which limited the amounts that could be collected by patients with malpractice claims.	32.3	21.2	22.6	9.9	13.8	2.52
A peer group review system in which a group of physicians reviewed malpractice claims and decided which ones should be taken to trial.	23.5	21.2	26.8	12.1	16.3	2.76
A release signed before a person is accepted as a patient agreeing not to sue for malpractice.	12.1	10.2	18.1	14.1	45.1	3.70
More time spent by your physician in explaining the risks or potential problems of your operation or medicine even though the charge for the doctor's services would be higher than now.	48.0	21.8	14.7	8.6	6.8	2.04
A state law which requires insurance companies to reduce malpractice rates to doctors in return for correspondingly higher rates on health insurance to the general public.	7.1	9.7	25.7	16.1	41.1	3.75
Countersuits by physicians against patients and their attorneys who sue for malpractice with no basis for the malpractice suit.	47.8	17.5	16.5	8.9	9.1	2.14

*The lower the number, the more support for the way of handling the malpractice problem.

Exhibit 28–10
Likelihood of Bringing Malpractice Suit under Alternative
Scenarios by Physician-Hospital Contacts

Classification of Respondents		Likelihood of Bringing Malpractice Suit for		
		Scenario A (64)*	Scenario B (407)	Scenario C (459)
Do you have a family doctor?				
Yes	(1343)†	3.9%‡	26.1%	29.6%
No	(152)	7.2	36.8	40.1
How many times were you, your spouse, and children living at home treated during the past twelve months by a physician?				
1-3	(315)	3.8%	27.9%	29.5%
4-7	(377)	3.7	29.4	31.6
8-11	(234)	2.6	29.9	35.0
12-15	(180)	3.9	17.8	23.3
16 or more	(309)	5.5	23.6	31.7
None or no response	(85)	9.4	38.9	31.8
How many days were you or members of your family in a hospital during the past twelve months?				
1-3	(119)	5.0%	30.3%	35.3%
4-7	(142)	3.5	30.3	37.3
8-11	(66)	4.5	24.2	25.7
12-15	(52)	1.9	28.8	32.7
16 or more	(85)	8.2	22.4	25.9
None or no response	(1036)	4.1	26.8	29.7

*Numbers in parentheses indicate number of respondents stating that they would be "very likely" or "somewhat likely" to bring a malpractice suit under the alternative scenarios.
†Numbers in parentheses indicate number of respondents in each classification.
‡Read: of the respondents in the data base who have a family doctor, 3.9 percent indicated that they would be "very likely" or "somewhat likely" to bring a malpractice suit under the conditions in Scenario A.

Scenario A: Doctor unable to determine a cure for you, and you thought your doctor might be at fault.
Scenario B: You developed a serious medical problem in which you thought your physician might be at fault.
Scenario C: Your spouse or parent died and you thought your physician might be at fault.

Exhibit 28–11
Likelihood of Bringing Malpractice Suit under Alternative
Scenarios by Various Classifications of Respondents

Classifications of Respondents		Likelihood of Bringing Malpractice Suit for		
		Scenario A (64)*	Scenario B (407)	Scenario C (459)
Sex:				
Male	(506)†	4.5%‡	32.0%	35.6%
Female	(994)	4.1	24.6	28.0
Age:				
Under 25	(187)	8.0%	41.2%	52.4%
25-34	(362)	3.9	31.8	39.8
35-44	(258)	4.7	23.6	27.1
45-54	(274)	3.6	24.5	24.1
55-64	(227)	3.1	23.8	21.6
65 and over	(185)	3.2	17.8	16.8
Education:				
Elementary/grammar school	(85)	3.5%	24.7%	21.2%
Some high school	(258)	5.4	20.5	25.6
High school graduate	(670)	4.8	28.4	31.8
Some college	(272)	4.0	30.9	34.2
College graduate	(144)	2.1	27.8	31.3
Post graduate studies	(69)	1.4	27.5	34.8
Income:				
Less than $8,000	(257)	3.9%	21.8%	21.4%
$8,000-$14,999	(498)	5.8	32.1	33.1
$15,000-$19,999	(261)	3.1	26.1	35.2
$20,000-$24,999	(128)	3.1	21.1	35.2
$25,000 and over	(143)	4.2	25.9	33.6
Family Size:				
1	(181)	5.0%	26.5%	25.4%
2	(420)	1.7	22.6	25.0
3	(290)	3.8	33.4	37.6
4	(314)	6.1	29.0	36.9
5	(161)	5.0	24.2	30.4
6 or more	(129)	7.0	27.9	25.6
Political Views:				
Very liberal	(85)	7.1%	27.1%	29.4%
Somewhat liberal	(319)	5.6	35.7	37.3
Middle of the road	(665)	3.0	20.8	27.8
Somewhat conservative	(315)	4.1	29.2	29.8
Very conservative	(94)	7.4	34.0	29.8

Exhibit 28-11 (continued)

Classifications of Respondents		Likelihood of Bringing Malpractice Suit for		
		Scenario A (64)*	Scenario B (407)	Scenario C (459)
Place of Residence:				
Rural area	(253)	4.7%	27.3%	26.9%
Small town	(429)	4.4	24.7	29.1
Urban area	(276)	5.1	30.8	33.7
Suburban area	(540)	3.5	27.2	32.0
Religious Identification:				
Catholic	(364)	4.7%	26.4%	32.1%
Protestant	(972)	3.9	27.5	29.6
Jewish	(16)	0.0	25.0	31.3
Other	(49)	4.1	16.3	24.5
None	(81)	8.6	32.1	40.7

*Numbers in parentheses indicate number of respondents stating that they would be "very likely" or "somewhat likely" to bring a malpractice suit under the alternative scenarios.
†Numbers in parentheses indicate number of respondents in each classification. Numbers may not add to the total sample due to non-response for that classification question.
‡Read: of the males in the data base (506), 4.5 percent indicated they would be "very likely" or "somewhat likely" to bring a malpractice suit under the conditions described in Scenario A.

Scenario A: Doctor unable to determine a cure for you, and you thought your doctor might be at fault.
Scenario B: You developed a serious medical problem in which you thought your physician might be at fault.
Scenario C: Your spouse or parent died and you thought your physician might be at fault.

Exhibit 28-12
Likelihood of Bringing Malpractice Suit under Alternative
Scenarios by Responses to Selected Health-Medical Statements

Classifications of Respondents		Likelihood of Bringing Malpractice Suit for		
		Scenario A (64)*	Scenario B (407)	Scenario C (459)
I have a great deal of confidence in my doctor.				
Agree	(1363)†	3.7%‡	26.2%	29.3%
Disagree	(46)	10.9	30.4	43.5
About half of the physicians in Ohio are not really competent to practice medicine.				
Agree	(198)	5.6%	30.3%	33.3%
Disagree	(855)	3.5	26.8	27.7
If I had a terminal illness, I would not want my physician to tell me.				
Agree	(136)	6.6%	29.4%	37.5%
Disagree	(1245)	4.4	28.1	31.1
Most doctors are overpaid.				
Agree	(595)	5.9%	31.9%	37.0%
Disagree	(552)	3.1	21.0	26.4
I wish there were brochures which explained things to me when a doctor treats me.				
Agree	(1149)	4.9%	29.4%	33.5%
Disagree	(216)	1.4	19.4	19.9
In most malpractice suits, the physician is actually negligent or in the wrong.				
Agree	(162)	6.8%	37.7%	49.4%
Disagree	(759)	2.2	22.9	24.4
My physician adequately explains my medical problems to me.				
Agree	(1291)	4.0%	26.0%	29.4%
Disagree	(123)	4.9	31.7	39.0
I generally do exercises (like push-ups or sit-ups or jogging) at least twice a week.				
Agree	(587)	3.9%	31.8%	33.7%
Disagree	(825)	4.2	23.2	27.9
I weigh about what my doctor says I should.				
Agree	(966)	4.0%	28.8%	32.9%
Disagree	(441)	3.9	23.4	24.5

Exhibit 28–12 (continued)

Classifications of Respondents		Likelihood of Bringing Malpractice Suit for		
		Scenario A (64)*	Scenario B (407)	Scenario C (459)
It seems that I am sick a lot more than my friends are.				
Agree	(143)	5.6%	24.5%	37.1%
Disagree	(1296)	4.2	27.2	29.6

*Numbers in parentheses indicate number of respondents stating that they would be "very likely" or "somewhat likely" to bring a malpractice suit under the alternative scenarios.

†Numbers in parentheses indicate number of respondents who "strongly agree" or "agree somewhat" with the statement, followed by the number of respondents who "disagree somewhat" or "strongly disagree" with the statement. The AGREES and DISAGREES do not equal the total respondent base of 1,500 because of neutral answers and non-responses to the statement.

‡Read: of the respondents who "strongly agreed" or "somewhat agreed" with the statement "I have a great deal of confidence in my doctor," 3.7 percent indicated they would be "very likely" or "somewhat likely" to bring a malpractice suit under the conditions described in Scenario A.

Scenario A: Doctor unable to determine a cure for you, and you thought your doctor might be at fault.
Scenario B: You developed a serious medical problem in which you thought your physician might be at fault.
Scenario C: Your spouse or parent died and you thought your physician might be at fault.

Case 29

Moody
vs. Sensenbrenner

On November 2, 1971, voters in Columbus, Ohio, went to the polls to elect a mayor to serve the city for its next four years. M. E. Sensenbrenner, the incumbent, was completing his fourteenth year as mayor, having held the city's highest office longer than any other person. Challenger Tom Moody, 28 years younger than the mayor, had served on the city council as a municipal court judge and as a common pleas court judge. As of July 15, the election committees for each candidate were actively involved in developing their final campaign strategies.

Situational Information

Politics and Marketing

Some might question whether marketing should be related to politics. The fact remains that today, whether by design or accident, marketing has a large role in politics. Techniques and skills developed in the marketing of goods and services are being increasingly applied to the political field through the use of television, radio, direct mail, telephone campaigns, opinion and image surveys, and many other methods of communication or information gathering.

The Selling of the President 1968 probably disseminated most widely the ways in which some marketing techniques could be applied to politics. These applications were also noted in *Newsweek*'s October 19, 1970, cover story on "The Selling of the Candidates, 1970."

Many of the famed "image makers" admit that they can neither guarantee victory over a long campaign nor accomplish the entire task by themselves. They point out, however, that political parties and their organizations do not have the same impact on the population of today that those of the 1800s and early 1900s did. This factor and others—like the growth of mass media, new computer techniques, a more sophisticated and mobile electorate, and the large amount of money in the political arena—have led to a marriage between certain marketing techniques and politics to regain some of that impact.

Politics has some aspects that challenge marketing experts. For example, a 30 percent market share for a soap account might be great, but in politics it takes a 51 percent market share to win (assuming there are only two candidates). In a two-party race a candidate is only a close second with 49 percent of the votes. Political candidates start each race with a certain base of support from party followers. The secret is to keep the "party faithful" happy and to attract support from the growing body of independent voters, while at the same time not offending the other party in such a way as to solidify opposition support.

The many diverse audiences make this task challenging. Young and old, men and women, rich and poor must all be reached. It is hard to gain the magic 51 percent by just appealing to one or two market segments. To make the task even more difficult, there is the final, absolute deadline of Election Day in November.

The City of Columbus

Columbus, Ohio, ranked as America's twenty-first largest city in the 1970 census, is something of a paradox compared to most large, midwestern or eastern cities. Situated on a large plain in the center of Ohio, Columbus has not been limited in its growth by any geographic factors such as rivers, lakes, or mountains. Being the seat of the state government and the site of one of the nation's major universities, Columbus has sustained a relatively prosperous and steady economy. The city has a mix of manufacturing, government, and white-collar employment with little pollution, low unemployment, and economic stability.

Columbus is not surrounded by layers of suburban communities concerned only with their own internal problems. Of Franklin County's 833,000 people in 1970, nearly 60 percent lived in the city. During the 1950s and 1960s Columbus maintained an aggressive annexation policy. Since the city operates the water and sewer system that supplies most outlying areas, it has more control and flexibility in planning, so it has not become an isolated work center and residence area for only the elderly and poor.

Blacks comprise 18.5 percent of the city population, while the foreign-born population is relatively small (comprises no major voting bloc). Because of the flat, relatively uniform development around the central downtown area, thoroughfares radiate like wheel spokes from the center of town. Freeways make it easy to reach most locations in the city within twenty minutes. The city government's major source of revenue is a 1.5 percent flat rate income tax that has grown with the prosperous economy of Central Ohio.

In summary, Columbus may have its problems, but most citizens, when contrasting their community environment to that of many cities, feel that Columbus is a good city in which to live.

The Candidates

M. E. Sensenbrenner: The Incumbent

Completing his fourteenth year as Mayor of Columbus, Sensenbrenner had served in the city's highest office longer than any other person. He first gained office in 1953 in a run-off election to fill an unexpired two-year term. A former state worker who had held a variety of jobs, Sensenbrenner was a colorful, civic-booster type of mayor. He narrowly gained reelection in 1955 but lost in 1959. Four years later he returned to office. In 1967, he swept to his biggest victory with a 71 percent margin.

Sensenbrenner maintained a flamboyantly patriotic style—proudly proclaiming his faith in God and Columbus as the "All-American City" and wearing a jeweled American flag pin in his lapel. Envisioning himself as an underdog, he was known for frequent battles with the city's largest newspaper and other established groups.

In 1971 Sensenbrenner was sixty-nine, but his highly energetic, peppery style belied his age. While holding the power as the city's chief executive, he delegated many of the day-to-day responsibilities to cabinet directors and others, giving himself plenty of time for ribbon cuttings, proclamations, and speeches that displayed his folksy, colorful style well.

In 1970, there were criminal indictments against several top-ranking police officers, and several officials resigned amid charges of corruption. Nothing, however, was linked directly to Sensenbrenner, and no police officers were ever convicted. There were other problems, but, in general, Sensenbrenner could rely on his record of experience and energy in a city that had prospered and grown during his tenure in City Hall. He was well known and, clearly, when people thought of Sensenbrenner, the title of Mayor came to mind.

Tom Moody: The Challenger

Not only was Tom Moody trying to unseat a well-known incumbent, but he faced the task without any real power base. The younger challenger also lacked the image appeal of the incumbent. A lawyer by profession, Moody was a cum laude college graduate who possessed an educated, articulate delivery. The contrast to the colorful Sensenbrenner was clear.

Moody had had some political experience (two years on the city council, five years as a municipal court judge, and two years as a common pleas court judge), but this public service had not made his name a popular household word. He had won all four of the political races he had entered and was well respected within the legal and business communities. Due to state law he had to give up his judgeship to run for mayor. Thus, Moody did not have a current office to use as a base for publicity or workers.

Political Parties

There were more registered Democrats than Republicans in Columbus. Democrats, however, were more likely to sit at home during an election, especially during an off-year municipal race such as the one in 1971. While Sensenbrenner was a Democrat and Moody a Republican, there were no party designations on ballots in Columbus municipal elections. Many people still knew the party of each candidate, however, and voted accordingly; but an increasing number felt more freedom to switch and vote for individual candidates.

The party issue was further complicated by the fact that the traditionally conservative Republican Party had a moderate-liberal candidate in Tom Moody, while the more liberal Democrats had a conservative one in Sensenbrenner. The question became which candidate would have the most impact on the voters—the deliberate, cool, scholarly Moody or the entertaining Sensenbrenner?

Research Data

Based upon the results of a telephone survey of 400 people in April 1971 and an additional 400 people in July 1971, certain conclusions were drawn concerning campaign issues, the ballot strength of each candidate, and geographical and demographic characteristics of potential voters.

Issues

The April 1971 research project included both an open-ended "most important issue" question and a closed-ended checklist for indicating the most important from a list of key issues. The results of this survey are compared with those of similar earlier studies in Exhibit 29–1. As can be seen, the general areas of crime and pollution drew the most attention in those years. Education also attracted concern, but it should be pointed out that by Ohio law neither the city nor the mayor has any power in the functions of the public schools. The schools are independent in taxing power and operate through a separately elected board. A mayor, however, can express his concerns as a community leader.

The Candidates

Additional survey data showed preferences for each candidate (see Exhibits 29.2 through 29.4). As compared with the April poll, the July survey showed two significant items: a large undecided vote and Sensenbrenner holding a small lead. Sensenbrenner's lead indicated at least two things. First, for an incumbent who won with a big margin in 1967, the smallness of the lead indicated potential problems and possibly a desire to "retire" a veteran office holder. Second, Moody, although not that experienced, was within striking distance and capable of winning.

Geographic Descriptions

The geographic data should be viewed according to the following generalizations regarding characteristics of each area's population:

Far north—includes both newer and older sections that tend to be white, Republican, higher income, and better educated.
Near north—includes areas changing from white to black, lower income, and mostly Democratic.
East side—includes many suburban-type residential areas of above-average income and education levels, leans Republican, mostly white with many affluent blacks moving into area, and major concentration of the city's Jewish population.
West side—mostly white, average income and education levels, many people employed in light manufacturing, and leans Democratic.
South side—smaller population than the other sections, has many long-time, older residents, recent influx of Appalachian poorer whites, movement of blacks into the area, average income and educational levels, and mostly Democratic.

The Need for Decisions

Traditionally, the summer months are slow ones politically—a time to organize, plan, make decisions, and raise funds for the final campaign strategy. With vacations over and school beginning, Labor Day serves as the usual starting point for intensive campaign efforts.

For each candidate, decisions had to be made as to major issues and the methods by which they would be emphasized. There was also a need for decisions concerning any additional research, including the timing and techniques of such research, the issues to be explored, and the methods of data analysis.

Candidates also had to decide how much emphasis should be placed on personalities in developing the positive or negative aspects for each side. Should Sensenbrenner's colorful style be emphasized or downplayed? How should his age be handled? Should he debate the lesser-known, more articulate Moody? How much credit should Sensenbrenner claim personally for the prosperity and success of central Ohio? Should Moody's lack of wide experience at city hall be attacked?

How should Moody's low-key, unglamorous style be handled? Should he attack his opponent's age and "circus style" directly? How much should he talk about specific, detailed changes at city hall?

Focal Topics

Assume the position of campaign chairman for either Moody or Sensenbrenner. Develop specific recommendations for your candidate, based on your judgments about the following:
1. Should campaigns for specific market segments be created? If so, which ones should be focused upon and how?
2. What issues should your candidate emphasize in the campaign?
3. Discuss the posture your candidate should assume toward his opponent.
4. What media should be utilized to best reach voters?
5. Should additional research be conducted? If so, indicate how it should be conducted, topics to be covered, and the types of analyses to be performed.

Exhibit 29–1
Comparison of April 1971 Poll with Earlier Studies

	Closed-Ended Question				
Issue or Problem	March 1970	June 1970	August 1970	October 1970	April 1971
Crime	41.0%	29.7%	28.8%	31.8%	28.6%
Pollution	22.0	24.3	25.7	22.6	17.8
Honesty in government	13.8	16.8	14.2	13.6	0.3
Campus unrest	8.6	23.4	15.4	16.8	12.9
Others	14.6	5.8	15.9	15.2	30.4

	Open-Ended Question			
Issue or Problem	March 1970	July 1970	September 1970	April 1971
Education, schools	27.5%	20.7%	27.8%	24.3%
Air and water pollution	31.5	24.7	19.7	22.9
Taxes	24.0	19.4	15.3	19.6
Crime in the streets	27.8	26.5	18.9	26.5
Racial problems	13.8	10.8	7.7	13.8
Student unrest	6.3	18.4	15.0	19.7
Honesty in government	3.0	12.5	9.4	9.9
Unemployment	4.9	9.7	10.9	5.3
Poverty	4.2	4.6	4.2	2.1

*Totals more than 100 percent due to multiple responses.

Exhibit 29–2
Name Recognition and Candidate Preference
(April and July 1971)

General Name Recognition

	April	July
M. E. Sensenbrenner	91.7%	90.2%
Tom Moody	67.6	81.4

General Ballot Strength-Preference

	April	July
M. E. Sensenbrenner	36.5%	34.2%
Tom Moody	32.5	32.3
Undecided	31.0	33.5

Exhibit 29–3
Candidate Preference by Geographic/Demographic
Characteristics (July 1971)

By Age	Sensenbrenner	Moody	Undecided
Under 25	32.8%	39.7%	27.5%
25-34	28.6	39.8	31.6
35-44	48.8	19.5	31.7
45-54	32.3	20.9	46.8
55-65	31.0	31.1	37.9
over 65	34.7	40.8	24.5

By Education	Sensenbrenner	Moody	Undecided
Primary	43.6%	27.3%	29.1%
Some high school	45.6	26.3	28.1
High school graduate	30.9	35.4	33.7
Some college	29.2	35.4	35.4
College graduate	15.6	34.4	50.0

By Geographic Area	Sensenbrenner	Moody	Undecided
Far north	28.6%	31.2%	40.2%
Near north	29.6	29.6	40.8
Central city	36.2	25.5	38.3
East side	25.0	45.5	29.5
West side	40.4	33.3	26.3
South side	46.9	30.6	22.5

By Sex	Sensenbrenner	Moody	Undecided
Male	30.2%	42.1%	27.7%
Female	36.9	25.1	38.0

By Political Party	Sensenbrenner	Moody	Undecided
Democrat	49.4%	29.4%	21.2%
Republican	29.6	40.7	29.7
Independent	26.4	33.6	40.0

Exhibit 29–4
Evaluation of Sensenbrenner's Performance (July 1971)

	Good	Average	Poor	Undecided
Far north	45.5%	33.8%	14.3%	6.4%
Near north	24.1	51.7	13.8	10.4
Central city	54.2	35.4	8.3	2.1
East side	56.8	40.9	2.3	0.0
West side	37.5	46.4	14.3	1.8
South side	55.1	26.5	14.3	4.1
Total city	46.8	37.1	12.0	4.1

Case 30

The National Foundation–March of Dimes

Since its beginning in 1938, the National Foundation–March of Dimes has invested more than $157 million in research activities and more than $480 million to aid more than 360,000 patients through its service programs. With full March of Dimes support the Salk and Sabin vaccines were developed to protect children against polio. By 1958, the victory over infantile paralysis was assured and the foundation redeployed its army of devoted volunteers and reconcentrated its capabilities against birth defects.

Background Information

Organizational History

The original National Foundation for Infantile Paralysis was founded in 1938 by Franklin D. Roosevelt. It was set up as a permanent, nonstock, nonprofit organization, incorporated under the Membership Corporation Law of New York. On June 9, 1958, it changed its name and enlarged its purposes: to carry on the fight against other diseases in addition to infantile paralysis.

Purposes of the Organization

The Certificate of Incorporation of the National Foundation, as amended June 9, 1958, provides that its purposes shall be:[1]

---

[1]From *Manual for Chapters*, published by the National Foundation, 1974, pp. 3–4.

1. To direct, unify, stimulate, coordinate and further the knowledge of, and the work being done on, any and all phases of infantile paralysis, including study and research into the cause, nature and methods of prevention of the disease and the prevention of harmful after-effects of the disease.
2. To initiate, promote, assist, encourage, develop, maintain, conduct and carry on, directly or indirectly, studies, investigations and research in any way relating to medicine and health and allied subjects, including the cause, prevention and treatment of any disease.
3. To initiate, promote, assist, encourage, develop, maintain, conduct and carry on, directly or indirectly, activities to increase the knowledge on all phases of any disease or diseases affecting human beings. Including the nature and causes of any diseases and the methods of their prevention and treatment.
4. To encourage, stimulate and promote the care and treatment by others of persons afflicted with any disease or suffering from the after-effects of any disease or injury.
5. To make voluntary contributions, grants or payments of money from the funds of the Corporation at any time and from time to time to individuals, partnerships, corporations, organizations or institutions to carry out or promote, in whole or in part, any of the purposes of the Corporation and, without limiting in any way the generality of the provisions of this paragraph, to make such voluntary contributions or payments to or on behalf of individuals who are afflicted with any disease or suffering from the after-effects of any disease or injury.
6. To do each and any one of the foregoing things alone or in conjunction with others.
7. To do any and all things necessary or incidental to the carrying out or promotion of the purposes of the Corporation.

Chapter Organization

Approximately 1,400 chapters function, within the framework of the organization's policies and programs, to assist patients, inform the public, accept responsibility for, and assist in conducting the March of Dimes in the territory assigned to each. Individual chapters do not duplicate the work of an essentially national character being done by the National Foundation, but each appoints a Medical Advisory Committee to advise it in the conduct of its local program and to assist it in interpreting the work of the National Foundation to the medical community and to the public.

Research Activities

A total of $157,040,028 in March of Dimes funds has been invested in research since 1938, including total financing of Salk and Sabin polio vaccine research. In 1977 over $8.7 million was allocated to grants to support birth defects research; $1 million is given annually to the Salk Institute to subsidize operating costs, while overall pledges for its construction now total $19 million. These research programs represent only a few of the projects presently supported by the National Foundation. Many other investigations are being conducted in a search for solutions to scientific problems directly or indirectly concerned with birth defects.

The Salk Institute

The Salk Institute in San Diego, California, is essentially a nondepartmentalized laboratory whose distinguished researchers in the life sciences are laboring to advance biological knowledge and to better understand the problems of humanity. The Institute gives its investigators an opportunity to exchange ideas and knowledge about human problems in an atmosphere fostering inquiry and complete freedom of thought. This unique laboratory is concentrating its research efforts on the molecular approach to cellular genetics, reproductive biology, autoallergic diseases, virology, the growth of normal and cancerous cells, and the very origins of life.

Institute scientists are applying their advanced insights and the techniques of their various disciplines to discover more about normal life processes. From the understanding of what is essentially normal in human growth will come understanding of the things that go wrong, including the defects attributable to hereditary or environmental factors or to both.

Fund Raising

The National Foundation does not participate in United Funds or any other locally oriented campaigns, since its program activities, which are now unified under central management, would be subject to control by individual committees in many different communities. Instead, an annual fund-raising appeal, called the March of Dimes, is held in January of each year to raise funds to maintain national and local programs.

This annual appeal is directed by the National Foundation, which appoints local directors to conduct fund-raising activities in their respective localities, in accordance with plans developed nationally. Each chapter appoints a March of Dimes Advisory Committee from among its members to assist the local campaign director in organizing and conducting a complete fund-raising appeal.

Each chapter sends 60 percent of its net campaign proceeds to national headquarters to support nationwide birth defects research programs and a wide range of medical service projects, professional and public health education, and public information services. The remaining 40 percent of the funds are used by local chapters to finance community projects.

As shown in Exhibit 30–1, a total of more than $57 million was raised during the 1977 campaign. A breakdown of the distribution of funds for various organization expenditures is presented in Exhibit 30–2.

Fighting Birth Defects

When the victory over polio was assured in 1958, the National Foundation had to decide whether the knowledge, experience, and volunteer leadership it had developed should be discarded or used to solve other health problems. Expert analysis indicated that the Foundation's specialized programs in research, patient services, and professional and public health education could be applied directly or with minor modification to the birth defects problem.

The mission of the National Foundation is to unify, direct, and lead the fight to prevent birth defects and their consequences. In its effort to protect the unborn and the newborn, it uses the same basic approach that led to victory over polio:

1. *Research* seeks causes and cures; faster, more accurate diagnostic methods; more effective treatment techniques; and, hopefully, preventive measures.
2. *Medical services* include a nationwide network of genetic and perinatal services designed to prevent birth defects and prevent problems arising for baby and/or mother during delivery.
3. *Professional education* helps to teach and train the many types of health personnel required in the prevention of birth defects.
4. *Public health education* relays to American families information that can help them help themselves in the prevention of birth defects.
5. *Community service* assists physicians, hospitals, health departments, and schools in providing services such as rubella vaccination and prenatal care to prevent birth defects.

What Birth Defects Are

A birth defect is any abnormality of body structure or function present at birth, whether inherited or caused by environmental interference during fetal development. Some abnormalities such as color blindness are so slight that they are but minor inconveniences. A baby born with only a rudimentary brain, however, or with multiple defects involving many organs, dies almost immediately. Between these extremes are many noticeable defects such as cleft lips and palates, shortened or missing hands, arms, or legs, and hidden ones such as diabetes, mental retardation, congenital heart disease, and faulty metabolism.

Extent of Birth Defects

Every year about 200,000 American children are born with some sort of defect. Another 50,000 babies have markedly low birthweight and therefore, organ systems too immature to function normally. Thus birth defects, including low birthweight, strike about one of every twelve newborns every year.

In addition, some 500,000 spontaneous abortions, stillbirths, and miscarriages each year are thought to be due to defective fetal development. Birth defects are either the direct or contributory cause of the deaths of over 62,000 infants, children, and adults each year.

Some birth defects can now be eliminated or greatly reduced in significance. For example, Rh blood disease can be prevented by a serum, and a vaccine against German measles (rubella)—a major cause of birth defects—is now in use. A number of other birth defects, such as PKU and water on the brain, can often be treated successfully with modern medical and surgical techniques, if detected early enough. In addition, prenatal care that instructs mothers-to-be about nutrition, exercise, physical hygiene, and medications can often reduce the risk of death or disability from birth defects and premature births.

The National Foundation's Educational Programs

An informed public is essential to the successful maintenance of the National Foundation's medical scientific research, medical service, and professional education programs. The national organization and its local chapters have been leaders in educating the health professions and lay people about developments in the prevention and treatment of birth defects.

Professional Education

One of the many services the Foundation performs is the prompt publication of new, authoritative information about birth defects, genetics, and perinatal health. Through the use of Reprint Series, Original Article Series, audiovisual programs, The International Directory of Genetic Services, and other publications, the Professional Education Department sees that new knowledge reaches medical schools, medical centers, physicians, nurses, and other health personnel. The National Foundation also sponsors medical conferences, symposia, and seminars to transmit and encourage discussion and exchanges of information and ideas concerning the study and treatment of birth defects.

A worldwide computer system to provide physicians with rapid diagnostic information about known birth defects is being developed through a joint effort of the National Foundation–March of Dimes, Tufts–New England Medical Center, and the Massachusetts Institute of Technology. The system, designed to help doctors everywhere to identify rare birth defect syndromes and relate them to unusual patterns in the occurrence of congenital disorders, will become operational after a period of clinical testing.

Public Education

In addition to educating professionals, the organization informs and educates the lay person about new developments in preventing birth defects, not only to arouse vigorous support for research but also to assure that the results of that research are applied as soon as possible to those who can benefit from them. To communicate with the public, March of Dimes volunteers annually distribute hundreds of thousands of pamphlets, resource booklets, posters, and newspaper and magazine articles. Examples of some of these are shown in Exhibit 30–3. The foundation also develops and distributes films, filmstrips, and slide shows to classrooms and other interested groups. Educational exhibits and programs for radio, television, theatres, and cable television are also utilized to achieve maximum awareness and understanding of birth defects and their prevention and treatment.

Focal Topics

1. What basic marketing concepts are being utilized by, or could be helpful to, the National Foundation–March of Dimes?
2. What advantages and disadvantages result from the National Foundation's conducting its own separate campaign for support instead of joining with some local organization like the United Fund? How can these advantages be maximized and disadvantages minimized?
3. What overall marketing strategy would you recommend for the National Foundation?
4. Indicate what strategy the organization should utilize in communicating its objectives, projects, results, and needs to its public.

Exhibit 30–1
Financial Information for The National Foundation–
March of Dimes

THE NATIONAL FOUNDATION
NATIONAL HEADQUARTERS AND CHAPTERS

Combined Balance Sheets, May 31, 1977 and 1976

	Current funds Unrestricted 1977	1976	Restricted 1977	1976	Land, building and equipment fund 1977	1976	Endowment fund 1977	1976	TOTAL ALL FUNDS 1977	1976
ASSETS										
Cash:										
Checking accounts (Note 2)	$18,249,279	$18,601,570	$ 61,787	$ 18,959			$ 393	$ 770	$18,311,459	$18,621,299
Savings accounts	8,544,847	6,973,235	65,210						8,610,057	6,973,235
Certificate of deposit (Note 2)	19,724,332	19,429,388	140,000	189,646			149,000	145,000	20,013,332	19,764,034
U.S. Treasury obligations — At cost which approximates market (Note 2)	15,608,404	14,621,443							15,608,404	14,621,443
Interest and other receivables	948,865	512,609							948,865	512,609
Bequests receivable (Note 1)	108,885	260,865							108,885	260,865
Supplies and educational materials — At cost	1,049,988	973,813							1,049,988	973,813
Prepaid expenses	267,807	136,532							267,807	136,532
Land, buildings and equipment — At cost—less accumulated depreciation (Notes 1, 4 and 6)	140,000				$3,718,839	$3,822,983			3,858,839	3,822,983
TOTAL ASSETS	$64,642,407	$61,509,455	$266,997	$208,605	$3,718,839	$3,822,983	$149,393	$145,770	$68,777,636	$65,686,813
LIABILITIES AND FUND BALANCES										
Grants and awards payable (Notes 1 and 3)	$ 9,501,284	$ 9,786,972							$ 9,501,284	$ 9,786,972
Accounts payable and accrued expenses	884,118	982,046.							884,118	982,046
Mortgage payable (Note 6)	76,852					$ 101,042			76,852	101,042
Total liabilities	10,462,254	10,769,018				101,042			10,462,254	10,870,060
Fund balances:										
Unrestricted:										
Appropriated for grants and awards (Note 3)	12,178,611	8,902,238							12,178,611	8,902,238
Designated by the Board of Trustees for other costs of program services and for related supporting services (Note 5)	40,561,826	38,277,474							40,561,826	38,277,474
Undesignated, available for program development	1,439,716	3,560,725							1,439,716	3,560,725
Total unrestricted	54,180,153	50,740,437							54,180,153	50,740,437
Restricted — For use in specific research and designated geographic areas			$266,997	$208,605					266,997	208,605
Land, building and equipment — expended					3,718,839	3,721,941			3,718,839	3,721,941
Endowment							149,393	145,770	149,393	145,770
Total fund balances	54,180,153	50,740,437	266,997	208,605	3,718,839	3,721,941	149,393	145,770	58,315,382	54,816,753
TOTAL LIABILITIES AND FUND BALANCES	$64,642,407	$61,509,455	$266,997	$208,605	$3,718,839	$3,822,983	$149,393	$145,770	$68,777,636	$65,686,813

Exhibit 30–1 (continued)

Combined Statement Of Financial Activity And Changes In Fund Balances
For The Year Ended May 31, 1977 With Comparative Totals For 1976

	1977 Current funds Unrestricted	1977 Current funds Restricted	1977 Land, building and equipment fund	1977 Endowment fund	TOTAL ALL FUNDS 1977	TOTAL ALL FUNDS 1976
PUBLIC SUPPORT AND REVENUE:						
Public support (Note 1):						
Campaign contributions	$55,688,679				$55,688,679	$52,430,966
Bequests	1,092,764	$116,662		$ 3,623	1,213,049	1,807,722
Other contributions	754,376	39,345			793,721	908,312
Total public support	57,535,819	156,007		3,623	57,695,449	55,147,000
Revenue:						
Investment income	2,473,589				2,473,589	2,211,770
Refunds of unexpended portion of grants authorized in prior years	662,077				662,077	727,253
Other revenue	12,874		$ 29,964		42,838	130,865
Total revenue	3,148,540		29,964		3,178,504	3,069,888
TOTAL PUBLIC SUPPORT AND REVENUE.	60,684,359	156,007	29,964	3,623	$60,873,953	$58,216,888
EXPENSES:						
Program services:						
Research support	9,259,968	53,875	16,462		$ 9,330,305	$ 9,249,820
Public health education	10,112,031	6,083	24,533		10,142,647	8,568,120
Professional health education	3,920,049	5,528	13,406		3,938,983	3,027,513
Community services	8,310,740		13,212		8,323,952	7,442,149
Medical services	9,904,413	32,129	115,078		10,051,620	10,599,355
Total program services	41,507,201	97,615	182,691		41,787,507	38,886,957
Supporting services:						
Management and general	4,118,960		57,483		4,176,443	3,566,577
Fund raising	11,392,582		18,792		11,411,374	10,517,028
Total supporting services	15,511,542		76,275		15,587,817	14,083,605
TOTAL EXPENSES	57,018,743	97,615	258,966		$57,375,324	$52,970,562
EXCESS (DEFICIENCY) OF PUBLIC SUPPORT AND REVENUE OVER EXPENSES	3,665,616	58,392	(229,002)	3,623		
OTHER CHANGES IN FUND BALANCES:						
Property acquisitions from unrestricted funds	(225,900)	208,605	225,900			
FUND BALANCE AT BEGINNING OF PERIOD	50,740,437		3,721,941	145,770		
FUND BALANCE AT END OF PERIOD	$54,180,153	$266,997	$3,718,839	$149,393		

Exhibit 30–2
Analysis of Functional Expenditures for the
Year Ended May 31, 1972

Combined Statement Of Functional Expenses For The Year Ended May 31, 1977 With Comparative Totals For 1976

| | Program Services | | | | | | Supporting Services | | | TOTAL | |
	Research support	Public health education	Professional health education	Community services	Medical services	TOTAL	Management and general	Fund raising	TOTAL	1977	1976
Grants and awards (Notes 1 and 3)	$8,879,761	$372,990	$1,483,673		$6,832,810	$17,569,234				$17,569,234	$17,288,964
Assistance to individuals					1,181,816	1,181,816				1,181,816	1,296,070
Equipment maintenance	5,153	97,422	27,009	$106,181	326,753	562,518	$75,949	$45,641	$121,590	684,108	566,371
Salaries	146,844	4,252,512	940,584	4,221,613	895,932	10,457,485	1,773,599	1,976,943	3,750,542	14,208,027	12,733,115
Employee benefits and taxes (Note 8)	24,285	661,320	163,603	676,006	147,407	1,672,621	318,301	229,515	547,816	2,220,437	2,032,155
Fees	28,668	214,298	165,817	203,231	31,997	644,111	740,001	657,004	1,397,005	2,041,116	2,175,755
Printing and supplies	33,434	1,653,063	415,769	699,984	67,952	2,870,202	171,349	4,023,641	4,194,990	7,065,192	6,073,417
Telephone	10,886	394,144	76,656	433,091	79,596	994,373	147,535	317,600	465,135	1,459,508	1,317,076
Postage and shipping	6,070	471,854	88,074	226,142	54,947	847,087	88,771	3,172,260	3,261,031	4,108,118	3,529,366
Occupancy	17,936	491,220	105,940	520,085	110,759	1,245,940	215,973	234,094	450,067	1,696,007	1,674,384
Travel and lodging	155,746	1,441,863	448,463	1,156,055	201,432	3,403,559	364,704	606,621	971,325	4,374,884	3,629,518
Subscriptions	1,172	3,782	1,330	1,016	1,313	8,613	16,178	1,118	17,296	25,909	23,671
Memberships	518	3,961	778	1,635	2,746	9,638	46,038	1,493	47,531	57,169	53,297
Other	3,170	61,396	8,340	67,880	7,091	147,877	179,959	127,580	307,539	455,416	325,957
Total expenses before depreciation	9,313,843	10,119,825	3,926,036	8,312,919	9,942,451	41,615,074	4,138,367	11,393,510	15,531,867	57,146,941	52,719,116
Depreciation of buildings and equipment	16,462	22,822	12,947	11,033	109,169	172,433	38,086	17,864	55,950	229,383	251,446
TOTAL EXPENSES	$9,330,305	$10,142,647	$3,938,983	$8,323,952	$10,051,620	$41,787,507	$4,176,443	$11,411,374	$15,587,817	$57,375,324	$52,970,562

See Notes to Combined Financial Statements.

Exhibit 30–3
Examples of Covers from Informational Booklets

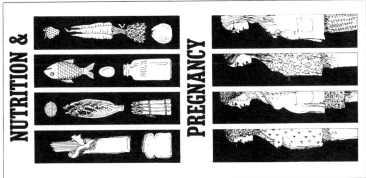

Part Six
Developing the Total Marketing Program

Case 31
Copsco, Inc.

Since the early 1970s considerable interest and activity have been directed toward energy conservation by government, business, and private sectors. One way in which the average homeowner, apartment dweller, or business person can reduce energy consumption is by turning the thermostat down during heating seasons and up during cooling seasons. Fuel savings can also be achieved by dialing down the thermostat at night when people are asleep and during the day if no one is around. The problem is that it is easy to forget to readjust the thermostat temperature when adjustment is needed.

Three doctors have designed a simple, inexpensive solution to the problem. Drs. Douglas Dachenbach, an optometrist who studied engineering, James Dindot, an anesthesiologist, and Edwin Jenkinson, a podiatrist, developed the Fuel Pacer device after several engineers said the project was "technically not functional and financially prohibitive."

The Product

Exhibit 31–1 presents specific details about the Fuel Pacer. The product is a solid-state electronic unit housed in a small plastic box. It heats the air inside its case to a constant temperature and automatically sets back any home thermostat eight to ten degrees when plugged into an ordinary household timer. It attaches to the wall directly beneath the thermostat by means of an adhesive strip.

A column of air is continually drawn through the device, and the heated currents are forced up to mix with the room air at the thermostat. This raises the temperature measured by the thermostat and "fools" it into thinking the room is actually eight to ten degrees warmer than it is. When the timer turns the Fuel Pacer off, the room temperature returns to the setting of the thermostat.

The automatic process has an advantage over manually turning down thermostats; no monitoring or adjustment is required unless a change in the timing of the setback is desired. To lower air conditioning costs, the strategy is reversed, with the thermostat set higher to reduce energy consumption. The Fuel Pacer will function on any wall-mounted thermostat with central heating or cooling and can be used with gas, electric, coal or oil heating systems. Production cost per unit in marketable quantities is approximately $3.83.

Potential Savings

A study by the Holifield National Laboratory in Oak Ridge, Tennessee, concluded that the total U.S. energy budget could be cut by 4 percent if homes usually heated at 72 degrees were heated to 68 degrees in the daytime and set back to 55 degrees at night. The fuel savings would be equivalent to about 25 percent of U.S. petroleum imports. The study also reported that, contrary to public opinion, the energy consumed to reheat a home is not as great as the energy saved by an eight hour setback. Energy savings are typically realized by any setback beyond four hours.

According to an energy conservation bulletin from the National Bureau of Standards, each one-degree reduction in the setting of the room thermostat will save about 1 percent of fuel in cold climates, and about 3 percent in moderate climates. Setting a thermostat back 10 degrees for an eight-hour period at night would be expected to yield a 10 to 15 percent fuel savings.

Initial Marketing Efforts

The three doctors, incorporated as Copsco, initially plan to market the Fuel Pacer via mail and telephone sales. The tentative price will be $19.95, which includes postage and handling. In anticipation of placing some print advertisements for the Fuel Pacer, the firm has developed the proposed layout shown in Exhibit 31–2.

Focal Topic

Develop a complete marketing plan for Fuel Pacer. Be specific in terms of:
1. Product design and packaging
2. Channels of distribution
3. Pricing strategy
4. Advertising and promotion
5. Marketing research

Exhibit 31–1
Fact Sheet for the Fuel Pacer

What Is Fuel Pacer?

It's a solid state device designed to reduce fuel consumption and costs through a systematic lowering of the thermostat temperature (or raising for air-conditioning systems).

How Does It Work?

Fuel Pacer utilizes a setback mechanism that automatically adjusts the thermostat at a specified time and for a certain number of degrees. The objective is to reduce use of fuel for heating and cooling during those times space is unoccupied or at night.

What Does It Do?

For one thing, it saves money—up to twenty percent monthly for residential users and as much as forty percent for commercial customers. In addition, fuel consumption is reduced astronomically.

How Is It Made?

The simple and sturdy Fuel Pacer is engineered to last. The solid state circuit eliminates repair and replacement problems. One per family per lifetime is the idea.

How Much Does It Cost?

The price is $19.95 and no installation cost is incurred. Peel off the adhesive backing and press to the wall; then plug it in to your household timer and set the timer.

What's Next?

So buy and enjoy. Saving money and our resources is not a bad deal for $19.95. Almost priceless, you might say.

Exhibit 31–2
Proposed Advertisement for the Fuel Pacer

Case 32
Merit Services, Inc.

The U.S. firm Merit Services, Inc., operating as Merit International, Inc. throughout the rest of the world, was founded to meet the need for technologically superior drilling fluids which can keep pace with today's requirements. Merit's principals, like its customers, are experienced oil field operators who became dissatisfied with the performance of competitors continuing to sell thirty-year-old products and ideas at a time when all other segments of the oilfield supply industry are marketing innovative products which reflect the rapidly changing technological state of the field.

The Company

Merit has adopted as its corporate motto "Performance is our most important product." This motto is based on the firm's desire to assure its customers that Merit will be first in product performance, engineering performance, and drilling cost performance. Toward this end, Merit provides its customers with technologically superior and cost effective drilling fluid products developed through extensive laboratory research and field testing.

Merit markets its proprietary drilling fluid chemicals under the "ULTRA" trademark to signify that the firm believes there are no better products available in the oil field today. The firm's field engineers are trained in the use of drilling fluids by an experienced group of staff engineers. Merit's field engineers are positioned as professionals in the industry; however, when a problem develops at a well drilling location, the entire expertise of the Merit organization is at the disposal of the customer.

Even though Merit was founded only two years ago, its principals have over twenty years of experience in oil field operations. The oil operators who founded the company recognize the need to minimize drilling costs. The firm, therefore, has focused its research and development efforts on designing drilling fluid systems which will maximize drilling rate, eliminate hole problems, and minimize third-party service costs.

The Product

Among its products, Merit has created and patented Ultradryl, which is revolutionary but, to date, relatively unknown in the marketplace. The product, used in drilling oil and gas wells, is a chemical low solids fluid system.

From the beginning of oil well drilling operations, almost all companies have used Wyoming bentonite based solids in solution called mud. Mud has a variety of purposes but serves primarily as a lubricant in the well bore to facilitate drilling operations. Although Ultradryl has many advantages over a high solids system, the liquid has received limited acceptance in the industry.

Specific advantages of using Ultradryl as opposed to using conventional drilling muds are as follows:
1. Penetration rates are greatly increased due to extremely low solids content.
2. Frictional coefficient is greatly reduced and hydraulics consequently improved and energy requirements to pump the fluids reduced.
3. Hole scouring is greatly improved.
4. Due to nonwetting characteristics of the fluid, the bedding planes and microstructures of sensitive shales are vastly inhibited.
5. Ultradryl is not sensitive to temperatures up to 435° F.
6. It is nonreactive to chemicals encountered in a drilling operation.
7. It creates a plastic film on the wall of the borehole or annular wall.
8. It enhances bit life. If ten bits are normally used, that number could be reduced to five.

The Market

The primary purchasers of drilling lubricants are oil field operators and drilling contractors. A key influence in the purchase decision is a person known as a "toolpusher," who coordinates the equipment and supplies used in the drilling operation.

Four major mud companies now hold over 50 percent of the market. Friendly relationships between salespeople and purchasers are a major basis for sales of almost all mud. Some observers have characterized the typical purchasing situation as one influenced by "wine, women, and song."

When introduced to Ultradryl, operators and contractors usually respond by saying that it sounds good and they feel they would like to test it. They go on to say, however, that they are somewhat afraid to stick their necks out and possibly lose their position due to foul-ups caused by testing something new. These operators and contractors admit that the muds used for many years are not that great but reason that they are proven and accepted throughout the industry, and therefore preferable because they do not present a possibility of failure.

On those occasions when Merit has been able to get Ultradryl used, the results generally have been quite favorable. The Appendix presents a representative use situation.

The management of Merit feels that if it could convince two or three of the major oil companies to use Ultradryl for some test cases, the other thirty-eight major companies would adopt the product for trial very quickly. Management is considering the possibility of a seminar or some type of meeting to reach influential contractors and operators.

Focal Topic

Develop a marketing program for Merit's Ultradryl. Be specific in terms of:
1. Emphasized product appeals
2. Personal selling techniques
3. Advertising programs
4. Other marketing activities

Appendix
An Example of Ultradryl Use

In anticipation of drilling the Tekxon #1 Wake Well located in Leavenworth County, Kansas, we transported forty sacks of Ultradryl via air transport to Lawrence, Kansas, at which point it was loaded in stacks of two sacks onto a small Ford van occupying perhaps half the length of the van. The van was then taken to the location where we were to drill the well.

At that time the toolpusher and several drillers were on location. The toolpusher asked where the mud was that we intended to drill the well with. I pointed out the fact that the mud was contained in the small van which had been pulled up on the location. He then uttered something to this effect, "Hell, man, you ain't got enough material in there to drill no well."

At that I took him over to the van and opened the back door, at which time he was even more perplexed. Rather than seeing a full van he saw a half empty van. He said something like, "You mean to tell me that you're going to drill that whole well with that stuff here in this truck?" I said indeed we anticipated so doing and walked over to talk with the engineer on location. At that time the toolpusher called over another individual or two and showed them the physical appearance of Ultradryl. When later engaged in a conversation, the toolpusher expressed disbelief that we would drill this well using that tiny bit of material.

The first day we started drilling, the crews added something on the order of four sacks of Ultradryl to achieve the viscosity and hole cleaning characteristics which I had expressed a desire to maintain. Then after drilling for another 24 hours the toolpusher and crews expressed amazement at the fact the hole was being properly cleaned and that they could easily identify penetration into different geologic formations. The geologist on the location was extremely pleased with the characteristics of samples achieved with the low viscosity typical while drilling with Ultradryl.

After the period of disbelief, the toolpusher, the crews, and the geologist said that they considered Ultradryl a more desirable drilling fluid medium than conventional mud systems.

Case 33
QUBE

On December 1, 1977, some consumers in Columbus, Ohio, became active participants in rather than passive viewers of the television medium, when a new media communication system was marketed by QUBE (a division of Warner Cable Corporation). The system permits two-way communications between subscribers and the company's computer-equipped production studios. By punching buttons on their QUBE console (a computer terminal device attached to the home television set), subscribers can receive thirty channels of video and other information. Subscribers can also take tests, participate in games, register opinions instantly, and actually take part in many programs and events scheduled on QUBE.

Background Information

QUBE is part of Warner Communications, Inc., a highly diversified corporation and a major innovative force in the entertainment and electronic communications industries. Warner Communications is involved with motion pictures, television productions, recorded music, publishing, toys, sports, and video games. Its Warner Cable subsidiary owns 138 cable systems throughout the United States.

Warner in Columbus
Before QUBE, 26,000 Columbus area homes subscribed to the basic cable service provided by Warner Cable. This service offered ten

channels of television to subscribers for a monthly rate of $7.50. The total area served by Warner in Columbus encompassed approximately 100,000 homes. In 1973, developmental plans began for what was to become known as QUBE.

System Description

Subscribers in the QUBE service areas are provided with a small, limited capability computer terminal and selector console, which open to the viewer thirty channels of entertainment, information, and education. The console's five response buttons allow the viewer to "touch-in" and respond instantly to material appearing on the home television screen through any of the thirty channels. The console, which is slightly larger than a hand calculator and is connected to the set by a twenty-five-foot cord, also controls channel selection and response.

Subscriber Services

Exhibit 33–1 illustrates the QUBE console and its basic operation. As can be seen, there are three columns of ten channels each. The T column lists traditional commercial and public television channels. Column C shows community and informational programming channels which originate through QUBE's studios and remote facilities. The P column contains a series of channels offering premium programming. Five buttons on the right side of the console enable the subscriber to communicate directly with the QUBE computer. Exhibit 33–2 presents a series of questions viewers ask most frequently, along with the respective answers.

Programming

In addition to traditional programming, QUBE offers viewers a variety of specialized entertainment and information shows on its premium and community channels. Exhibit 33–3 presents a brief description of each of the channels listed in the P and C columns as taken from QUBE's promotional brochures.

All programs on QUBE's nine premium channels are presented without commercials and are scheduled at a variety of times each month for the convenience of the viewer. Consumers pay on a per-program basis and are billed by computer each month, just as they would be billed and pay for long-distance calls.

First-run movies during QUBE's first month of operation included *A Star Is Born* with Barbra Streisand and Kris Kristofferson, *Silent Movie* with Mel Brooks, *Demon Seed* with Julie Christie, Federico Fellini's *Amarcord*, *The Enforcer* with Clint Eastwood, *Raggedy Ann and Andy,* and *Midway* with Charlton Heston and Henry Fonda. Movie greats included *The Maltese Falcon* with Humphrey Bogart, Boris Karloff in the original *Frankenstein, A Streetcar Named Desire* with Marlon Brando, Marilyn Monroe in *The Seven Year Itch,* Gary Cooper in *High Noon, Marriage Italian Style* with Sophia Loren, Burt Lancaster as *Jim Thorpe—All American,* Doris Day in *Pajama Game,* Humphrey Bogart in *Sahara,* and Peter Sellers in *The Mouse That Roared.*

First month presentations on QUBE's Premium Performance Channel included *Madame Butterfly, Marriage of Figaro, Sleeping Beauty, Swan Lake, Bach's Christmas Oratorio* and *Brahms Symphonies No. 2* and *4.* Also featured were music programs with Frank Zappa, The Beatles, Johnny Mathis and Roberta Flack. Also, a new theatrical British rock group, The Deaf School, made its first United States video appearance on QUBE.

QUBE's Sports Channel presented a variety of games and events, including a live high school basketball game during its first month. Other sporting events included professional basketball and hockey games and a series of events from New York's Madison Square Garden. In that same time, QUBE's Special Events Channel presented the play *Scapino,* featuring Jim Dale; *Spice on Ice,* a musical comedy review produced in Las Vegas; and *Cafe Manhattan,* a contemporary version of the Ed Sullivan Show. David Hoy, a psychic of world renown, appeared live on QUBE to demonstrate his extrasensory perception, using QUBE's unique response buttons to answer questions from subscribers. Hoy also made his annual yearly predictions during this program.

The Columbus Alive and Pinwheel Channels offer subscribers a variety of specialized programming. Columbus Alive contains individual shows for all age groups, while Pinwheel is directed to the preschooler and is presented without violence or commercials.

A two-hour live interactive television show that uses all of Columbus as its stage and all of its citizens as its cast is the primary component of the Columbus Alive Channel. QUBE's Studio C with its huge front windows (allowing for staging inside and outside) is the central headquarters for all the acts. Two cohosts talk with a wide variety of guests and participants in all kinds of action events. Outside the window a police helicopter might land for a demonstration on rescue work or a college sorority might show how to build a floral parade float. The umbrella format of the show allows for a number of other features, such as *Talent Search.* Undiscovered amateur entertainers of Columbus perform, and the at-home audience rates the performers using the response buttons.

Other programs on the Columbus Alive Channel include (1)

Columbus Goes Bananas—a flexibly structured kaleidoscope of teenage happenings such as dancing, talent showcases, celebrity interviews, and games; (2) *Flippo's Magic Circus*—a children's participation show combining the best in magic, competition between children's teams, and various stunts and antics; (3) *Celebration*—an afternoon entertainment program originating from QUBE's remote studio in a local shopping center and focusing on the achievement of Columbus area residents, among other things; and (4) *Columbus Then and Now*—a relaxed and casual program which centers on quality of life, people's attitudes, and the cultures of today and the past.

The setting for *Pinwheel* is a Victorian-style rooming house run by a life-sized puppet named Aurelia, a fortune-teller with a thoroughly modern touch-tone crystal ball. She and all the folks who live in her household create a world of fun and fantasy for the preschooler, uninterrupted by commercial messages. There are also award winning animated firms from all over the world; games to entertain and instruct; and music, art, poetry, and dance. There is no beginning, middle, or end to the program, so children can move in and out as they wish. Program segments average three minutes in length and are self-contained units.

Each month all QUBE subscribers receive a free program guide, which outlines in detail programs, events, classes, and courses scheduled for that month. Exhibit 33–4 shows the cover of March's guide.

Pricing

Present Warner Cable subscribers pay $9.95 for installation of the system; new subscribers are charged $19.95. The monthly charge for QUBE service is $10.95. If the consumer elects to pay for eleven months of service in advance, the twelfth month is free. Other costs depend on how much the premium channels are used.

For example, the movie *Network* cost viewers $3.50; a Frank Sinatra concert, $2.00; the La Scala productions of *Pagliacci* and *Cavalleria Rusticana*, conducted by Herbert von Karajan, $2.50; a course in real estate or the performing arts, $2.00 a session; *The Seven Year Itch*, $1.00; sporting events, $2.00 and $2.50; and adult movies, $3.00 to $3.50.

Other Services

QUBE programs five channels of stereo music—classical, country, mellow rock, golden oldies, and beautiful music. This stereo music service is wired directly to the consumer's existing stereo system, providing commercial-free music twenty-four hours a day, seven days a week. Certain premium performances are programmed simultaneously through the television and through the subscriber's stereo system. Programs on the Columbus Alive Channel are also simulcast in stereo. There is a one-time $10.00 installation charge for this service, and there is no monthly fee.

QUBE also plans to offer security services to its subscribers in the near future. Consumers will be able to choose the combination of home and personal security systems which best fits their individual needs. Fire, smoke, and burglar detection, and panic and medical alerts all wired to central receiving and dispatching points will be available. Installation charges and monthly monitoring fees for such security systems have not yet been determined.

Services to Advertisers

New forms of immediate response television advertising—*Qubits* and *Infomercials*—can be run on the Columbus Alive channel. In the entertaining and informative programs on this channel, the advertiser can establish two-way direct interaction with the viewer. A commercial can be integrated within, and become a part of, the live programming in which it is scheduled.

A Qubit is comparable to a traditional television spot commercial, but can be of variable length (up to two minutes long) and allows interaction with the home audience. An Infomercial is an *INFOrmative comMERCIAL* message which is integrated with the program content. Infomercials also allow audience interaction and can last up to five minutes. Possible examples of Infomercials include:

- A travelogue on the Bahamas by a travel agency
- A microwave oven demonstration by an appliance store or manufacturer
- A survey of reader attitudes by a newspaper
- A fashion show by a clothing store
- A discussion of family expense budgeting by a bank
- A cooking demonstration by a food producer

Programs on the Columbus Alive channel contain no more than four Qubits and no more than one Infomercial per hour. Advertisements are not double or triple spotted.

Advertising on QUBE can achieve results never before possible through the television medium. For example, through viewers' use of the response buttons, advertisers can be provided with:

- A list of qualified prospects with name, address, and phone number for advertiser follow-up and closing
- A list of viewers who want to sample an advertised product (Advertiser follows up by direct mailing samples to the viewers' homes)

• A list of viewers who respond to a discount coupon opportunity from an advertiser (Advertiser is supplied with list of respondents for mailing coupons or making them available at a place of business)

Advertisers can also research and analyze viewer opinions realistically and speedily through interactive questions and answers concerning identification of product users and nonusers, product awareness, reaction to proposed traditional radio/television commercials, and competitive product information. A hard-copy printout of responses is made available to the advertiser the morning after the advertisement appears on the Columbus Alive Channel. Advertising rates include the cost of programming the QUBE computers and the resultant printout of responses. Exhibit 33–5 gives the rates for Qubits and Infomercials.

Advertisers may elect to reach only a very specific audience, such as physicians, attorneys, nurses, union members, or Democrats through the use of a "narrowcast" channel. A client alerts the desired audience by phone or direct mail to tune in this channel at a specific time and day. The client provides QUBE a list of those homes which should receive the program to be "narrowcast." QUBE's computer sends the program at the agreed time and day only to those households designated by the client. No other QUBE household can receive that special programming on Channel 9 during that time.

Programs run on this channel can be interactive, with the instant give and take of questions and answers. Physicians or nurses may take medical quizzes or union members may vote using the response buttons. Results are tallied by QUBE computers and delivered to the client.

Promotional Strategy

Initial promotional efforts were designed simply to create awareness of and interest in QUBE. Later advertisements focused on more information about QUBE—its advantages and capabilities. Print, radio, and television advertising was used to inform consumers about this new communications phenomenon. Exhibits 33–6 and 33–7 are illustrative of the introductory advertising for QUBE.

An intensive direct mail campaign was used to reach Warner Cable's 26,000 subscribers and encourage them to sign up for QUBE. Exhibit 33–8 shows the cover of an elaborate and attractive twenty-four-page, full-color brochure sent to each of these subscribers. Two days later each of these households received a copy of the first month's forty-page QUBE guide with complete programming and pricing information.

Current Situation

As of the middle of February, after two and a half months of operation, QUBE had over 13,000 subscribers. Severe weather conditions seriously hampered and delayed installations. QUBE has not yet commenced door-to-door and other marketing techniques to encourage other Warner cable subscribers to convert to QUBE. In addition, no special marketing efforts have been directed to the 75,000 other homes in the areas served by Warner.

QUBE subscribers have adapted readily to the concept of purchasing video programs on an individual basis. Certain live sports events, such as Ohio State University basketball games, are being purchased (at $2.50) by 10 to 15 percent of the subscribers. In January, new motion pictures were being purchased at an average rate of over two per home per month. In the first three weeks of availability, fifty-five students enrolled for credit in tuition courses being offered by local colleges and universities.

Initial advertising support and interest in QUBE, both national and local, has been substantial. Advertisers include American Express, Paine-Webber, Jackson & Curtis, stockbrokers, Lazarus Division of Federated Department Stores, and some major local businesses. National pharmaceutical companies and a number of trade associations are preparing to provide closed-circuit programs to doctors and other selected audience groups in the QUBE area.

On the basis of this initial response, Warner is also actively seeking cable television franchises in other urban markets where QUBE service can be offered. The company recently made a franchise proposal in Fort Wayne, Indiana, and expects to make a similar proposal to Pittsburgh, Pennsylvania. Warner is also considering the extension of QUBE to Akron, Ohio, where it operates a normal cable television system.

While all of the initial results seem favorable, QUBE management is naturally interested in expanding its subscriber base in Columbus, increasing the utilization of the premium channels, attracting more advertisers to its community channels, and enlarging its service offers to consumers and businesses. The firm is currently evaluating a number of marketing strategies consistent with these interests.

Focal Topics

1. What marketing strategy do you think QUBE should adopt in attempting to add to its subscriber base?
2. Discuss the alternatives open to QUBE in the area of increasing premium channel usage. What are your recommendations?

3. How would you go about getting more advertisers to avail themselves of QUBE's services?
4. What other services do you think QUBE should offer consumers
   and businesses?
5. What types of marketing research should QUBE undertake at
   this point?

Exhibit 33–1
QUBE Console and Its Operation

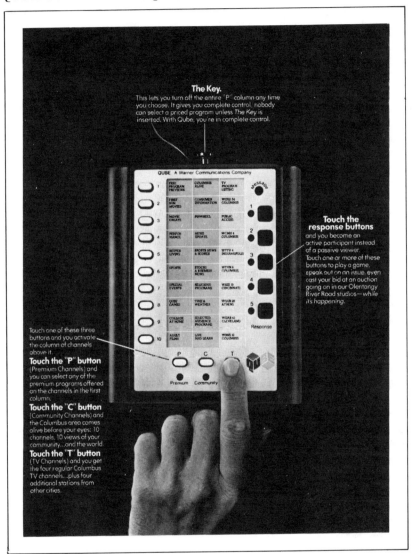

Exhibit 33–2
Questions and Answers about QUBE and Its Operations

Will I get a good clear picture?

Yes. The Qube converter has been designed with both automatic frequency control (AFC) and automatic fine tuning (AFT). Once Qube is installed, you need not adjust the fine tuning or color adjustments on your television set. Each time you select any of Qube's 30 channels, your converter will automatically adjust for variation in transmission from channel to channel.

How does Qube work?

When Qube is installed in your home, you get the Qube console. In addition, a small on-line computer terminal is installed in an inconspicuous location. The terminal is wired to both the Qube console and to your television set. Every time you touch a Qube button—whether a Program Button or a Response Button—the terminal "reads" your choice and relays it to the main Qube computer in our Columbus studios. Automatically the program you selected is sent to your home by Qube, or your response is registered.

What about my privacy? Does somebody know everything I watch?

Our Qube computer makes no record of individual home viewing other than the record of Premium Channel purchases for billing each subscriber. This record is strictly confidential.

Individual home responses to interactive programs are not recorded unless called for as part of the program format. In such cases, the viewer will have been appropriately advised.

Can I count on getting reliable service?

Expert professional technicians are as close as your telephone. Qube has studios and offices based right in Columbus with a large and competent staff.

Suppose I don't want the Adult Movie channel at all. How can I prevent it from coming into my home?

Unless you specifically order Premium Button #10 to be activated, you'll receive no programming on that one channel. In addition, The Key lets you turn off all of the "P" column.

Exhibit 33–2 (continued)

**What happens if I press the wrong
Premium Button by mistake?
Will I be charged?**

You will have a two-minute grace period in which to correct your
error by selecting another channel.

**How can I budget my viewing so I
won't run up an unexpectedly high
Premium Channel bill?**

You can call our office any day, and we'll give you a current report
on your total costs for the month.

**How can I be sure I won't get charged
for Premium Shows I didn't watch?**

Computerized monthly billing will itemize by date and program
every Premium Program you have been charged for. It's as reliable
as your monthly bank statement.

Exhibit 33–3
Description of Premium and Community Channels

P-1. *Free Program Previews.* A continuous program of previews so you'll know at all times what's available on each Premium Channel, the exact time each program is scheduled, and how much it costs.

P-2. *First Run Movies.* Each month you can see the best of the recent films; complete, uncut, and never before shown on television. First rate first run films at a single-admission price.

P-3. *Movie Greats.* You'll be able to tune in Gary Cooper in "High Noon," Humphrey Bogart in "Casablanca," Marlon Brando in "On the Waterfront" ... an exciting lineup of different films every month, uninterrupted by commercials.

P-4. *Performance.* "Swan Lake" with Nureyev and Fonteyn; "Madame Butterfly" from La Scala; concerts from Artur Rubinstein to Roberta Flack. With The Stereo Option, frequent simulcasts bring the sound to your stereo system.

P-5. *Better Living.* Personal skills, job advancement, and how-to courses you always thought about. Take courses like Beginning Guitar, Speed-reading, or an S.A.T. prep course, and participate from your home, using the Response Buttons.

P-6. *Sports.* OSU sports, and high school, too. Professional sports from everywhere ... the events commercial television doesn't bring you.

P-7. *Special Events.* Major entertainment extravaganzas and performances you'd never see on television ... from Manhattan, Paris, Las Vegas, and Columbus, too.

P-8. *Qube Games.* For the first time ever, match your skills against your Columbus neighbors from the comfort of your home. Win prizes in an exciting variety of Qube Games using the Response Buttons.

P-9. *College At Home.* You can enroll for certificate and credit courses offered by Columbus area colleges and universities and communicate with your instructor without leaving your home, using the 2-way Response Buttons.

P-10. *Adult Films.* If you don't want this channel, you won't get it. If you do want it, you can always deactivate it with The Key when necessary.

C-1. *Columbus Alive.* This is the pulse of your home town. It's an entire channel where every day the nitty-gritty, the unusual, and the big happenings in Columbus come together ... come alive. Columbus Alive ... is alive with Columbus.

C-2. *Consumer Information.* Comparative prices for the same items in Columbus stores, compiled by Ms. Consumer, Qube's "in the field" expert. Items from supermarkets to service stations will be surveyed to save you money.

Exhibit 33–3 (continued)

C-3. *Pinwheel.* The first channel ever designed for pre-schoolers. Its modular format lets the child join in at any point without missing any of the fun. Puppets, films, music, stories . . . without violence, without commercials, all day, every day.

C-4. *News Update.* A constant source of Columbus area, state, national, and worldwide news presented in printed form on the screen 24 hours a day. You get the news at the same instant that newsrooms across the nation are getting it.

C-5. *Sports News & Scores.* All day, all night continuous reports covering up-to-the-minute local, national, and worldwide sports news and scores.

C-6. *Stocks & Business News.* Latest stock prices plus financial news and market summaries around the clock.

C-7. *Religious Programs.* A channel totally devoted to religion. Inspirational programs from different religious denominations.

C-8. *Time & Weather.* Continuous printed local, state, and national weather reports and forecasts. And the correct time any time you need it.

C-9. *Selected Audience Programs.* Special programs for special audiences—doctors, lawyers, teachers, union members—can be shown on this channel. Only those authorized by prior notification will receive these programs.

C-10. *Live and Learn.* Visit the Canadian Rockies or let Pele show you the secrets of winning soccer. Also, specially captioned programs for the hearing impaired. This is a community channel featuring informational and educational programming.

Exhibit 33–4
Cover of QUBE Guide for March

Exhibit 33–5
Rate Card for Advertising on QUBE

Time Classifications: (Monday through Friday)

Day*	11:00 A.M. to 4:00 P.M.
Afternoon	4:00 P.M. to 8:00 P.M.
Night	8:00 P.M. to Midnight

Qubits: Interactive commercials, variable length up to two minutes.

Qubits per Week:	9x	6x	3x
Day	$ 55	$ 60	$ 65
Afternoon	$100	$120	$140
Night	$160	$190	$220

Infomercials: A commercial message integrated with program content in a five minute segment.
Double the Qubit rate

DISCOUNTS:

13 Weeks	10 percent
26 Weeks	20 percent

Agency commission included @ 15 percent

---

*Except for Celebration! which takes night rate.

Exhibit 33–6
Introductory Advertisement for QUBE

Exhibit 33–7
Introductory Advertisement for QUBE

Exhibit 33–8
Cover of Introductory Brochure for QUBE

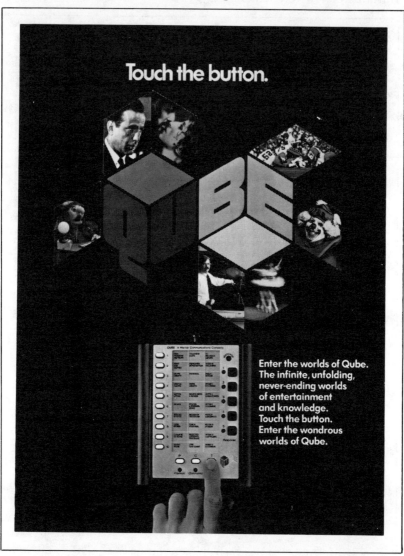

Case 34

M-tron Industries, Inc.*

In April 1971 the management of M-tron Industries attempted to develop a marketing plan for E-Z Breathe, a portable electronic air cleaner for home use, which management made several attempts to market. Total factory sales since April 1970 had been between 5,000 and 6,000 units, only around one-third of a full year's production capacity. Mr. Kornelius (Kase) Mooibroek, marketing manager of M-tron, believed 2,500 to 3,000 units were still in the channels of distribution in the inventories of distributors and dealers.

Background Information

M-tron Industries, Inc. was founded in 1965 through the efforts of Greater Yankton Industries, Inc., a development company in Yankton, South Dakota. Manufacturing operations began in April 1965. The company began with approximately 30 employees, most of whom were administrative and supervisory personnel. By 1970 it employed 190, most of whom lived in the Yankton vicinity.

M-tron's primary product is a piezo electric quartz crystal component used for frequency control in all military and commercial com-

*Modified for inclusion in this text with the permission of James D. Taylor and Bert C. Nyman, University of South Dakota, authors of the original case.

munications equipment. Some commercial quartz crystal applications are citizen band, industrial, taxi, police, and aircraft radios; air navigation systems; television receivers; and radio-controlled model aircraft and boats for hobbyists. The military uses the components in all types of radios and communications equipment.

Mr. William Liggett, president of M-tron in 1968,[1] felt the company needed a product or group of products that would balance the sales market in case of variations in demand for quartz crystals and allow M-tron to grow. About that time management was approached by a person with an idea for a product that seemed to fit both needs. The product—an electronic air cleaner for home or office use—would probably enjoy an expanding market in the future because of the increased severity of air pollution.

Handmade models were demonstrated and reworked until, by October 1969, M-tron had developed a model of the air cleaner that was ready for home testing. The E-Z Breathe trademark was applied for and hand-assembled test units were placed in local homes at a nominal cost to the user.

Product Description

The E-Z Breathe electronic air cleaner measures 12 inches by 12 inches by 6 inches and weighs only twelve pounds. It can be plugged into any 110 volt outlet and is available in two finishes—walnut woodgrain in washable vinyl and stainless. It removes up to 99 percent of all airborne particles, including pollens, lint, fog and mist, fly ash, dust, mold spores, bacteria, oil smoke, and tobacco smoke, and can completely filter the air in a 15 by 25 foot room three to five times per hour. (See Exhibits 34–1 and 34–2.)

The E-Z Breathe removes particles in the air through a process known as "Electrostatic Precipitation." Air drawn into the filter cell passes through a series of ionizing wires, which impart a positive charge to the particles. The air then passes between a series of parallel aluminum plates which are alternately charged positive and negative. The positively charged particles are repelled by the positively charged plates and attracted to the negatively charged plates in the same way iron is attracted to a magnet.

To keep the unit operating effectively, the electronic filter cell needs to be pulled out once or twice a month and soaked in a dishwasher detergent solution or washed in an automatic dishwasher. After the filter cell has been thoroughly dried, it can easily be

---

[1]Mr. Liggett left the firm in January 1971.

reinserted into the unit. Since each unit has only one moving part (the fan), the only additional maintenance required is to place a drop of oil on the fan once a year. M-tron provides a one-year guarantee against defects in materials and workmanship, during which time the factory or authorized service station will repair the unit free of charge.

Competitive Situation

When M-tron developed and began selling E-Z Breathe, there were competitive air cleaners on the market. Dome Laboratories sold an air cleaner based on the same principle for $150 through medical and therapeutic devices marketing channels. S.C.S., a company in Minneapolis, had a portable model on the market, as did Minneapolis Honeywell. Emerson Electric and Sears & Roebuck marketed models but never put forth much effort to sell them. In 1970 Hoover began selling an air cleaner which also deodorized for $119 retail. M-tron management believes these models are less attractive to buyers, however, because they are large, bulky, unattractively designed, and difficult to maintain (cleaning the electronic plates where particles collect often requires removal of bolts and disconnection of circuitry). It believes E-Z Breathe's compactness, design, and convenience provide a competitive advantage.

Marketing Experience

Initial marketing efforts for E-Z Breathe began in 1969, when a few salesmen who distributed other products became convinced that E-Z Breathe had a good future and agreed to act as its distributors. Attempts to market E-Z Breathe through heating and air-conditioning dealers in South Dakota and Nebraska were not successful. One dealer's attempt at selling through direct mail failed. A Texas distributor attempted sales to doctors and consumers through Sunday supplement advertising but discontinued the effort. A Des Moines, Iowa, firm attempted to set up a house-to-house selling organization, but without success. M-tron rented a booth at a home show in Sioux City, Iowa, and sold only three machines at $69.95. During this initial sales period, prices ranged from $69.95 to $99.95.

In February 1970 M-tron contracted with an independent marketing research analyst to conduct a study to determine consumer reaction to E-Z Breathe and to help M-tron decide how to market the product.

In early April of 1970, before the results of the research were available, M-tron decided to test market E-Z Breathe through a department store. Through contact with an Ohio distributor, Rike's Department Store in Dayton was selected to stock E-Z Breathe in its major appliances department.

An advertising agency in Dayton was engaged to develop TV commercials and set up the TV schedule. The agency recommended a thirteen-week program at $10,000 as the minimum necessary to gain adequate sales for E-Z Breathe in the Dayton area. The campaign was scheduled to begin in late April. Print ads were run in the *Dayton Daily News*. Rike's advertised a price of $99.50. A local distributor was also found to establish other dealers in the area; Rike's received their stock of E-Z Breathe cleaners; and the ads were run off on schedule.

In the first week Rike's reordered twice. The second week the ads were not run. The third week the ads were again run and Rike's reordered once. Subsequently, Rike's reordered once after a considerable length of time. After eight weeks the advertising was pulled off the air, since sales had apparently fallen off too far to warrant continuation. M-tron figured the cost of selling the units (that is, the ratio of advertising to sales) was $50 per unit.

Meanwhile, M-tron placed an ad in *Salesman's Opportunity* magazine, and attracted several distributors, some of whom were still selling E-Z Breathe nearly a year later. The ad in *Salesman's Opportunity* ran in the April, May, and June 1970, editions. One East Coast distributor who was attracted by the ad gained some department store distribution. A dealer using small ads in the *Denver Post* to get sales leads followed them up with a direct sales demonstration in the home. She was able to sell the product successfully.

Distributors were also obtained in various cities thinly scattered throughout the nation. In Atlanta, a medical personnel agency sold some to medical people. Another medical supplier, who had good connections with doctors, ordered his fourth dozen E-Z Breathe cleaners for his rental-purchase plan.

A distributor on the East Coast used in-store demonstrations in several major department stores and in some cases was able to sell from twenty-five to forty per two-day demonstration period. These sales fell soon after demonstration ceased. Housewares representatives (agents) were used to try to gain distribution through some department stores. Beauty supply representatives were used to try to gain sales to beauty salons for the stainless model, priced at $129.

In December 1970 Brandeis Department Store in Omaha sold the product, which M-tron advertised for Brandeis in newspapers and on TV. The price was set and advertised at $99.50. The results, just as in the past, were good initial sales which then tapered off.

Marketing Research Data

In early May 1970, during the campaign through Rike's in Dayton, M-tron received the market research results contracted for in February. Interviews with groups of men, groups of women, and individual families were used in the study, whose major findings are summarized as follows:

1. Women sinus sufferers are as conscious of air pollution in the home as they are of the general air pollution problem outside the home.
2. Interviewers agreed that sleeping in clean air would be beneficial to health, especially for people with "breathing problems" such as asthma, sinus problems, hay fever, and allergies.
3. E-Z Breathe would be used in the bedroom at night and in the kitchen and living room during the day.
4. (a) One-third of the interviewees were enthusiastic about wanting an E-Z Breathe in their home.
   (b) One-third had reservations about having one in their home.
   (c) One-sixth would not want it in their home, because there was no one in the family with a respiratory problem, they would rather have a central unit for the whole house, or they believed air-conditioning filtered the air sufficiently.
   (d) Those who were enthusiastic about wanting E-Z Breathe wanted it for relief of breathing problems—sinus, hay fever, bronchitis, and emphysema, in that order.
5. E-Z Breathe would be bought primarily for health reasons (respiratory problems). It would also be bought to help keep a clean house.
6. The women urged the importance of a home demonstration lasting several days to demonstrate its value.
7. E-Z Breathe would be bought primarily for the family. Protecting babies and small children from health hazards was frequently given as a reason for buying.
8. The wife became interested in E-Z Breathe before the husband in two-thirds of the family interviews.
9. The buying decision would be a joint decision in two-thirds of the cases, and the wife's decision alone in about one-fourth of the cases.
10. "If I did not buy an E-Z Breathe it would probably be because the price is too high" was given as the reason for not buying by two-thirds of the families. Other reasons were lack of need and the belief that furnace filters and air-conditioning would do the job. (In the interviews no price information or sales promotion

had been presented.) Some people were disappointed that it was not an odor remover also.
11. Most respondents indicated they would expect to buy E-Z Breathe in department stores. Some named appliance, hardware, and discount stores.
12. The appearance and compactness are features that people liked about E-Z Breathe.
13. Consumers expected to pay from $60.00 to $75.00 for E-Z Breathe.
14. The E-Z Breathe had a very broad consumer market appeal—greatest in large urban areas, particularly in residential districts located near industrialized areas or in areas of heavy traffic flow, and where household incomes are relatively high.

Potential Name Change

On the basis of previous experience with its electronic air cleaner, M-tron felt that the E-Z Breathe name might restrict its market to those customers who bought the product for health reasons. In a brainstorming session, the firm and its advertising agency developed a list of potential brand names for the product. Exhibit 34–3 lists these alternative names.

Focal Topics

1. Should M-tron continue to sell under their own brand name or should they manufacture air cleaners for private brands?
2. If they continue to sell under their own brand, should they adopt a new brand name? What procedure would you recommend to select the appropriate name?
3. What name would you recommend? Why?
4. Should any additional research be undertaken at this time? If so, what type of research should it be?
5. What marketing plan would you recommend for E-Z Breathe?

Exhibit 34–1
Portions of a Brochure for E-Z Breathe

CAN'T BREATHE?

Get comfortable with **EZ·BREATHE**
ELECTRONIC AIR CLEANER

...reduces discomforts of asthma, hay fever, emphysema and other respiratory illnesses

EZ·BREATHE

space age compactness

Electrostatic filter traps 99% of airborne particles.

Quiet 2-speed fan circulates up to 120 cubic feet of air per minute through purification chamber.

Efficiently handles rooms up to 15' x 25'.

Only one moving part. Operates trouble-free for pennies a month.

Lightweight—can be carried and plugged in anywhere you have a 110 A.C. outlet. Underwriter's Laboratory Listed.

Filter never needs replacing—cleans easily with little effort.

Handsome woodgrain and brushed aluminum finish. Only 12" wide x 6" high x 12" deep.

Exhibit 34–2
Operating Characteristics of E-Z Breathe

POLLUTED AIR CLEANED IN SECONDS

| E-Z Breathe is placed in plastic hemisphere. | Cigarette smoke is pumped into hemisphere. | E-Z Breathe is turned on. | In less than 10 seconds, pollutants from smoke are trapped by E-Z Breathe filter, leaving air clear and pure. |

In any room in your home, an E-Z Breathe Air Cleaner can effectively remove dust, dirt, pollen, smoke, grease and other airborne particles, down to 1/2.5 millionth of an inch (.01 micron) in size—so small that 5000 would fit on the period at the end of this sentence. Rooms where an E-Z Breathe is used are easier to clean, more pleasant to live in—and healthier.

EZ·BREATHE
operates like this   and gives results like this

Air drawn into the E-Z Breathe filter cell passes through a series of ionizing wires. These wires impart a positive (+) charge to particles suspended in the air. The air then passes between a series of parallel aluminum plates which are alternately charged positive (+) and negative (–). The positively charged particles are repelled by the positively charged plates and attracted to the negatively charged plates in the same way iron is attracted to a magnet. Simple, foolproof—yet so effective that 99% of all airborne particles stay in the filter and out of your lungs!

■ *"I am bothered by hay fever, asthma and emphysema but feel so much better after using the E-Z Breathe Air Cleaner. Hay fever bothers me in the day but, when I turn on the unit in my bedroom, my pollen irritation is gone in about half an hour. I'm sleeping better than I have for 20 years."*

A. W. Eggert
Norfolk, Nebraska

■ *"I have less general congestion and take much less oxygen since I have been using the E-Z Breathe Air Cleaner."*

D. Myers
Snyder, Texas

■ *"Using an E-Z Breathe Air Cleaner in my bedroom has made it possible for me to sleep soundly all night long without having to get up and take decongestant pills."*

W. D. Inman
Lincoln, Nebraska

Exhibit 34–3
Potential Brand Names for Electronic Air Cleaner

Nature-Aire	Relieftronic	Vista-Aire
Sani-Aire	Electro-Fresh	Vistatronic
Fresh-Aire	Airtron	Ultraronic
Cleer-Aire	Electro-Airtron	Electromatic
Crystal-Aire	Micro-Tronic	Air Guard
Tropic-Aire	Mini-Tronic	Air Stream
Islandaire	Electropure	Spring Air
Ecolo-Aire	Environmenta	Spring Time
Airalator	Refreshaire	Air Pac
Aller-Out	Recycle-Aire	Alpine
Allergex	Futuraire	North Woods
Electro-Breeze	Smog-Ex	The Nordic
Electro-Kleen	M-Tronic-Aire	The Viking

Case 35
Franklin Mint Corporation

After twelve years of exceptional and uninterrupted growth, Franklin Mint Corporation had a difficult year in 1977. Sales declined to $289.8 million from $306.9 million in 1976. Net income was $7.2 million, or 85 cents per share, compared to $24.7 million, or $2.92 per share, in 1976.

Some analysts suggest that Franklin Mint's problems stem from its ambitious expansion of product offerings beyond collector's medals, a business it knows inside out. In order to diversify, the company decided to go into a wide range of other collectibles—from books to porcelain and crystal—with different kinds of customers, costs, and promotional requirements.

The firm has indicated that its emphasis in 1978 will be on improving the profitability of its collectible business rather than increasing collectible sales. Accordingly, it has reduced the number of programs scheduled to be offered in 1978 by about one-third. It has also decreased the number of higher-priced, single issue programs and has put more emphasis on moderate-priced single offerings and series programs with lower monthly prices.

The Franklin Mint is also intensifying efforts to diversify into noncollectible areas. It has projects under development in several consumer product fields where the firm believes there is the potential for significant sales by direct marketing.

Situational Information

What Is the Franklin Mint?

The Franklin Mint, founded in 1964, is the only nongovernment mint in the United States that produces legal tender coin for foreign countries. Foreign coins, however, represent just a small part of its work. The firm is best known for its many series of commemorative medals, which are usually struck in solid sterling silver and issued in limited editions.

The Franklin Mint specializes in proof-quality coins and medals. Proofs bearing the FM hallmark are characterized by flawlessly minted detail on a brilliant, mirror-like background and are highly prized by collectors around the world. It has been appointed the official minter for many important series of commemorative medals. It has minted and distributed medals for such eminent sponsors as the National Trust for Historic Preservation, the White House Historical Association, Postmasters of America, the United States Olympic Committee, the United Nations, the National Audubon Society, and the Royal Ballet.

Operating Subsidiaries

The Franklin Mint Corporation has subsidiaries in fifteen foreign nations. Its French subsidiary, LeMedaillier, S.A., is the sole manufacturer of the Janvier engraving machine, a basic piece of diemaking equipment used by most of the mints of the world. The principal operating division of the corporation, however, is the Franklin Mint, which has the distinction of being the world's largest private mint.

Corporate Performance

Exhibit 35–1 shows comparative financial statistics for the years 1968 through 1977. As can be seen, growth in all aspects of financial performance had been steady up to 1976. Earnings grew an average of 40 percent annually for 1972 through 1976. In 1977, however, there was a substantial decline in financial performance at all levels.

Total subscription and order backlog, adjusted for expected attrition, amounted to $440 million at the end of 1977, compared with $482 million at the end of 1976. The U.S. backlog accounted for $286 million and the international for $154 million of the $440 million; approximately $158 million was scheduled for shipment in 1978, $93 million in 1979, and the balance thereafter.

The number of collectors worldwide did increase during 1977 by 103,000, bringing the total at year-end to 1,868,000. Of this total, the number of U.S. collectors was 1,041,000, while collectors abroad totaled 827,000. A sizeable number (almost 130,000) of the firm's collectors belong to the Franklin Mint Collectors Society, the largest such group in the world.

The Art of Minting

The creation of coins and medals brings together the talents of many artists—including designers, sculptors, and engravers. The designer begins by developing a variety of concepts, from which the final design is selected. Frequently, the designer is also a medallic sculptor, but in many cases two different artists are involved. Working in clay, the medallic sculptor models the design about four to six times larger than the finished piece, blending artistry with carefully learned technical skills. Insight and artistic discipline come into play as he or she strives to convey the feeling and flavor of the subject, as well as its substance.

The clay model is cast in plaster and the sculptor continues refining the work in this harder material. Eventually, when the work is complete, it is cast in an even harder form and then cut into steel by the Janvier engraving machine. The hand engraver, artistic partner of the medallic sculptor, now takes up the task and sees that every minute detail of the sculptor's design is faithfully engraved in the steel dies from which the finished coins and medals will be minted.

The Product Offering

When asked to describe Franklin Mint Corporation's role in society, Charles L. Andes, President and Chief Executive Officer of the corporation, responded:

I'd begin by saying this company occupies an unusual position in the business world. Our products are essentially art objects. Creating them involves the inspiration and creativity of artists, the skills of the best craftsmen, and unusually high standards of quality.

The result is an object whose principal reasons for being is to be admired for its beauty and then passed along to children and grandchildren for them to enjoy. In an age when true craftsmanship is scarce, there is great satisfaction in the continued pursuit of excellence. In an age where everything seems to wear out too quickly, producing objects that will go on giving pleasure for generations is almost unique. Our collectors seem to understand what we are trying to do and appreciate it. I guess you could say that's why we're here.

With this in mind, a major purpose of Franklin Mint can be viewed as producing series of coins and commemorative medals for general sale or for sale to members of specific societies. In addition to coins and medals, other collector's items produced by the Franklin Mint include miniature silver ingots, coined zodiac jewelry, collector spoons, and medallic greeting cards. In 1970, the firm introduced the first in a series of original, sterling silver Christmas plates designed by Norman Rockwell, titled "Bringing Home the Tree," and has since produced several other collector's plates by major artists.

Some of the Franklin Mint's major issues include The Franklin Mint History of the United States, The White House Historical Association Presidential Medals, The Franklin Mint History of the American Revolution, Norman Rockwell's Spirit of Scouting, The Genius of Michelangelo, The Centennial Car Ingot Collection, The 100 Greatest Masterpieces, Official Big Game Medals, Patriots Hall of Fame, The Fifty-State Bicentennial Medal Collection, Treasures of the Louvre, Kings and Queens of England, Roberts Birds, and a medallic history of the American presidency. This latter program, involving 100 medals, was offered in selected markets late in 1977 and introduced nationally in February 1978. A representative grouping of the firm's offerings is illustrated in Exhibit 35–2.

While some Franklin Mint issues are available individually, most are part of a monthly series and are issued only to subscribers of that particular series. When a new series is announced, attractive mailings describing the offering are sent to selected segments of the firm's present collectors. For certain series or individual items the company occasionally makes use of newspaper and magazine advertisements to reach a broader potential market.

When a new series is introduced, the subscription rolls are usually open for just a brief period of time, and only applications postmarked on or before the subscription deadline are accepted. In most cases, the total edition is limited to the exact number of original subscribers. For commemorative plates, the edition is enlarged somewhat for a limited sale in retail stores. The limited edition policy is designed to help establish the rarity of each Franklin Mint issue at the outset. To further assure rarity and hopefully enhance the value of an edition, the minting dies are actually destroyed after all authorized specimens have been safely delivered.

Most Franklin Mint editions number between 5,000 and 20,000. More than 102,000 Americans, however, ordered the silver Apollo 14 medal. A total of 9,500 subscriptions were received for the 36 plates (each priced at $150) in the Presidential series.

Franklin Mint limited edition issues are not available through retailers. The firm reaches customers either through direct mail or advertisements in newspapers, magazines, Sunday supplements, radio, and television. In this way, the firm has full control over the way it communicates to customers.

The Franklin Mint Collector

People from all walks of life have become Franklin Mint collectors in recent years. Most of these people never previously considered themselves collectors. In fact, many never collected anything before. Their reasons for collecting its issues are almost as diverse as their socioeconomic characteristics. While some individuals have acquired collections for their investment potential, the firm has found through research that most collectors purchase the products primarily for other reasons: to become more knowledgeable about a particular subject, to systematically accumulate a personal collection for posterity, and often just to enjoy the beauty of the collection.

Even though there are limited secondary markets for trading Franklin Mint's collectibles, some issues have gone up substantially in value since their initial issue. For example, the 1970 sterling silver Christmas plate designed by Norman Rockwell originally sold for $125 but now commands a price around $500 in the open market. Nevertheless, survey research indicates that the overwhelming majority of Franklin Mint customers view collecting as an enjoyable long-term hobby, not a short-term investment for profit. Only 3 percent responded that they plan to sell any of their collections in the next few years and 85 percent stated that they do not plan to sell at all.

Certain new issues are offered exclusively to the 130,000 members of the Franklin Mint Collectors Society through its monthly magazine, *The Franklin Mint Almanac.* Annual dues of $12.00 entitle a member to a dated sterling silver membership medal, use of the Society's private clubroom at the Franklin Mint, a subscription to the *Almanac,* special insurance rates for Franklin Mint Collectibles, and other special benefits.

Expanding Market Potentials

After three years of developmental work, the international operations of the Franklin Mint Corporation began to contribute profitably to the company in 1972. During the developmental period, the company tested foreign collector tastes, developed mailing lists in many countries where direct mail marketing still is in its infancy, and established relationships with renowned artists and organizations. By the end of 1977, more than 800,000 people outside the United States had become Franklin Mint collectors.

International operations experienced a record sales year in 1977, but profits were down, primarily because of increased advertising, general, and administrative costs. International sales were $107 million in 1977 and profits were $2.2 million. Pretax margins were 7.6 percent compared with 11.3 percent in 1976.

While operations in most countries were profitable, the division encountered losses in England, Italy, France, Sweden, and Switzerland (in the latter country, principally because of start-up costs). Major organizational changes in the division were implemented during the year to achieve operating economies. German and French manufacturing facilities were consolidated into the United Kingdom location. International headquarters personnel relocated from London to company headquarters in Franklin Center. Nine European companies were organized into four groups to provide better utilization of management talents and realize cost savings.

Many crystal, porcelain, and philatelic offerings were well received, and jewelry products proved especially popular. Japanese flower vases, a pewter tankard, an ornamental Easter egg, and Japanese wood block prints were among products successfully introduced in international markets in 1977.

Product Diversifications

In 1972 Franklin Mint announced its first major initiative outside the field of silver collectibles: The Franklin Mint Gallery of American Art. This new program offers limited editions of signed prints by both established and new artists in an innovative manner. The first print offering, a collection of ten award-winning Western paintings issued in signed, limited edition prints, drew a response of well over $2 million in subscription commitments, more than double the original sales forecast.

In this same year, the firm introduced its first collection of collector spoons in sterling silver. The following year, Franklin Mint commissioned Andrew Wyeth to design his first work in fine bone china. The success of the Wyeth bowl and the subsequent Hans Christian Andersen plate collection confirmed expectations concerning the worldwide appeal of procelain-based collectibles.

A Celebrity Art Portfolio was offered to those owning established Franklin Mint Collections in 1973. This collection was comprised of paintings by ten of America's entertainers: Tony Bennett, Candice Bergen, Richard Chamberlain, Duke Ellington, Henry Fonda, Peggy Lee, Kim Novak, Dinah Shore, Red Skelton, and Elke Sommer.

A 1974 collection of thirteen colonial figures cast in pewter represented Franklin Mint's first sculpture offering. Since that time, the firm has produced sculptures in silver, pewter, bronze, crystal, silver with 24-karat gold, and porcelain. Later that year it took a bold step outside the familiar line of minted and metallic products and formed

The Franklin Library. In slightly over three years, the library revived the art of deluxe, leather-bound book production by combining classic literature with fine art to please the eye as well as the mind.

In 1975 the firm established The Franklin Philatelic Society, which emphasizes first day covers and cachets featuring illustrations as beautiful as the stamps themselves. The society has attracted thousands of new collectors, both in the United States and in international markets.

After increasing its porcelain and crystal offerings in 1976, the firm continued its diversification program in 1977 by introducing a variety of jewelry collectibles and forming two more divisions—Franklin Heirloom Furniture and The Franklin Record Society.

Franklin Heirloom Furniture recreates masterpieces of eighteenth century American furniture at prices well below the originals. Its first offering was a $4,800 re-creation of the 1765-labeled Townsend Chippendale Desk, which currently stands in the diplomatic reception room of the U.S. Department of State in Washington and is valued at $250,000. The division also plans to offer re-creations of celebrated clocks, chests, and highboys.

The Franklin Record Society offers proof-quality recordings of the greatest recorded works of music. Although its first program consists entirely of classical music, future offerings could embrace such musical styles as jazz, popular, opera, and folk.

Recent Developments

The Franklin Mint

Reduced demand for The Franklin Mint's commemorative medals and monetary coins adversely affected 1977 operations. Apart from medallic products, however, a wide range of collectibles—particularly new product forms—achieved good customer acceptance. Notable examples included The American Military Sculpture Collection, a hundred miniature sculptures honoring Americans of every military service and era; Main Street America, four pewter tableaus depicting life at the turn of the century; Silver Car Miniatures, the first collection of silver miniatures ever offered by the company; and Coast of Maine, a framed silver etching created by artist Jamie Wyeth.

Jewelry product offerings were expanded considerably, with encouraging collector response. Products were made available in several price ranges and included a wide selection of pendants, one of which featured a 100-franc Monte Carlo Casino silver chip; a love bracelet; a gold ring designed by Gilroy Roberts; and a first recreation of museum jewelry, the coronation scarab of Tutankhamun.

New luxury product forms introduced by the company were well received. These included a chess set in pewter and gold, hand-enameled flower arrangements designed by Gloria Vanderbilt, sculptured silver plate napkin rings, and a zodiac watch in gold-on-silver.

The Franklin Library

The Franklin Library, which offers deluxe, leather-bound books, achieved its highest sales and profits in 1977. However, the library experienced higher-than-expected attrition on certain book programs and, accordingly, the subscription backlog was reduced by $34 million. At year-end, the library had a subscription backlog of $140 million, adjusted for expected attrition, and had 80,000 collectors.

Programs introduced in 1977 were: The World's Best Loved Books; Great Books of the Western World, a program produced with the cooperation of Encyclopaedia Britannica; and Signed Editions, the greatest books of our time autographed personally by their authors, including Leon Uris, John Kenneth Galbraith, James Baldwin, Norman Mailer, and others. Portions of a promotional piece of the Signed Editions are shown in Exhibit 35–3. The books, issued at the rate of approximately one per month for four years, are priced at $45 each.

While these programs were successful, the number of subscriptions was lower than for programs promoted in previous years; therefore, the firm is evaluating additional marketing techniques to increase book sales.

The Franklin Philatelic Society

The Franklin Philatelic Society increased sales and profits in 1977. The society, founded in 1975 to develop and market stamp-related proprietary products, maintained its position as a major philatelic organization. More than 150,000 collectors are society members, including 60,000 in the Franklin Mint International division.

The society offers commemorative stamps on first-day cover cachets, most of them postmarked in countries throughout the world on their first day of issue. Offerings in 1977 included The Stamps of All Countries First-Day Cover Collection; The Heritage of America Stamp Collection; The Official First-Day Covers Commemorating the 20th Anniversary of the Space Age, which featured original illustrations by Russian cosmonaut Alexei Leonov; and the Postmasters of America First-Day Covers, a collection featuring all of the new commemorative stamp issues by the United States Postal Service.

Franklin Porcelain

Franklin Porcelain markets a wide variety of handcrafted, finely detailed collectibles, including decorative plates, sculptures, and wall plaques as well as such innovative products as thimbles and pendants. Porcelain products attained record sales in 1977, and worldwide operations were profitable, although domestic operations experienced a small loss as a result of start-up costs at the manufacturing facility at Rockdale, Pennsylvania.

This new facility, one of the most modern porcelain plants in the world, is now operating efficiently and producing high-quality plates and figurines. The company also utilizes outside porcelain producers, and delivery problems with some of these suppliers reduced 1977 sales and profits. The division now is scheduling longer lead time in the development of products supplied by outside producers in an effort to alleviate this problem.

Porcelain continues to show promise as a collectible form. Because of the popularity of its collectibles, in 1977 Franklin Porcelain increased the number of its offerings from three to eleven. These programs included its first Mother's Day plate; baby animal sculptures; the official Mark Twain plate collection; and songbirds of the world porcelain plate collection, an official issue of The National Audubon Society.

Franklin Crystal

While increasing its offerings of engraved plates, sculptures, and paperweights in full lead crystal during the year, Franklin Crystal operated at a loss in 1977. Collector response was lower than anticipated, primarily because of the relatively high price of crystal offerings. Shipment delays caused by manufacturing problems also affected the division's performance.

The division, established in 1976, shares facilities with Franklin Porcelain and has its own design, engraving, and etching capabilities. The number of offerings will be reduced in 1978 and most of the products will be redesigned to achieve lower price offerings.

The Future

From the beginning, Franklin Mint developed in three clear directions, each contributing to the other two. First, the company grew in terms of what it marketed, which can be referred to as *product growth.* Second, growth occurred in terms of how it marketed products, called *merchandising growth.* Third, Franklin Mint grew in terms of where it marketed its products, which can be labeled *market growth.*

In 1977, however, the usual rate of growth in sales was not realized. Had the success of Franklin Mint, which attracted a number of other companies into the business, led to product saturation? Had the firm ventured into areas of product diversification in which it lacked the necessary expertise to attain the same profit returns?

In its assessment of some of the causes behind the disappointing performance in 1977, management offered the following observations:

The principal reason for the profit decrease was much lower-than-expected response to our 1977 promotions. Nothing in our previous experience prepared us for such a sudden and prolonged underachievement of our planned sales and order generation. Because incoming orders and shipments were under expectations, advertising and promotion expense was significantly greater as a percentage of sales in 1977 than in 1976.

We believe we have identified most of the reasons for the lower-than-expected order response. These include too frequent offerings of programs, particularly in the first half of the year; a product mix that was somewhat more expensive than in prior years; and a decline in interest in our numismatic products. Other reasons for the profit decrease included increased selling, general and administrative costs, which had been budgeted at higher levels than in 1976 in anticipation of additional volume, and greater depreciation and interest expense.

Product costs increased as a percentage of sales because it was necessary to write off the cost of outside sourced products in connection with certain programs where our commitments exceeded requirements as a result of lower-than-planned sales. In addition, some elements of our manufacturing overhead are relatively fixed and cannot be reduced quickly when sales volume falls short of plan. There were delays in shipping certain of our new product forms to customers, and this affected profits.

Income also was affected because customer withdrawals in some programs occurred at higher rates than in the past, requiring us to accelerate the amortization of promotion and advertising expenditures. Increased customer attrition occurred primarily on programs where the monthly payment is relatively high and on orders which are secured through such widely circulated advertising media as freestanding newspaper inserts. The attrition was most significant in recently promoted book programs.

As the problems of 1977 became apparent, we took a number of actions in an effort to improve profitability. We priced new programs to produce acceptable profit contributions in spite of the higher advertising-to-sales ratio being experienced. We decreased as much as possible the number of programs to be offered, given the time constraints. We also accelerated test marketing efforts in the last half of 1977 so that now all major corporate programs are pretested in the marketplace.

Focal Topics

1. What is the real product being marketed by the Franklin Mint? What consumer needs are satisfied by this product?
2. Should Franklin Mint continue its diversification moves? If so, should the company concentrate on collectibles or expand into other product areas? What specific categories of collectibles or other product areas would you recommend?
3. Discuss any specific types of research that should be undertaken by the Franklin Mint.
4. What long-range marketing strategy would you recommend for the Franklin Mint?

Exhibit 35–1
Comparative Financial and Other Statistics for 1968 through 1977

Ten-Year Review of Performance

Dollar amounts and shares expressed in thousands except figures on a per share basis	1977	1976	1975	1974	1973	1972	1971	1970	1969	1968
Summary of Operations										
Net sales	$289,795	$306,898	$233,909	$166,736	$112,676	$80,156	$62,782	$48,128	$29,001	$10,258
Costs of products sold	127,946	130,611	98,609	71,242	44,739	31,762	26,680	25,824	16,949	6,730
Interest expense	4,952	2,701	1,429	1,867	501	307	453	730	226	200
Income tax provision	8,230	26,990	20,400	13,605	10,130	6,820	5,440	2,563	1,745	594
Net income	7,158	24,718	19,148	13,012	9,138	6,733	4,533	2,473	1,688	630
Per Share Information*										
Net income per share	$.85	$2.92	$2.28	$1.58	$1.12	$.83	$.61	$.35	$.25	$.11
Cash dividends per share	.63	.65	.45	.30	.20	.125	.034	.028	.023	.006
Price range of shares	29¼-7¼	35¾-23¼	32⅜-13¼	20-10	23⅝-9⅜	25¼-17⅛	19⅜-9⅛	12⅝-3⅛	13⅝-7⅛	9⅝-1
Price earnings ratio	35-9	12-8	14-6	13-6	21-8	30-21	32-15	36-9	55-29	87-9
Performance Indicators										
Return on sales	2.5%	8.1%	8.2%	7.8%	8.1%	8.4%	7.2%	5.1%	5.8%	6.1%
Return on average "total capital employed"	8.7%	31.2%	24.2%	27.9%	31.7%	14.7%	25.9%	26.9%	16.3%	22.7%
Return on average shareholders' equity	8.2%	32.6%	33.6%	30.4%	27.6%	26.3%	28.2%	28.8%	27.2%	19.4%
Established collectors	1,868,000	1,765,000	1,359,000	1,115,000	810,000	575,000	425,000	300,000	200,000	75,000
Subscription and order backlog	$440,000	$482,000	$359,000	$322,000	$139,000	$68,000	$64,000	$50,000	$30,000	$29,000
Deferred promotion/ backlog ratio	14.3%	11.9%	10.2%	8.3%	7.5%	7.4%	8.1%	5.4%	2.0%	2.3%
Financial Position										
Working capital	$ 59,470	$ 68,785	$ 30,133	$ 16,152	$ 14,538	$10,874	$ 9,557	$ 2,887	$ 4,487	$ 2,559
Property, plant and equipment (net)	35,314	29,789	23,530	22,842	20,890	18,755	14,732	12,587	9,380	2,684
Other assets	44,545	43,099	25,166	21,076	10,152	6,468	3,277	2,693	1,053	387
	139,329	141,673	78,829	60,070	45,580	36,097	27,566	18,167	14,920	5,630
Long-term debt	32,058	40,495	4,180	4,504	4,878	4,986	3,915	6,861	7,295	–
Deferred income taxes	18,534	14,881	9,287	7,020	3,653	1,986	1,593	1,261	510	320
Shareholders' equity	$ 88,737	$ 86,297	$ 65,362	$ 48,546	$ 37,049	$29,125	$22,058	$10,045	$ 7,115	$ 5,310
Other Information										
Employees	3,020	3,388	2,513	2,369	2,001	1,633	1,325	1,193	947	739
Shareholders	14,832	10,437	10,475	11,006	10,435	8,230	5,354	5,657	4,450	2,550
Shares outstanding*	8,404	8,383	8,299	8,213	8,081	8,028	7,866	7,042	6,912	6,672

*Ajusted for all stock splits

Exhibit 35–2
Representative Products of the Franklin Mint

Exhibit 35–3
Portions of a Promotional Brochure for the Franklin Library

Case 36
Wendy's International, Inc.

"Does America need another hamburger chain?" was the question being asked as R. David Thomas opened the doors to his first Wendy's Old Fashioned Hamburgers restaurant at 257 East Broad Street in downtown Columbus, Ohio, on November 15, 1969. At that time many food industry experts and some skeptical observers had commented that the fast food growth curve had already peaked during the late 1960s and that the rapid expansion of the industry was over.

On March 21, 1978, after only eight years and four months, the thousandth restaurant in the Wendy's chain opened at 1000 Memorial Boulevard in Springfield, Tennessee. Never before had such an accomplishment been achieved in such a short period of time.

Company Background

Wendy's was founded by R. David Thomas, who was previously associated with Kentucky Fried Chicken and Arthur Treacher's Fish and Chips. Thomas presently serves as chairman and chief executive officer. Robert L. Barney, presently president and chief operating officer, joined Wendy's in 1970. He started in the fast food business in 1962, when he became an owner of a Kentucky Fried Chicken franchise, later becoming a regional vice-president in charge of 135 stores. For a short period of time before joining Wendy's he was vice-president of operations at Arthur Treacher's Fish and Chips.

Much of Wendy's growth has come from rapid expansion of the franchise system. At the end of 1977, Wendy's had 905 restaurants open to the public. Of these, 712 were franchised units with the remaining ones operated by the company. In 1978 Wendy's expects to open approximately 500 new restaurants and to expand out of continental North America for the first time, beginning with Hawaii. The firm is also involved in active negotiations for the granting of franchise rights in Japan and plans to move into other international markets in the near future.

Franchises are assigned for twenty years on an area basis. The cost for a franchise is $10,000 per unit with a continuing 4 percent of sales service fee paid monthly to the parent company. Most of Wendy's franchises are owned by operators who have had previous experience in the food service field.

Wendy's is also directing considerable attention toward expanding the number of company-owned outlets by buying back existing franchises and by constructing its own units.

The typical Wendy's building is about 30 × 76 feet, seats 90 to 100 people, and has a parking area for 30 to 45 cars. Most units are built on a half- to three-quarter-acre lot as opposed to a typical McDonald's or Burger King, which usually occupies an acre or more. Wendy's needs less land than the other two operations because a drive-in window accounts for 45 to 50 percent of a unit's total sales. Those customers who use the pick-up window obviously do not require parking spaces or inside eating areas. Exhibit 36–1 shows pictures of a typical Wendy's unit.

An average investment of $350,000 is required to construct a Wendy's unit. Of this total, about 40 percent goes for the building, another 40 percent for real estate, and the remaining 20 percent for equipment. The typical Wendy's outlet averages $609,600 in annual sales.

Product Offering

Wendy's places primary emphasis upon consistent quality in all areas of food preparation and presentation. The firm uses 100 percent pure beef, which is delivered in bulk and pattied fresh every morning in each of its restaurants. The patties are cooked slowly so that they retain their natural juices and flavors. Whether the customer orders the quarter-pound single (79 cents), the half-pound double ($1.39), or the three-quarter triple ($1.89), the hamburger is served directly from the grill. By mixing and matching the eight available condiments, a Wendy's customer can specify one of 256 different ways to have a hamburger served. Current sales break down into approximately 70 percent singles, 25 percent doubles, and 5 percent triples.

Chili is also on the menu at 79 cents. In addition to being popular with customers, this product serves a unique secondary purpose. To keep the hamburgers fresh for customers, no cooked patties are kept on the grill for more than four minutes. In order to eliminate this potential meat waste factor, hamburgers not served within the four-minute time period are steamed in a kettle and used for the next day's chili.

French fries, Frostys, coffee, tea, milk, and soft drinks round out the menu. The Frosty, a Wendy's exclusive, is a thick, creamy blend of chocolate and vanilla (much like a very thick milkshake) served with a spoon. An illustration of Wendy's product mix is shown in Exhibit 36–2.

Financial Performance

As shown in Exhibit 36–3, Wendy's has experienced substantial growth in revenues, expenses, and net income during the eight-year period ending December 31, 1977. Operation of additional company-owned restaurants was the most significant factor in increased revenue and expense. However, as indicated by the average annual revenues of company-owned restaurants open twelve months or more, growth is also attributable to increases in volume per restaurant. As indicated earlier, each franchise pays an amount equal to 4 percent of gross sales to the company as a franchise royalty. Royalty income was 2.8 percent of gross revenues in 1973 and 11.5 percent in 1977. Management expects royalties to continue to increase as a percentage of total revenues.

To gain a better understanding of the relative costs associated with running a Wendy's restaurant, Exhibit 36–4 presents a typical pro forma statement of annual operating expenses for two levels of gross sales. These figures would vary with certain localized factors and are not meant to represent any particular operating unit. They are used here for illustrative purposes only.

Marketing Strategy

Wendy's has designed its product, restaurant, and promotion to reach the adult market, and through the adult, to reach the family. In terms of overall market positioning, the firm seems to be a step above fast-food hamburger operations like McDonald's, Burger King, and Burger Chef but a step below inexpensive steak outlets like Bonanza and Ponderosa.

Communications with Consumers

A great obstacle facing Wendy's in any new market is that the consumer is likely to view it as another McDonald's, Burger King, or Burger Chef. As a result, Wendy's must educate the consumer as to how and why it is different than other hamburger restaurants. The following four points outline the areas in which Wendy's management perceives the firm to be different from its competition:

1. Wendy's hamburgers are made the "Old Fashioned" way with fresh beef that is never frozen. They are cooked slowly on the grill and prepared to the customer's order with an unlimited choice of condiments. In addition, each sandwich is served on a warm bun. Sandwiches are never cooked or wrapped ahead of time. They are served directly from the grill.

2. Wendy's provides the ultimate in take-home food convenience by providing the customer with Pick-Up Window service. While others may have a drive-thru window, none can provide the speed of service and consistent high-quality product that Wendy's is famous for. This adds up to a big benefit to the consumer, namely, fast, high-quality stay-in-the-car service.

3. Wendy's offers a full menu of top quality products. The chili is made fresh every day with almost a quarter pound of beef in each serving. Wendy's offers a consistently crisp and golden french fry that is served moments from the fryer. Wendy's has an all-natural dairy product dessert, the "Frosty." It's cool and creamy with a rich chocolate/vanilla flavor that's better than ice cream. And it's so thick you have to eat it with a spoon.

4. Finally, Wendy's offers a family dining room that's warm, inviting, bright, and cheerful. The turn-of-the-century decor includes Tiffany lamps, Victorian parlor beads, bentwood chairs, and table tops printed with turn-of-the-century advertisements. Additional touches of wood paneled walls, colorful carpeting, and low music complete the setting.

Marketing Objective

The firm's basic marketing objective is to dominate local markets and to educate the consumer about Wendy's advantages over its competition. The firm identifies its target market as men and women between 18 and 49 years of age. Wendy's attempts to achieve its marketing objective by actively pursuing the following four points:

1. To introduce and promote the Wendy's Old Fashioned concept in the new market.

2. To provide a sales building plan for each market, whether franchise or home office.

3. To provide each market with the necessary materials and counsel.

4. To promote the pick-up window until it reaches a satisfactory percentage of volume.

Advertising Objective

Wendy's basic advertising objective is to consistently attract and retain new customers and to form favorable attitudes and opinions toward Wendy's products. Put more basically, the firm wants the consumer to feel that Wendy's products are better than those of the competition. Wendy's attempts to achieve its advertising objectives by actively pursuing the following five points:

1. To sell Wendy's theme of quality, choice, and freshness. To create positive attitudes toward the Wendy's concept.
2. To sell the pick-up window as highly convenient for "hurry" situations.
3. To sell the unlimited choice of condiments.
4. To sell the size of the hamburger.
5. To sell Wendy's features of rich, meaty chili, and thick Frosty.

To accomplish these objectives, Wendy's makes extensive use of advertising, sales promotions (usually couponing), and publicity/public relations. Each Wendy's outlet spends at least 3 percent of sales of local advertising activities and contributes an additional 1 percent of sales to the national advertising program.

In 1977 Wendy's system-wide advertising budget amounted to $15.6 million. Of this total, $12.6 million went into network ($3.6 million) and local ($9 million) television advertising. The remaining $3 million was spent on radio, outdoor billboard, newspaper, and direct mail advertising and promotional effects.

Wendy's national advertising program is administered by a twelve-member committee made up of six franchisees and six company officials. Advising the committee is Dick Rich (of the Alka-Seltzer "Stomachs" campaign and the Benson & Hedges "Long Cigarette" campaign), who produces Wendy's network and spot television commercials and is the creator of Wendy's "hot and juicy" hamburgers theme. Exhibits 36–5 and 36–6 are sample storyboards for Wendy's television commercials. Types of television programs used for the firm's national advertising are shown in Exhibit 36–7. An example of radio commercials which are supportive of the television advertising is given in Exhibit 36–8.

The company's local advertising and promotional materials are prepared by Stockton-West-Burkhart, Inc. This firm also makes available to Wendy's franchisees and their local advertising agencies reproductions of Wendy's television and radio commercials, newspaper advertisements, discount coupons, direct mailers, and other advertising materials. Exhibits 36–9 and 36–10 present examples of various print advertisements, billboards, and point-of-purchase materials.

Coupons serve as a promotional device, increasing sales or heightening awareness on a short-term basis (a phenomenon which the firm hopes will retain some residual benefit in return customers). They provide an opportunity for consumers to save money and also may encourage them to try new products. Coupons used by Wendy's generally offer a free item with the purchase of another one or two menu items at regular price or a discount off a regular price item. From test situations Wendy's has found coupons distributed through newspaper advertisements and direct mail are most frequently redeemed, because of the greater selectivity of saturation per dollar spent.

Wendy's also focuses on cultivating a good relationship with the public in each store's market. Local restaurants are encouraged to take part in public activities and community programs. Examples of such participation include joining in local parades, sponsoring a queen in a pageant, and making tickets available for local sporting and cultural events.

Marketing Research

To learn more about the relative importance of various restaurant characteristics and how Wendy's compares with other hamburger restaurants on those characteristics, a marketing research project was undertaken in several of Wendy's primary markets. Potential respondents were randomly selected from city directory lists by a firm specializing in mail questionnaires. In addition to the standard demographic variables such as age, income, occupation, sex, education, etc., respondents were asked the following questions:

How *important* is it to you that a fast food restaurant satisfy you on the following characteristics? Circle "1" if the characteristic is very important or "6" if the characteristic is very unimportant, or somewhere in between depending on how important it is to you that the restaurant satisfy you on the characteristic. [Eleven characteristics were presented to the respondent, each with a six-point scale to measure the level of importance.]
Please indicate how much you think each of the fast food restaurants *has* of the following characteristics. Circle a "1" if you think the restaurant is high in the characteristic, a "6" if you think it is low in the characteristic, or somewhere in between depending on how much of the characteristic you think the restaurant has. Please give your opinion of every restaurant on each characteristic even if you have to guess. [Seven characteristics were presented to the respondent, along with a six-point

scale to measure Burger Chef, Burger King, McDonald's, and Wendy's on each of the characteristics.]

Following are a series of questions regarding your attitudes toward fast food restaurants. To each question please indicate whether you STRONGLY AGREE, AGREE, DON'T KNOW (NEUTRAL), DISAGREE, or STRONGLY DISAGREE. There are no right or wrong answers: We only want to know what YOU think. [Respondents were then presented with a series of specific statements, along with a five-point scale to indicate their degree of agreement with each statement.]

How important do you consider each of the following as sources of information about fast food restaurants? Check one for each item listed. [Respondents were then presented with seven information sources and asked to indicate if each was important, somewhat important, or not important.]

From a total mailing of 5,000, 1,720 respondents returned questionnaires which were usable for most of the analysis. The actual number of respondents varied for each question due to incompleteness and omissions. Results for each question are presented in Exhibit 36–11 in terms of percentages of respondents giving each of the possible answers.

Focal Topics

1. Based on your analysis of the case and your knowledge of the existing marketing environment, what do you see as the basic problems likely to face Wendy's in the future?
2. Wendy's philosophy is to direct the promotion, motif, and product toward the adult market, and through the adult, get the family trade. Do you agree with this philosophy? Why or why not?
3. Evaluate Wendy's advertising strategy. Be specific in terms of objectives, media, and creative strategy.
4. What can you learn from the research given in the case? What other types of analyses would you recommend? What other types of research should Wendy's undertake at this point?
5. Considering your analysis of the case and statement (in 1) of the problems Wendy's may face, what specific marketing recommendations would you make to Wendy's and why?

Exhibit 36–1
Pictures of a Typical Wendy's Restaurant

Exhibit 36–2
Wendy's Product Offering

Exhibit 36–3
Historical Financial Summary of Wendy's International, Inc.

Financial Summary—Eight Years Ended December 31

	1977	1976	1975	1974	1973	1972	1971	1970
Revenues	$114,231,146	$65,637,321	$34,233,583	$13,555,800	$4,540,931	$1,834,118	$683,967	$257,308
Cost of Sales	53,134,772	32,706,268	17,501,392	6,983,055	2,372,883	979,602	391,894	145,125
Operating Expenses	32,184,505	18,255,810	10,260,801	4,003,478	1,449,157	649,184	226,357	97,890
Interest Expense	1,943,983	2,001,931	893,415	394,409	135,434	23,134	9,878	9,003
Income Before Income Taxes	26,967,886	12,673,312	5,577,975	2,174,858	583,457	182,198	55,838	5,290
Net Income	14,061,886	6,610,312	2,918,875	1,160,125	327,257	108,498	45,570	2,290
Earnings Per Share	2.12	1.19	.63	.26	.08	.04	.02	—
Dividends Per Share	.25	.0075	.0019	.0019	.0013	.0013	—	—
Total Assets	92,161,826	71,411,439	25,904,360	13,028,128	4,900,835	1,788,700	508,165	273,000
Shareholders' Equity	57,996,850	44,842,409	7,163,129	3,069,157	1,572,761	949,534	151,417	15,847
Number of Shares Outstanding	6,584,956	6,508,185	4,487,630	4,285,490	4,198,157	3,700,000	3,000,000	1,650,000
Pre-Tax Margin	23.6%	19.30%	16.29%	16.04%	12.85%	9.93%	8.16%	2.06%
Return on Equity (1)	27.4%	28.80%	57.10%	50.00%	26.00%	19.70%	54.49%	15.58%
Sales—Company-owned and Franchised	425,847,900	187,683,200	74,462,600	24,232,900	6,263,800	2,014,500	681,804	255,610
Number of Restaurants in Operation	905	520	252	93	32	9	4	2
Company-owned	193	151	83	44	17	7	4	2
Franchised	712	369	169	49	15	2	—	—
Average Annual Revenues of both Company-owned and Franchised Restaurants (2)	609,600	511,400	489,800	429,900	368,400	335,700	255,600	230,200

(1) Based on average Equity Employed (2) Based on weighted average number of days open

Exhibit 36–4
Franchise Pro Forma Statement of Operations for One Year

Sales	$300,000	100.00%	$400,000	100.00%	$500,000	100.00%
Cost of Goods Sold:						
Manager or owner	$ 14,000	4.67%	$ 14,000	3.50%	$ 14,000	2.80%
Co-manager	11,500	3.83	11,500	2.87	11,500	2.30
Crew and manager						
Trainee	31,500	10.50	46,500	11.63	59,500	11.90
Total labor	57,000	19.00	72,000	18.00	85,000	17.00
Food	111,000	37.00	148,000	37.00	185,000	37.00
Paper	12,000	4.00	16,000	4.00	20,000	4.00
Laundry	1,050	.35	1,400	.35	1,750	.35
Total cost of goods sold	$181,050	60.35%	$237,400	59.35%	$291,750	58.35%
Gross profit	118,950	39.65	162,600	40.65	208,250	41.65

Exhibit 36–4 (continued)

Operating Expenses:

Rent	$ 28,800	9.60%	$ 28,800	7.20%	$ 28,800	5.76%
Royalty	12,000	4.00	16,000	4.00	20,000	4.00
Insurance	2,100	.70	2,500	.62	3,000	.60
Taxes—payroll	3,900	1.30	5,000	1.25	6,000	1.20
Taxes—real estate	2,000	.67	2,000	.50	2,000	.40
Taxes—other	1,000	.33	1,000	.25	1,000	.20
Supplies	3,750	1.25	5,000	1.25	6,250	1.25
Utilities	10,250	3.42	12,000	3.00	15,000	3.00
Repairs and maintenance	5,000	1.67	6,000	1.50	7,000	1.40
Telephone	500	.17	500	.13	500	.10
Trash removal	1,500	.50	1,500	.37	1,500	.30
Advertising & promotion	12,000	4.00	16,000	4.00	20,000	4.00
Office expense	1,200	.40	1,200	.30	1,200	.24
Miscellaneous	250	.08	250	.06	250	.05
Total operating expenses	$ 84,250	28.08%	97,750	24.44%	$112,500	22.50%
Cash flow	34,700	11.57	64,850	16.21	95,750	19.15
Depreciation	7,200	2.40	7,200	1.80	7,200	1.44
Pretax profit	$ 27,500	9.17%	$ 57,650	14.41%	$ 88,550	17.71%

Exhibit 36-5
Example of 30-Second Television Commercial

Exhibit 36–6
Example of 60-Second Television Commercial

Exhibit 36–7
National Television Used by Wendy's during the
Second Quarter of 1977

Exhibit 36–8
Example of Continuity of Radio Commercial for Wendy's

THE
**WENDY'S
NATIONAL
ADVERTISING
PROGRAM,**
INC.

RADIO CONTINUITY

Wendy's International
Radio   :60
"LINES"

(Music: "Wendy's Tune")

(woman):   There are two great things about Wendy's
                           hot and juicy hamburgers. They're hot.
                           And they're juicy.

(burley guy):   I love my mustard, and I love my relish,
                           but Wendy's hot and juicies are good enough
                           to eat straight.

(black woman):   Do you know why I love hot and juicy
                           hamburgers? Because I've had so many that
                           weren't.

(Manager):   We make 'em as juicy as we can. If they
                           trickle down your chin a little, we're
                           sorry.

(Announcer):   At Wendy's, hot and juicy is not a slogan.
                           It's the way we make our hamburgers.

                           If you're not too thrilled with dry, chewy
                           hamburgers, come on in to Wendy's Old
                           Fashioned Hamburgers. We've got juicy meat,
                           juicy toppings, and lots of napkins.

Tag:

Exhibit 36–9
Examples of Print Advertising

Exhibit 36–10
Examples of Billboards and Point-of-Purchase Materials

Exhibit 36-11
Results of Consumer Research on Selected Fast-Food Restaurants

Importance of characteristics in the selection of fast-food restaurants.

	Very Important 1	2	3	4	Very Unimportant 5	6	Average Score
Speed of service	55.2%	23.5%	11.1%	4.9%	2.1%	3.2%	1.41
Variety of menu	24.8	23.2	25.7	12.2	7.5	6.6	2.58
Popularity with children	20.5	12.1	12.9	9.1	10.8	34.5	3.99
Cleanliness	82.2	8.2	1.9	1.2	.8	5.8	1.11
Convenience	65.6	17.5	8.0	3.2	1.9	3.9	1.26
Taste of food	79.1	10.4	2.7	1.0	1.6	5.1	1.13
Price	48.4	20.2	16.3	5.5	3.9	5.7	1.58
Drive-in window	14.6	13.2	17.6	13.1	14.3	27.1	3.85
Friendliness of personnel	45.1	23.5	16.3	6.7	3.2	5.3	1.71
Quality of french fries	45.5	19.5	14.5	5.6	5.6	9.4	1.73
Taste of hamburgers	68.4	16.6	5.5	1.8	1.5	6.1	1.23

Ratings of selected restaurants on specific characteristics.

	Food Tastes Very Good 1	2	3	4	Food Tastes Very Bad 5	6	Average Score
Burger Chef	8.0%	14.9%	39.6%	24.6%	7.5%	5.4%	3.18
Burger King	25.0	28.1	27.8	13.0	3.6	2.4	2.39
McDonald's	29.5	32.3	22.2	9.0	4.5	2.5	2.14
Wendy's	40.0	24.7	18.7	9.5	3.7	3.4	1.90

	Extremely Clean 1	2	3	4	Extremely Unclean 5	6	Average Score
Burger Chef	11.6%	26.5%	39.1%	16.7%	4.0%	2.1%	2.81
Burger King	23.6	38.9	27.8	7.4	1.7	.6	2.18
McDonald's	43.5	36.2	15.3	3.3	1.2	.6	1.68
Wendy's	42.4	35.6	17.0	3.3	1.0	.8	1.71

	Close to Where I Am 1	2	3	4	Out of the Way 5	6	Average Score
Burger Chef	15.7%	10.1%	13.9%	10.9%	10.5%	38.9%	4.45
Burger King	29.8	17.9	15.0	10.0	10.0	17.3	2.65
McDonald's	54.6	22.9	12.0	4.3	2.7	3.6	1.42
Wendy's	49.6	21.2	13.9	5.7	4.0	5.7	1.52

Exhibit 36–11 (continued)

	Low Cost Menu					High Cost Menu	Average
	1	2	3	4	5	6	Score
Burger Chef	12.0%	21.6%	42.0%	16.9%	4.1%	3.4%	2.89
Burger King	13.6	26.1	35.9	15.7	6.6	2.1	2.79
McDonald's	31.7	26.8	25.6	10.8	3.7	1.3	2.18
Wendy's	12.2	21.1	29.5	18.2	12.9	6.2	3.07

	Very Fast Service					Very Slow Service	Average
	1	2	3	4	5	6	Score
Burger Chef	15.5%	22.6%	36.4%	18.3%	4.4%	2.7%	2.83
Burger King	28.4	31.3	26.4	9.9	2.5	1.5	2.19
McDonald's	43.3	32.2	14.9	4.4	2.9	2.2	1.71
Wendy's	41.0	31.0	19.8	5.6	1.4	1.1	1.79

	Children Like the Food Very Much				Children Don't Like the Food at all		Average
	1	2	3	4	5	6	Score
Burger Chef	17.5%	22.7%	32.7%	17.4%	4.9%	4.9%	2.80
Burger King	32.3	29.3	23.9	9.7	2.6	2.2	2.10
McDonald's	65.7	20.2	10.0	2.6	.6	.9	1.26
Wendy's	32.7	27.2	23.9	10.2	3.5	2.6	2.14

	Wide Variety Menu					Narrow Variety Menu	Average
	1	2	3	4	5	6	Score
Burger Chef	6.9%	14.8%	36.3%	23.3%	12.4%	6.3%	3.28
Burger King	12.4	19.5	32.7	19.8	10.8	4.8	3.05
McDonald's	22.6	25.5	26.7	13.0	8.0	4.2	2.57
Wendy's	13.8	18.8	30.2	17.0	13.0	7.2	3.08

Exhibit 36–11 (continued)

Degree of agreement with selected statements about fast-food dining.

	Strongly Agree 1	Agree 2	Don't Know 3	Disagree 4	Strongly Disagree 5	Average Score
I personally don't like fast-food hamburger restaurants.	7.0%	13.1%	7.1%	46.4%	26.3%	3.99
It costs me more to make my own hamburger than to buy one at fast-food restaurants.	10.9	15.3	16.0	29.5	28.2	3.77
I eat at fast-food restaurants more now than in the past.	19.4	30.6	10.4	24.2	15.4	2.50
Adults like to take their families to fast-food restaurants.	13.5	38.8	24.7	14.5	8.5	2.44
All fast-food hamburgers taste the same.	5.0	10.5	7.7	39.4	37.4	4.18
The way a fast-food store is decorated is important to me.	8.4	33.8	17.6	26.5	13.7	2.94
I tend to go to the same fast-food restaurant all the time.	10.6	30.3	7.0	40.6	11.5	3.55
I prefer a fast-food restaurant that has an atmosphere.	17.8	33.9	19.3	22.6	6.4	2.45
I would rather specify what toppings I want on a hamburger than buy one that is pre-cooked and pre-wrapped.	54.8	27.5	5.4	10.3	2.0	1.41
As long as the food tastes good and I can get what I want, a place does not have to be nice.	5.0	11.8	6.5	37.0	39.8	4.22
Fresh meat makes a better tasting hamburger than frozen meat.	41.3	22.8	25.1	8.7	2.1	1.88
I prefer fast-food restaurants that have a drive-in window.	13.9	22.4	23.8	28.9	11.0	3.08

Importance of sources of information about fast-food restaurants.

	Important 1	Somewhat Important 2	Not Important 3	Average Importance
Television	36.1%	35.0%	28.9%	1.91
Radio	19.3	39.1	41.6	2.29
Newspapers	30.4	38.1	31.4	2.01
Magazines	7.9	31.3	60.8	2.68
Billboards	13.7	36.7	49.6	2.49
Friends or relatives	46.7	31.8	21.6	1.61
Mail	12.5	29.9	57.6	2.63
Community involvement	15.3	30.5	54.1	2.58